BULBS

The WI Creative Gardening Series
BULBS

Christine Skelmersdale

WI BOOKS

This edition specially produced for WI Books
Limited, 39 Eccleston Street, London
SW1W 9NT by Unwin Hyman Limited.

UNWIN HYMAN LIMITED
15–17 Broadwick Street
London W1V 1FP

Allen & Unwin Australia Pty Ltd
8 Napier Street, North Sydney, NSW 2060,
Australia

Allen & Unwin New Zealand Pty Ltd with
the Port Nicholson Press
Compusales Building, 75 Ghuznee Street,
Wellington, New Zealand.

British Library Cataloguing in Publication Data
Skelmersdale, Christine
  Bulbs.
  1. Gardens. Plants. Bulbs
  I. Title   II. Series
  653.9'44

  ISBN 0–04–440377–1

Designed by Julian Holland

Typeset by Latimer Trend & Company Ltd,
Plymouth
Printed in Great Britain by Butler & Tanner Ltd,
Frome

Acknowledgements
For Louise and Yvonne, and with grateful
thanks to Kath for making sense of my
handwritten notes and to my family for
their long-suffering understanding and
patience.

Contents

Foreword

Ornamental gardening is undergoing a revolution as significant as the demise of the parterre, the rise of the woodland garden or the advent of the Wardian case. The difference between this and other revolutions is that whereas they could be summed up in a very few words, the present one cannot. Instead, it needs to be defined and, once that has been done, its central theme must be named.

The gardening population has grown enormously in numbers which has led, in turn, to a growing demand for the availability of a wider variety of plants. These people have come to be highly discriminating and aesthetically aware about what they wish to grow. They are now ready to realise that specialisation in gardening can be a dead end and that plants do not have to be segregated, one group from another, in some sort of horticultural apartheid.

Modern Creative Gardening is the art of appreciating the qualities of plants – including those that are to be seen when flowers are absent – and putting them in the context of inter-related beauty. It is gardening become art, and it is an art that is accessible to everyone.

This series of books does not address the subject of Creative Gardening directly. It is rather a primer, in which the prevailing conventions are used as starting points from which the reader may progress further. The books follow the divisions in which garden plants are (sometimes arbitrarily) put, but they endeavour to lead you, the reader, towards a feeling that such distinctions hold our gardening imaginations back.

The authors are people who really do garden. They may be specialists in their field, or like me, generalists with particular favourites and individual ways of looking at things. However, they have all been driven to tears by failure, made joyful by success and been rendered bereft of any explanation for the contrariness and sheer mystery of Nature. What we all have in common is a love of plants and of the gardens in which we grow them. Our motivation in writing these books has been a desire to share such things with those who read us.

John Kelly

Series Editor
Abbotsbury, Dorset, 1989

1 Creative gardening with bulbs

This book is designed with the creative gardener in mind. Someone who wishes to be more adventurous in their planting and, by the clever use of bulbs, to add another dimension to their gardening. It is not intended to be an authoritative botanical guide, the bookshelves are already awash with these, but a layman's guide to using bulbs imaginatively in the garden in order to create 'The happy combination of some two kinds of flowers that bloom at the same time and that make either kindly harmonies or becoming contrasts', as Miss Jekyll so aptly put it in 1904.

As gardens decrease in size, so the limited space remaining must be made to work overtime. We cannot delight in the luxury of the 'The Spring Garden', 'The Lime Walk', or 'The Orchard', areas to be visited during March and April, but largely ignored for the rest of the year. The one cherry and two apple trees in the lawn have to double for all these. Likewise, for many of us the herbaceous border is a luxury now precluded by space or labour. For town dwellers shade can be a real problem, but many woodlanders will tolerate deep shade so there is scope for bulbs there too.

As we have created our own garden so I have become very much aware of the lack of imagination that is often encountered regarding the use of bulbs. They are something that is bought in the autumn, and pushed in where there is a gap. There may be a little basic consideration and thought about simple requirements of sun or shade perhaps, but often there is little awareness of how the bulbs will look in late spring in relation to their surroundings, and, even more important, their neighbouring plants. Too often one sees unsympathetic, solid planting (of daffodils and tulips particularly) which may be striking on their own but do not relate to their situation and often cause unsightly problems as they fade, whereas the careful planting of the same bulbs (they can be the cheapest 'special offer' on the market, not necessarily very special varieties) could so easily enhance the whole ambience of the garden. Bulbs can also be used to extend the flowering season, especially into the winter months, or to provide a specific touch of colour and texture to a border.

Rather than approach the subject bulb by bulb, I have chosen to look at areas of the garden and possible associations that may be considered for them. The usual approach is to buy some bulbs and then wonder where to put them. I want to reverse this process and consider the garden first and then choose the bulbs that will enhance that uninspiring border or add a spot of interest to a drab lawn in February. The two approaches are not, of course, mutually exclusive but I feel that my method may encourage experimentation with new varieties.

Throughout this book the term 'bulb' is used in the loosest sense to mean a swollen underground storage organ – corms, true bulbs, tubers, and rhizomes, etc. All are adapted to withstand adverse conditions of heat, drought, or cold and have one thing in common – for part of the year they are completely dormant. In order to withstand this time of inactivity, the bulb must build up its reserves while it is growing, for which the leaves are vital. The importance of this cannot be stressed too much.

Bulbs are essentially ephemeral. Their flowering period can be as long as a few weeks in the early part of the year when the weather is cold, or as short as a few days, but normally they last for about one week to 10 days, depending on the weather. However, their leaves, unlike their flowers, persist for many weeks and very few of these are ornamental in their own right. Severe frost, unexpectedly hot conditions, or more especially, strong winds, can quickly devastate the flowers, leaving an untidy heap of leaves in their place.

However, it is essential that they are left to die down naturally in order to create a strong bulb for the following season, even if they are, to quote Reginald Farrer's graphic description 'flopping in masses of yellow decay'.

It is this mass of slowly dying vegetation littering the border and delaying the cutting of the lawn until it is almost necessary to use a haymaker that has given bulbs a bad name, and in extreme cases gardeners have been known to banish them from the garden altogether. However, if the bulbs are placed with care this need not be an insurmountable problem.

It is impossible to make generalizations about soil type, conditions, alkalinity, etc. preferred by bulbs. They have such disparate requirements that this aspect will be discussed in later chapters in relation to specific bulbs when it is of importance. However, one point should be stressed, and cannot be stressed too often, that of drainage. Most bulbs are found in the areas of the world that experience a Mediterranean climate of winter rainfall and warm, dry summers. Thus they are adapted to withstand long periods without rain. In Britain, in contrast, we have rain throughout the year and often the bulbs do not receive the summer baking they need. In extreme cases, some bulbs are better grown in an alpine house or bulb frame where the watering can be very carefully controlled, but the provision of good drainage overcomes much of the problem. There are, of course, exceptions to this. Our native Lent lily *Narcissus pseudonarcissus*, for example, has adapted to our damp climate and dislikes a hot, dry summer. Indeed, the effect of these on flowering is very noticeable. Our stocks of Lent lily flower poorly the first year they are planted after an artificial dry summer caused by storing the bulbs, but perform well in subsequent years unless there has been a long dry period. Snowdrops behave in a similar manner, as do many woodland bulbs.

Thus the prime consideration when planning a planting scheme must be the compatibility of the plants and their situation. It is impossible to combine the woodland peat-loving trilliums with the sun and limy clay-loving tulips for example. There are tables at the end listing bulbs suitable for each location which give a wide range of compatible bulbs to choose from.

Bulbs are not particularly prone to pests and diseases but, the ubiquitous slug apart, many of the problems are specific to certain genera and are best discussed where appropriate. A general outline of the main problems will be found on page 145.

In any book on creative gardening and associations, colour is of course the single most important factor after compatibility of location. I feel strongly that effects should be planned and schemes that do not work, or plants that do not mix, moved. This does not mean single-colour gardening, although I might give that impression occasionally, nor am I suggesting the opposite. Indeed, I have planned colour borders myself but frequently long to break my own rules and add a contrasting colour to deepen and emphasize the pattern. I have three 'Iceberg' roses into which the blue *Linaria purpurea* has seeded. This tall toadflax can be a dreadful weed but here, in the middle of my white–yellow border, I now let it stay. Its long season of small blue–purple flowers enhance the intense white of the roses so much that it seems churlish to remove it for the sake of purity.

Indeed, the same bed can have two completely different colour schemes at different times of the year. Take, for example, a bed of pink roses underplanted with pink and blue geraniums in summer. In spring, the emerging leaves of many roses are reddish shades and make a good foil for clumps of bright yellow tulips, the whole bed edged perhaps by red and yellow polyanthus or blue grape hyacinths. Thus there is a 'hot' scheme for mid-spring when all the garden seems full of fresh yellow–green, and a softer pink–blue scheme for midsummer.

The simplest and safest planting scheme must be, of course, the single-colour one, such as the beautiful White Garden at Sissinghurst. However, we do not all have the genius of Vita Sackville-West in combining plants of one colour to make an interesting rather than a monotonous picture. Even that garden, wonderful though it is, has its off moments. An easier, simple plan is to mix shades of the same colour – yellow, cream, and white, for example, all combine well in early spring to create a warm, pleasing effect. For a more dramatic picture contrasting colours should be used – blue with white and yellow, scarlet with yellow, pink with white, but try and avoid pink with yellow or orange, the result is discordant – very!

Blue is a superb colour, usually intense

in bulbs such as *Scilla*, *Chionodoxa*, and *Muscari* but, as anyone who arranges flowers will tell you, it is a colour that recedes when viewed from a distance. It therefore requires another lighter, contrasting colour to enhance it. Blue with pink, as in hyacinths, is a soft harmonious combination, reminiscent of sunny summer afternoons, of delphiniums and roses, whereas blue with white or yellow is more vibrant – blue Dutch irises planted among pure white peonies, or yellow irises hovering among blue aquilegias, for example.

Colours also change through the seasons. Not only does the range of colours alter but the same colour changes according to the intensity of the light and the amount of competition from other plants and consequently other colours. Early in the year, when there is little true colour, intense yellow daffodils are at their most magnificent, seeming to glow even on the dullest day. As spring progresses, however, and the trees and shrubs come into leaf, so the predominant background colour switches to shades of yellow–green. Against this background, yellow loses its intensity. White daffodils are now much more striking and yellow ones tend to look rather tired. Thus a colour combination that is dramatic at one season may completely fail at another. Who would ever notice snowdrops in July?

In Taunton there is a fine Georgian house which is painted terracotta. It is most attractive, but not worthy of a second glance until April when the double pink cherry trees in the garden flower. The resultant combination, or rather clash of colours, must surely be one of the most unattractive possible. No amount of planned, sympathetic planting under the cherry trees will ever improve it. Although an extreme case, it does emphasize the importance of the background to any planting scheme. Superb combinations against an unsympathetic backdrop can totally ruin the desired effect. I once saw a simple example of this in a botanic garden. A fine clump of orange crown imperials carefully placed amongst the emerging leaves of sweet rocket (*Hesperis matronalis*) and the grey foliage of common sage (*Salvia officinalis*) was very dramatic when viewed against a chaemaecyparis hedge, but when approached from the other direction the background changed from the dark-green of the conifer to the pink of the flowering currant in the next bed. Immediately the picture changed. What had been a simple effective planting became a muddle of colours.

I am not for one minute suggesting that you should rush out and paint your house white, pink or some other colour to match the latest flower shades, rather that some consideration be made of the background, especially when it is a permanent solid colour, such as brick. Soft pink plants do not look their best against orange–red bricks, as I know from experience. This may not stop us from choosing them, indeed, it may be the only place to plant some of the sun-loving bulbs such as *Nerine* or *Amaryllis* (why is it that they all seem to have pink flowers?) but when it comes to choosing some of the more common bulbs, such as tulips, it is possible to enhance the effect by incorporating the background into the scheme, rather than fighting against it.

The appearance of the garden from inside the house is also of the utmost importance and is an aspect that is frequently overlooked. In most cases there is no clash between the inside decor and the garden beyond, but there are instances when it is possible to enhance the view outwards. For example, when choosing a rose to frame a window it is worth bearing in mind the colour of the curtains or paintwork. The resultant sympathetic combination may be of short duration, but for that time it adds another dimension to the room. We inherited a rather blowsy Victorian rose round the dining-room window which is coincidentally, entirely by accident, exactly the same shade of pink as the pattern on the curtains. In June this serendipity makes the room part of the garden and vice versa. I have noticed a similar phenomenon where a clump of burnished coppery red *Tulipa kaufmanniana* 'Showwinner' was planted beyond French windows, which had a deep red Persian carpet in front of them.

Scent is another very important and often neglected factor to be taken into consideration when planning a planting scheme. It is one of the most difficult things to write about, being virtually impossible to describe, but our lives would be very impoverished without it, and never more so than in the garden. Indeed, it is often the scent drifting on the breeze that prepares the mind for what the eye will see.

Above: Bulbs are very useful for extending the season of interest as at Sissinghurst Castle, where the peony beds are underplanted with the spring-flowering *Ipheion uniflorum* whose pale blue flowers form a pleasing contrast to the deep red peony stems

Left: Herbaceous borders need not exclude bulbs. Here a wide border is edged by a gentle mixture of cream and white to create Gertrude Jekyll's 'kindly harmonies'. *Tulipa fosteriana* 'White Emperor' is mixed with hyacinths, polyanthus, *Euphorbia polychroma* and lemon daffodils

Left: Bulbs are very effective to add depth to a border. Here the planting of *Tulipa* 'Goudoshnik' emphasises the planting around the bird bath and draws the eye towards it

One of my favourite pastimes when taking the dog for his bedtime walk along the lane is to guess what is in flower on the other side of the wall. The scent is often the first indication I have that a particular plant has come into flower.

Much has been written about essential oils in a scientific explanation of scent but an understanding of *how* does not enhance our pleasure in the heavy scent of hyacinths, or the delicate perfume of a jonquil.

Although I do not choose my plants primarily for their scent there are one or two I would not be without. Except for the cream and white ones, I am not very partial to hyacinths, unless they are in bowls indoors, as I find the stout flowers rather top heavy. However, I do adore their perfume and, being congenitally unable to throw anything away, I banish all my ex-indoor bulbs to the depths of a large mixed border where they may flower unseen, but certainly not unnoticed.

Scents are often magnified by the cool air at night, indeed some only appear at night, and this should be remembered when planting near the house or around the patio, etc. I always plant clumps of lilies near my dining-room window and fill a couple of tubs with them for the terrace, in the fond hope that we will have a few fine evenings when their heady scent can be fully appreciated both inside and out.

Bulbs, therefore, cannot be seen in isolation, except perhaps when they are planted in grass. They must form part of the whole picture at any one season, and all have some unique character – shape, colour, texture, or just flowering time – to add. Therefore, most of the associations mentioned in this book will be between bulbs and other plants rather than between bulb and bulb, although, of course, this will happen.

What is a bulb?

So far, little mention has been made as to exactly what I am writing about when I use the word 'bulb'. We all use it in its widest sense to include crocuses, which are corms; anemones, with tubers or rhizomes; as well as the true bulbs of tulips, daffodils, and lilies, each with a very different appearance.

The common factor linking all these disparate plants is that part of them has become modified and swollen to form a store of food so that they can withstand a long period of dormancy during inclement weather, which may be heat, drought, or cold. Bulbous plants are frequently found in areas with relatively extreme climates, where there is only a short favourable growing season, often spring, and this store enables them to grow and flower rapidly.

True bulbs – daffodils, tulips, lilies, fritillaries, nerines, etc. – have a basal plate from which rise two or more fleshy scales which are formed at the base of the leaves. Some bulbs may have a few large scales, like many fritillaries, while the scales of others may be tightly packed in rings, as in daffodils. In the case of lilies, the scales are only loosely attached to the base. In subsequent years these scales are either replaced or move out towards the sides of the bulb where they dry and harden into the 'tunic'. These hard scales are designed to protect the bulb against adverse conditions, and tend to be thickest on bulbs that are natives of the harshest climates, such as tulips.

Some bulbs come from areas of regular rainfall where a protective skin is not so necessary, and it may be completely absent as in the case of lilies, fritillaries, and erythroniums, which makes them very vulnerable, particularly during storage.

Unlike true bulbs, a corm is not a permanent structure but is replaced each year by a new one. In some cases the corms may build up in layers over the years, as is frequently encountered in crocosmias. In the case of crocuses, the old corm shrivels completely and is replaced by new ones on the top.

Corms are swollen stems, usually flattened in shape with a solid centre and covered by a protective tunic. This is formed from the base of the old leaves, and may be smooth or fibrous. If you cut a corm in half, you will see that there is no basal plate and that the growing point is at the top. *Crocus, Colchicum, Crocosmia, Gladiolus*, and *Brodiaea* are all corms.

Tubers are less simple to classify as they may be either swollen stems (*Anemone*) or swollen roots (*Corydalis*), or both (*Cyclamen*). Basically, they are solid structures without tunics, that are not replaced each year. In some genera it is possible to trace the development from thin rhizomes to rounded tubers, depending upon the dryness of the summer. Our native wood anemone has long, thin rhizomes, whereas the anemones of Greece have round tubers to withstand the dryness of their summers.

Rhizomes are swollen stems that creep along the ground, as in the case of irises, or below the ground, as in the case of wood anemones or trilliums.

Very occasionally a plant may combine two methods of storage. The Juno irises have bulbs with thick .tuberous roots which supplement them. Both are necessary. The South African *Eucomis* are similar.

Bulbs can be found in all parts of the world, from the Arctic to the tropics, but in this book I propose to discuss hardy bulbs that are dormant for part of the year. Thus I will not include the half-hardy *Ixia, Tigridia*, etc. that require lifting each autumn, although I have made an exception for *Gladiolus* as it is so popular and the genus does include some hardy members. The word 'hardy' is very difficult to define accurately without resorting to scientific measures. For this book it will be taken to mean a bulb that can survive out of doors in Britain with only the minimum of protection. Most of the bulbs discussed will survive quite happily anywhere in the British Isles, others may be limited to the milder counties, but all will stand a certain degree of frost.

There is also a group of bulbous plants that are evergreen and behave more like herbaceous perennials than bulbs. These are plants like *Dierama* and *Schizostylis* and, once again, these are not covered by this book as there is no season during which they are completely dormant.

I make no apology for the fact that this is a very personal selection from the many hundreds of varieties to be found in catalogues and on garden centre shelves.

Planting bulbs

When to plant

The choice of bulbs depends very much upon the final garden site and, of course, personal preference, but once having made that decision the actual bulbs must be purchased. As with all plants the ultimate performance is closely linked to the quality of the material bought. When buying from a reputable mail-order nursery the bulbs are stored under perfect conditions and will be sent out at the correct time, but buying from shops may be a little more difficult. Bulbs start to appear in the shops from the middle of August for autumn and spring varieties or winter and early spring for the summer-flowering ones. They should be purchased as soon as they are available as the conditions under which they are stored are often not ideal. Other factors, such as direct sunlight, high humidity, or the presence of other vegetable matter, notably fruit, can all cause deterioration in the bulbs which may lead to a subsequent poor performance.

Gardening writers often quote recommended or ideal planting times for bulbs but it is very noticeable that these times have tended to move earlier and earlier in the autumn and are often no more than a convenient time, suiting a lull in trade rather than the bulb's requirements. Most bulbs are designed by nature to withstand a long dormancy and, after all, who wants to dig up their summer bedding in August to plant spring bulbs?

Provided that they are stored in cool, dry conditions the traditional spring bulbs such as crocuses, grape hyacinths, and daffodils can be planted at any time during September and October. We even found, one January, a tray of *Narcissus* 'Sweetness' that had been overlooked. The bulbs, although sprouting, were still firm, so we planted them and had a fine display of golden flowers, albeit a month late.

Tulips do not produce their roots until late in the autumn and are best if planted in a cool soil. They can, therefore, be delayed until late October and even November without harm, even though they may have been received much earlier.

Bulbs that flower during the autumn, notably colchicums, have a very short dormant period and should be planted as soon as they are available, normally from mid-

Left: The stately flowers of *Fritillaria imperialis* are best appreciated on their own

Right: Pure white hyacinths mixed with *Tulipa* 'White Emperor' are used to add lightness and scent to a dark border

August to early September. With many of these autumn-flowering bulbs the first sign of growth is flower production, which can happen before they produce roots or leaves, and frequently occurs in the parcel while it is in the post. This does not harm the bulbs, although it is disappointing to lose one season's flowers, and they should be planted immediately they are received.

Although most bulbs like the dry dormancy of the supermarket shelf that echoes their native dry summers, some, particularly the woodland bulbs, dislike this enforced dry period and it can lead to a poor performance or, in extreme cases, the demise of the bulb. There are two possible solutions to this problem. One is to buy the bulbs as growing plants. Cyclamen and snowdrops are examples of bulbs ideally bought in growth at any time from the autumn to the spring, and they are increasingly offered as such by the many specialist nurseries.

However, some, such as erythroniums and wood anemones, are not suitable for transplanting like this as their shoots are very fragile and are easily damaged. They can be successfully moved in the autumn provided they have been properly stored in damp peat or, best of all, left in the ground and only lifted when required and not left dry in packets or boxes.

There are a few bulbs, especially the Lent lily daffodil and its near relatives, that survive the usual conditions but, resenting the artificial dry dormancy, will refuse to flower until well established in a suitable location. This lack of flowering may occur in other bulbs as well but this is usually due to other factors. Although it is usually present in the bulb when you buy it, the bud will only develop and flower if the subsequent growing conditions are suitable. A check to its growth, especially extremes of temperature or a period of drought, will cause the bulb to abort its flowers and concentrate its energy on replenishing the bulb for the next season. This is very noticeable in late-flowering subjects, such as pheasant's eye daffodils, crown imperials, fritillaries, and lilies, all of which must have ample moisture during late spring. However, most bulbs, woodlanders apart, will flower well in their first year, although their subsequent performance will depend upon your horticultural conditions.

Summer-flowering bulbs do not finish their growing season until late in autumn and are therefore not available until the winter months. They can be divided into those that are hardy, such as lilies, crocosmias, nerines, crinums, and galtonias, and those that need to be lifted each autumn and stored in a frost-free place. These include gladioli, ixias, and many others that do not concern us in this book. The hardy bulbs should be planted as soon as they are available and there is an open period in the weather. Should the weather continue frozen for a long spell, then it is probably best to pot up the bulbs and keep them in a frost-free environment, but not warm, until the weather conditions improve and it is possible to plant them out. Laying the bulbs in a tray, and covering them with peat is an alternative, but they should not be left in a warm atmosphere for too long, or the bulbs exposed to frost. This is especially important for lilies that do not have a protective outer tunic and easily dry out.

Other bulbs that are not completely hardy, nerines, *Amaryllis belladonna*, crinums, and the true non-hardy bulbs such as gladioli, should only be planted when the worst of the weather is past. In cold districts where the growing season is short and late frosts may damage the emerging foliage, the bulbs should be planted out in spring and then protected by a cloche or a mulch of straw or bracken.

Choosing bulbs

Although reputable mail-order nurseries should always supply top-quality and top-sized bulbs, picking out the best, when faced by a vast array in a garden centre or shop, may be a daunting task. Size is difficult to specify as a top-sized miniature variety may well be smaller than the smallest offset of a larger variety. This is especially true of daffodils, where they range from tiny species with bulbs little bigger than a bean to the tall hybrids with bulbs larger than an egg. Tulip bulbs also vary from the small species such as *Tulipa pulchella* to the large Darwin hybrids. If possible, top-sized bulbs should always be purchased as they will usually give better performance than the smaller sizes, and it is worth bearing in mind that some very cheap offers may be of second-size bulbs designated for growing on, and may well take a couple of seasons to settle and flower.

All bulbs, unless actively in growth, should be firm and free from blemishes. The bases especially should be checked for any sign of rot or softness. During storage, bulbs are handled frequently and this can cause bruising which may damage the tissues and lead to attack by fungus. Bulbs without tunics, such as erythroniums and fritillaries, are prone to dry rot, and any bulbs with patches that are dry and corky should be avoided, as should those with areas of soft rot. All bulbs should be clean and dry, but sometimes the conditions can become too warm and humid and if there is insufficient ventilation a surface mildew may appear. Grape hyacinth and scillas are especially prone to this, particularly when they are sent through the post. However, it is unsightly rather than damaging, provided the bulbs are planted immediately.

Whereas many bulbs have very firm protective tunics, others have partial or brittle tunics that are easily dislodged. This is especially true of some of the tulip hybrids and the nanus group of gladioli but it does not matter provided that the underlying bulb is still firm and undamaged.

If it is not possible to plant bulbs as soon as they are obtained, then they should be stored in cool, dry conditions with ample ventilation. Parcels of bulbs received through the post should be opened to allow the air to circulate. Bulbs that require a cool, shady position should be put into damp peat to prevent them from drying out. This is also advantageous for small species daffodils that root early in the autumn.

Some authorities recommend soaking the bulb before planting as a means of breaking the dormancy of very dry bulbs. Whereas this is unlikely to have much effect upon very desiccated ones, for certain bulbs it can be very efficacious, notably for lilies, where there is no tunic to protect the bulb and anemones. These bulbs are very prone to drying out during storage and should be soaked in clean, cold water for one hour prior to planting. All bulbs should be watered once they have been planted if the ground is dry, as their roots are formed immediately and the quality of these will determine the subsequent flowering.

How to plant

Most bulbs, given correct growing conditions, should give as many years' pleasure as perennial plants, and therefore it is worth spending a little time preparing the ground thoroughly before planting. The text, and the tables in particular, give detailed information about planting, but I feel that it is worth outlining the principles.

It cannot be stressed too often that good drainage is essential for all bulbs; even those that require moist conditions cannot survive in waterlogged soils. If your soil is heavy, the addition of sand will aid both rooting and drainage, whereas peat will increase moisture retention on light, sandy soils. For most bulbs the acidity of the soil is not important, but there are one or two exceptions – *Lilium speciosum* needs an acid soil, whereas tulips thrive on an alkaline soil, for example – so it is advisable to check with the tables. These will also indicate the nature of the soils and the situation suitable for each bulb. Those requiring a hot, dry, sunny position will not thrive in a cool, peaty soil in semi-shade and vice versa.

Once having chosen bulbs for a particular location and having prepared the soil thoroughly, some consideration should be given to the ultimate appearance of the bed. Here the single most important fact is height. With early flowering varieties this is not so important as few herbaceous plants are in growth and bulbs can therefore be placed almost anywhere in the border. However, as spring advances so the bulbs must compete with the growing herbaceous plants and it is best to place tall varieties towards the back of the bed with low ones at the front. Late-flowering varieties can be planted in front of early ones to help hide their dying leaves.

It is difficult to make generalizations about planting depths as some bulbs have very disparate requirements. The size of the bulb is often quoted as a guide to planting depth but this can be very misleading. Take, for example, the large tubers of *Cyclamen hederifolium* which need to be planted just below the soil surface, whereas the small bulb of *Iris reticulata* should be 6–8 in (15–20 cm) deep. The tables at the end of the book give detailed information for each species, but the general rule of thumb for the more

ordinary bulbs – scillas, daffodils, crocuses, tulips – is 4 in (10 cm) deep for small
bulbs and 8 in (20 cm) deep for large ones.

The actual method used to plant the
bulbs depends very much upon personal
choice and there is no correct procedure.
Provided that your method works then
there is no reason to change it. The trowel
is probably the quickest and easiest way
for small numbers, although there is a
danger of making the hole insufficiently
deep. This method can be used both in
borders and grass. However, when planting large quantities some other way may
be considered. When planting large groups
in a border it is probably best to excavate
an area to the overall required depth,
loosen the soil at the base, and then press
in the bulbs and refill the hole. This
method has the advantage of avoiding
spearing the bulbs, a thing I frequently do
when planting with a trowel. A similar
method can be followed for large clumps
in the grass, only in this case the turf is
rolled back and then the bulbs planted.
Many people favour bulb-planters, but
unless a good, long-handled one is used
this can be very laborious. However, with
a good planter, two people, one making

the holes, the other planting, can plant a
large number of bulbs in a relatively short
time and it does allow the overall design to
be seen clearly. Careful attention should
be paid to the outline of the clumps, particularly in grass, if they are to appear
natural. It is also advisable to mark each
clump with a stick and label to avoid
spearing the bulbs, especially when weeding later.

It is, of course, not necessary to plant
the same variety in any one area. Although
it is more attractive to have clumps of one
variety in flower at any one time, it is
possible to plant early bulbs with late ones
so that the same area is continually in
flower. Thus, autumn crocuses, snowdrops
with spring crocuses, daffodils, and finally
bluebells could all be planted at the same
time, and even in the same hole if it was big
enough. However, although this succession sounds, and indeed can be, very attractive you must take care that the bulbs
are compatible. Many tulips, for example,
produce large leaves relatively early in the
year which may swamp daffodils before
they flower.

Once the bulbs are planted they should
be watered to encourage the production of

Above: Bluebells should
be kept to the wild areas
of the garden where they
can be mixed with other
woodland plants such as
euphorbias and hellebores

Right: White daffodils
such as 'Geranium' can be
used effectively to draw
the eye along a border

the strong root system that is vital for later performance, and it should also be remembered that water is required throughout the period that they are in active growth. Should a dry spell occur they must be watered regularly otherwise they may become prematurely dormant or abort their flowers.

Most bulbs are completely hardy and require no protection during the winter, but certain half-hardy ones, such as crinum and nerine, especially when newly planted or in colder districts, should be protected with a layer of ashes, straw, or bracken.

For various reasons you may have to lift some bulbs and store them, as when remaking a bed for example, or when growing gladioli. If this is necessary, it should be carried out after the foliage has completely died back. It is advisable to clearly mark the clumps while they are in growth to make this easier. The bulbs should then be spread out, preferably on a wire rack, to dry in a cool well-ventilated place such as a garage. When they are completely dry the soil should be rubbed off, the bulbs checked for any visible sign of damage, and they should be stored so that the air can freely circulate until the correct planting time. Half-hardy bulbs such as gladioli must be kept frost-free. Before replanting, the bulbs should be checked for firmness or rot.

Although the bulbs at the time of buying contain sufficient food for that season's growth, subsequent performance depends upon a replenishment of this store, and they therefore require feeding as do any other plants. However, high-nitrogen fertilizers, especially organic ones such as manure, cause the bulbs to produce soft leaves, which are vulnerable to fungal attack, in preference to flowers. High potash fertilizers (such as the ones produced for tomatoes) are preferable. They can be applied as slow-release granules in the autumn or as a foliar feed during the spring. Bulbs in grass benefit from the application of bone-meal, at the rate of 1 oz per sq. yard (100 g per sq. metre) during the autumn every two or three years.

Provided that care is taken over the initial planting, most bulbs are trouble-free and should give many years of pleasure.

2 Sunny borders

The word border conjures up different pictures in different people's minds. This chapter considers the primarily sunny beds in a garden where bulbs can be combined with a wide range of other plants. They may be the traditional herbaceous border or beds where shrubs or roses and plants are mixed, but the linking factor is that they all receive sun for much of the day. However, I will not include very dry, sun-baked beds beside the house as these will be dealt with in Chapter 5.

The types of bulbs that can be used in these borders vary seasonally and with soil type, but they must all be able to tolerate competition. Early in the year when herbaceous plants are only just emerging, crocuses or other small bulbs are suitable, but as the seasons progress so taller bulbs will be needed – narcissus, tulips, camassias, culminating in the lilies.

When I first began gardening my image of the ideal border in winter was of neat plants and bare, mulched, or well-manured soil. An overriding impression of brownness, which only reached its real glory in midsummer before fading gradually into autumn, and thence into neatness again. Although not always achieved, this is still the ideal for many gardeners. However, if bulbs are included then colour can be added and interest extended, especially if the necessary tidying and mulching is carried out during late autumn. So often I visit a large public garden in late winter or early spring and, while admiring the industry that has been expended, I long for a little more imagination and a touch of colour and interest that could so easily be added by the judicious use of early bulbs. By spring the whole border can be enhanced by careful associations of bulbs and early foliage plants. Many of the summer-flowering bulbs – *Gladiolus*, *Camassia*, *Eremurus*, and galtonias have narrow spikes which are useful to add yet a further dimension and complement the flat heads of many herbaceous plants.

The value of foliage can very easily be ignored, but as flowers are often fleeting it can be almost as important. Some plant associations will inevitably involve true foliage plants such as hostas, but many bulbs flower early in the year before foliage plants emerge and such combinations are consequently not possible. Therefore, bulbs must rely on contrast of texture between plants that are normally considered flowering plants rather than foliage plants. It is quite surprising what a wide range of greens are present in any border in spring. The new foliage of the day lilies (*Hemerocallis*) is a soft yellow–green, whereas the young leaves of roses are frequently red, as are the emerging stems of peonies and phlox. Others, such as *Dicentra*, have soft, ferny foliage which forms an ideal, carpet for bulbs. Bulbs continue to flower well into the autumn and as the true herbaceous flowers decrease in number so their foliage once again plays an important part. Some herbaceous plants take on autumn hues, as do many of the smaller shrubs, opening up the possibility of more combinations.

For the best effect, bulbs should be planted in clumps and not dotted throughout the border. With certain ones, scarlet tulips for example, the effect may be striking, but it is usually a muddle, especially if the border is full of other colours. A single well-placed clump is much more effective and also provides scope for you to add other complementary schemes at a later date. The number of bulbs per clump cannot be dictated as it will vary not only with the stature of the bulbs and the time of year but also with the size of the border. Early in spring, large clumps of *Crocus* and *Narcissus* can be used, but later small numbers will be just as effective. As a rule of thumb, the minimum should be ten bulbs of *Crocus*, *Muscari*, and *Chionodoxa*, five of *Narcissus* and tulips, and three of large alliums, *Camassia*, and lilies.

The main disadvantage of adding bulbs to herbaceous borders is the problem it causes when it comes to forking over the bed in autumn. As the bulbs are normally dormant, it is easy to spike them. Labels are the best method of marking the clumps but I always find that these disappear. However, if bulbs are planted at a sufficient depth, 6–8 in (15–20 cm) or more, then the surface can be lightly forked without damaging the bulbs. Another problem is that of feeding the border, as an excess of manure (which is high in nitrogen) can be damaging to bulbs, causing excess leaf growth and possibly blindness. For this reason I use only a little manure and add a potash-rich fertilizer in spring and a dusting of bone-meal every other autumn. I mulch with composted bark, peat, and my own well-rotted grass cuttings. I may not grow prize delphiniums but I do have colour in the border for nine months of the year.

It is a good idea to observe your garden regularly and note where bulbs could be added to give a lift to a dull patch. One of the best methods is to visit other gardens and borrow ideas. Never be ashamed to copy ideas that work, especially if they are in local gardens with a similar soil and climate. However it can be very difficult, faced with a sad autumn border, to remember exactly where the bulbs already are and where the new ones should go. Ideally, notes should be made and even lables pushed in to mark the spot, as it is only too easy to see a space and think that a clump of pink tulips would look good under that ceanothus and to forget that by the time the tulips flower the following spring the delphiniums in front will completely swamp them.

Remembering just where the existing bulbs are is another major problem when it comes to adding new bulbs, or even plants, in the autumn. In a single-tone bed it doesn't really matter if yellow tulips pop up in the middle of a clump of cream or white ones. Although the effect may not be what you planned, it may be even better. However, brilliant orange tulips in the middle of a soft blue and pink scheme would not be so welcome.

One tempting possibility is to buy bulbs in pots. This overcomes the problem of what and where but it is not really to be recommended for most bulbs. The main disadvantage is the size, or rather lack of it, of the pot in which the bulbs are grown. The pots are usually far too small to provide an adequate root run or for the bulbs to be planted at the correct depth without completely covering them. A depth of 2 in (5 cm) is not deep enough except for the smallest scillas or crocuses, and even these would prefer to be deeper. I have successfully planted *Muscari*, fritillaries, *Crocus*, and *Narcissus* this way, but I would not choose it for preference as

they may not flower for a couple of seasons following transplanting.

It is, of course, possible to plant entire beds solely with bulbs. The traditional method is to mix one variety of bulb with an annual in the manner of many parks departments. This kind of planting can be very effective, if rather formal, in small beds where the bulbs will be replaced in the summer by bedding plants. There are many possible combinations to choose from, some simple and traditional, such as red tulips and blue forget-me-nots, but they could be much more dramatic. Two good examples are the beautiful lily-flowered tulip 'China Pink' rising from a bed of silver and white *Lamium maculatum* 'White Nancy' or pure white daffodils, 'Mount Hood' or 'Ice Follies', above the bronzed purple leaves of *Heuchera* 'Palace Purple'. In each case the planting lasts for a relatively brief period before being replaced. This usually necessitates the removal of the bulbs while they are still in growth and obviously they must be replanted, and well watered, elsewhere in the garden if they are to be kept for another year. Once the leaves have fully died back the bulbs can be lifted and stored. However, they rarely perform quite as well a second year so it is probably advisable to discard them and buy new ones the following autumn. The discarded bulbs can, of course, be planted elsewhere in the garden.

Another less formal type of garden, relying almost exclusively upon bulbs, is the true bulb garden where different varieties are planted in sympathetic clumps to create a succession of flowers from late winter through to early summer. The Lime Walk at Sissinghurst Castle is probably one of the finest examples of these. Here a whole garden is devoted to bulbs, with only a few perennials such as polyanthus and pulmonarias to provide a foil. Although basically a very simple idea, these borders only really work if the colour and flowering sequences and, particularly, heights are very carefully chosen. There is also the problem that for much of the year the soil is left bare, and few modern gardens have the space to create such a seasonally exclusive garden, but it may be an idea to try in a bed around a small tree.

An awareness of the overall picture is very important. Here, *Tulipa* 'Rosy Wings' complements the pink cherry blossom

Winter–early spring

Once the main tidying up has been carried out, many borders remain looking much the same until May, with only the gradually emerging and growing mounds of herbaceous plants to mark the changing season. Judicious use of bulbs can add colour throughout much of this period without disrupting the cultivation too much. The prime fact to remember is to plant the bulbs deeply, so that not only do they often perform better but they are also well below fork level when the border is weeded.

Very few bulbs flower in true winter but as spring approaches so more appear. The earliest to flower are the snowdrops and, although I would not recommend large quantities of the common snowdrop (*Galanthus nivalis*) in the true herbaceous border, in a mixed one they could be planted right under a deciduous shrub, a hydrangea for example, which does not have an attractive naked shape. However, a few clumps of the bolder double snowdrop are very effective towards the back of the herbaceous border. We always mulch the beds with old potting-compost which inevitably includes a few bulbs, and in this way many chance associations have occurred. One that I find particularly attractive is where a few common snowdrops annually pop up through *Stachys lanata* edging a path; the snowdrops look most charming above the grey, felted leaves of the stachys. In the same way, a clump of double snowdrops have put themselves under a large patch of *Lamium maculatum* 'Beacon Silver' used as ground cover at the back of the border. In both these places the situation is not too dry for the snowdrops, and they are remarkably tolerant of disturbance and do not seem to mind summer watering.

In a similar way, snowdrops are most attractive peeping through clumps of heather, either providing interest above one that flowers at a different season or complementing winter-flowering heathers such as *Erica carnea* 'Springwood Pink'. Surprisingly perhaps, snowdrops are even more attractive when mixed with *Erica carnea* 'Springwood White' or other white

heathers. The heathers must be clipped regularly in order to maintain their neat, low shape, otherwise the snowdrops will be invisible amongst the shaggy branches.

One bulb that revels in a dry position is the delightful winter aconite whose bright, golden cups above a ruff of leaves appear in February. I always plant a few clumps at the front of the border to come through the edging plants and add colour early in the year. Their leaves are most attractive and disappear early and relatively neatly. They also don't seem to object to being accidentally dug up during the autumn tidying session. The best time to divide and move clumps is during spring, just after flowering. The North European *Eranthis hyemalis* is more tolerant of damp than the Turkish *Eranthis cilicica*, which needs a hotter, drier position. I try to mix *Eranthis* with clumps of *Crocus* to continue the colour scheme.

Tucked in, like the aconites, among and through edging plants, such as *Geranium* and *Helianthemum*, *Crocus* can be very charming in the early spring border. Its leaves, although lengthening quite considerably after flowering, are not untidy and do not detract from the overall picture or swamp their neighbours. It is among the first true plants of spring and as such is always welcome in every garden, but it must be planted where it receives sun in the middle of the day otherwise the flowers will not open and display their full beauty. This is especially important for bi-coloured crocuses where the outer petals that completely enclose the inner ones are often rather insignificant. It is not until the sun opens them wide that their striking inner colours are revealed. This is especially true of *Crocus corsicus* which is always ignored and overlooked until it opens and is transformed from a discreet cream to an intense lilac. The January-flowering *Crocus imperati* is another that needs sun to reveal its presence.

Sunshine is the main requirement for crocuses, most being very tolerant of soil conditions, although they cannot cope with waterlogged soil. Some of the species crocuses, however, are a little more demanding and require a well-drained position such as a rock garden (q.v.) or raised bed. They should all be planted 4–6 in (10–15 cm) deep and the soil well firmed afterwards to discourage mice.

The yellow of *Crocus*, particularly

Dutch varieties with their strong orange cast, is a difficult colour to associate comfortably with other bulbs, but they are very reliable and most attractive if used on their own. I have seen them in a cottage garden lining a path under deciduous shrubs to create a very striking sight in February. They should be planted 2–3 in (5–8 cm) apart in quite large groups. The first year they are rather thin but they soon fill out to form enormous tightly packed masses that need no disturbance until such time as they fail to flower.

I plant clumps of many yellow crocuses along the edge of my borders, such as the large yellow Dutch crocus, *Crocus chrysanthus* 'E. A. Bowles', *Crocus angustifolius*, etc. The popular *C. ancyrensis* (sometimes called 'Golden Bunch') only really does well in a sunny, well-drained position.

Large clumps of a single variety can be especially effective in a small garden where space is at a premium. I have a friend with a tiny garden that is the epitome of careful planting, each plant having been chosen to complement its neighbours at a particular season. She has made very effective use of two varieties of *Crocus chrysanthus* – 'Snow Bunting' and 'Cream Beauty'. Now increased far beyond the 30 original corms, they form a striking patch of colour in a bed that would otherwise be naked except for the emerging leaves of the herbaceous plants, and the bare twigs of low shrubs.

Some of the soft lavender crocuses are particularly good with silver foliage plants such as *Artemisia schmidtii* or *Lamium maculatum* 'Beacon Silver'. A good variety to use is *Crocus etruscus* 'Zwanenburg' which has small, rounded flowers with a delicate silver sheen to the outer petals. It increases well and does not seem to be attractive to birds. However, as with all crocuses, care must be taken that the surrounding plants do not swamp them. The first appearance of the crocus leaves should be noted and the lamium pruned accordingly. Blue polyanthus added to the group would enhance the blueness. One of the best blue crocuses that I know is *C. chrysanthus* 'Skyline' as it really is sky blue, delicately veined in a darker shade. Its relatively large flowers are well rounded and I mix it with primroses at the foot of a ceanothus. Other reliable blue-shaded crocuses are *C. sieberi* 'Firefly' and *C. s.* 'Vio-

let Queen'. These are virtually indistinguishable, having beautifully rounded flowers in a lovely shade of soft blue–purple with a golden throat. They increase well and are virtually indestructable.

I would not recommend the delicate *C. tommasinianus*. One or two clumps are quite charming but they set copious amounts of seed as well as producing large quantities of tiny offsets, and can soon choke a border with their foliage.

I often plant out old show pots of crocuses but those that have been used in the house can also be used in this way, especially the *C. chrysanthus* varieties with their two-tone flowers and neat rounded shape. Provided they are planted sufficiently deeply, they seem to move very satisfactorily just after flowering, and, of course, it is then possible to tell exactly where a particular clump would be best, something which is not always easy to imagine in September or October when there is still so much other colour in the garden.

One charming mixture is of shades of blue–purple crocuses – *Crocus sieberi* 'Firefly', *C. etruscus* 'Zwanenburg', and *C. chrysanthus* 'Skyline' – with primroses and *Narcissus* 'Dove Wings' under a ceanothus, the whole picture softened by the grey leaves of *Geranium renardii*. As the crocuses fade they are replaced by the large *Hyacinth* 'Delft Blue' which had started life as prepared hyacinths for Christmas flowering and had been planted out some years ago. Their flowers are now much smaller but they have grown into quite a sizeable clump and look very natural among the soft foliage as well as adding their delightful scent.

Blue is very much a colour that is found in late spring but there are two invaluable early blue blubs – *Anemone blanda* and *Scilla tubergeniana* (more correctly and unpronounceably *S. mischtschenkoana*). The scilla is a soft, china blue, almost grey in colour, with a darker stripe to each petal. It is ideal for the front of the border where it can push up through a low carpeting plant such as *Dianthus*, but because the flowers open as soon as they appear above ground, the stems only gradually elongating to 4 in (10 cm), care must be taken that it is not destined to flower unseen. However, it flowers in February and is therefore a most welcome and cheering sight tucked between the plants at the front of

Crocus chrysanthus
'Skyline' with primroses

the border where it will increase quite happily provided it is not too wet in summer. It is also a most welcome meal for slugs who can eat all the flower stems, so precautions must be taken.

Anemone blanda, on the other hand, is never attacked by slugs. It is not an ideal plant for borders, but it can be effective in slightly unusual positions – such as planted on the top of peonies, where it looks most attractive with the new red stems pushing through them. In mild winters established colonies begin to flower in February and they can be tucked with other small bulbs, under deciduous shrubs in a mixed border where their finely divided leaves provide a good contrast to the sword-like leaves of other bulbs. *Anemone blanda* also comes in various shades of pink, magenta, and white, the latter 'White Splendour' being more useful in borders where its large pure white flowers make a bold splash. These normally flower later than the blue form.

Mid-spring

With the advent of March, the general stature of bulbs increases to keep pace with the burgeoning herbaceous plants and daffodils begin to dominate the spring garden.

No plant so epitomizes the end of winter than the first daffodils. They are a welcome sign that finer weather should at last be on the way. Indeed, there is a splendid planting of daffodils on an embankment near Bristol that never fails to cheer me as it literally spells out, in yellow daffodils, 'spring is sprung' in 10-foot-high letters.

Few gardens are without daffodils and their intense colour is most welcome early in the year. The principle colour is at first golden and this luminous warm yellow seems to glow, even on dull, overcast days, and is most effective if used sparingly in borders. One or two clumps thoughtfully placed are much better than the random dotting about of twice the number of bulbs which, even if only one variety is used, still creates a muddled impression.

Daffodils are often banished from herbaceous borders because, as with all bulbs, their leaves continue to grow after flowering. If the bulbs are to continue to flourish and flower vigorously in future years, the leaves must be allowed to die down naturally and, inevitably, untidily. Some gardeners try to overcome this by tying the leaves in knots or bending them over and tying with string. This may make them tidier but is actually harmful as it damages the tissues and prevents the nourishment in the leaves from replenishing the bulbs for the next season.

This problem means that in the border and other more formal schemes care must be exercised when planting daffodils, bearing in mind that for at least six weeks after flowering the leaves could be a nuisance. However, it should be possible to arrange clumps so that the emerging foliage of other plants will obscure the leaves or, by flowering, distract attention from them. Daffodils are very effective if planted in groups at the back of the border, especially early varieties that flower before many plants have made much growth, where their dying leaves will be hidden by the growing plants in front. You must also remember to remove the seed-heads, as most daffodils are hybrids and do not come true from seed, especially as tests have shown that leaving the seed head detracts from the ultimate bulb size. The faded heads also attract attention to themselves, whereas once they are removed the leaves blend into the background and become virtually invisible.

Early varieties are particularly welcome, and well-placed groups serve to draw the eye along the often bare border, adding depth as well as interest. The *N. cyclamineus* hybrids are of particular value in this situation as they flower early and have delightful, delicate flowers, often with narrow trumpets and swept back petals, and their small stature and tolerance of early spring weather make them ideal for use in all borders. 'February Gold' and 'Peeping Tom' are amongst the earliest to flower, but I find the strong yellow colouring a little harsh and prefer to use them in mixed borders among evergreen plants such as hebes. A clump of either can be used to soften architectural features such as gates or seats, where they look most attractive early in the year.

I must admit to a particular fondness for 'Dove Wings' with its lemon cup and white petals, and the similar 'Jenny' where the whole flower fades to a uniform cream. Both of these daffodils have a soft, delicate colour, a neat shape, and, perhaps most important, they increase well. In certain lights they have an almost ethereal grey appearance, particularly when viewed in twilight. They are especially effective in clumps at the back of a border which is backed by a dark hedge or wall, or tucked in under the variegated sea buckthorn, where their creamy flowers match the grey variegated leaves beautifully.

It is always difficult to advise on the size of clumps to be planted, but ideally they should not be too small, 10 or 15 bulbs being best for the smaller border but correspondingly larger groups will be necessary in large beds. It is much better to limit yourself to a sensible quantity of one or two varieties each year rather than buy a few bulbs of many varieties, especially as it is always possible to add a new variety in subsequent years to increase the range. I always try, often unsuccessfully I must admit, to study the garden and note any dead areas that need filling and the type of daffodil – its colour, height, or flowering time – that would be most suitable, for it is much easier to do this while the daffodils are in flower than to wait until the autumn and then try to remember just which variety would look best, and where.

Although it is difficult to be precise with such a diverse genus, most daffodils should be planted 4–6 in (10–15 cm) deep and about 2–3 in (5–8 cm) apart, depending upon their size. On light soil it is advisable to plant the bulbs deeper still, at 6 in (15 cm). Within three years the clumps should fill in and they can then be left alone for about 10 years with no further attention, until they become so congested that flowering is impaired, when they must be lifted, divided, and replanted. This is traditionally done in the autumn, but should it be necessary it can be carried out in late spring when the leaves have turned yellow but not quite disappeared. In this way it is easy to spot the clumps, and any damage to the roots will be of little importance. Replanting need not take place immediately and the bulbs can be stored in a well-aired place, such as a garage, and planted out in the autumn in the usual way. Alternatively, they can be immediately replanted back in the same place, but the ground should be well dug first and any damaged bulbs must always be discarded as they may lead to fungal attacks. A handful of bone-meal can be

beneficially incorporated into the planting hole. The dwarf varieties of daffodils (hybrids not the species, which have special cultural requirements), can be effectively used towards the front of the border. Although their leaves grow much longer after flowering, they tend to be much narrower and more grass-like and are therefore not so intrusive. In semi-shaded positions that are not too dry the golden 'Tête a Tête' and 'Jumblie' are enchanting in early March, followed by 'Sundial' and 'Lintie' in April for sunnier spots. I am particularly fond of the slightly taller 'Jack Snipe', which has delicate flowers of pure white and lemon and is very good with variegated plants such as a small-leaved *Hebe glaucophylla* 'Variegata' or *Astrantia major* 'Variegata'. I always mix cream and yellow polyanthus with it and, by adding the later-flowering *Tulipa fosteriana* 'White Emperor' ('Purissima') to the group, extend the flowering season well into April. This tulip, with its enormous flowers on 12 in (30 cm) stems, opens a creamy yellow but gradually fades to pure white, and in the cool days of spring can last for a long time.

Some of the golden daffodils are rather harsh in colour and are not always easy to place satisfactorily, although I have seen them looking good with *Brunnera macrophylla* – a classic mixture of blue forget-me-not flowers and yellow daffodils that is still very pleasing. Lemon shades are much softer and associate well with the acid green that frequently characterizes the new herbaceous foliage – especially that of day lilies. I once saw the beautiful pale lemon 'Binkie' planted right through a bed of day lilies and tall bearded irises, the whole forming a lovely soft picture. The taller, similarly coloured 'Spellbinder', could be used in the same way. For a slightly shorter daffodil with a more intense lemon colour 'Liberty Bells' could be used. It is a *N. triandrus* hybrid, usually having two nodding flowers per stem, and it forms most attractive clumps and has the almost luminous quality shared by primroses in twilight. I plant it by my front door where it is a joy beside the grey wall, but it might not be so good against red brick.

There are many white triandrus hybrids available which are ideal for associating with the rather intense pink that begins to dominate the garden in April as bergenias, *Prunus* (cherry), camellias, and some of the

The creamy cyclamineus
hybrid daffodil 'Jenny' is
very useful for early colour
in the border

early rhododendrons burst into flower. 'Rippling Waters' is a particularly fine white with a lovely, stiff grey foliage. 'Tresamble' is one of my favourites and it is very similar to 'Rippling Waters' but the cup is more creamy. Both are excellent with the grey leaves of rosemary and lavender.

While on the subject of pink in the spring garden, I feel strongly that daffodils and camellias or rhododendrons do not mix. The rather harsh yellow of the daffodils tends to make the camellias appear anaemic, and white ones provide a rather stark contrast. It may be possible to mix the pink cup varieties such as 'Foundling', but so often the pink-cupped daffodils have a touch of orange and the result is a colour clash rather than a harmonious blend. One of the problems with tall daffodils is that most rhododendrons and camellias have flowers almost down to ground level and therefore they are much better underplanted with low-growing bulbs. There are many bulbs that are much more suitable than daffodils for mixing with rhododendrons (see Chapter 3).

Coinciding with the peak of the daffodil season is the emergence of what I loosely term the 'blue' bulbs – *Chionodoxa*, *Scilla*, *Muscari*, and *Hyacinthus*. These all have intense blue flowers which are useful to provide good contrasts to the yellow of daffodils.

The much maligned grape hyacinth genus contains many fascinating and unusual members that are just as easy to grow and that do not suffer from the prodigious increase normally associated with them. However, the humbler *Muscari armeniacum* can be used to great effect as few other bulbs give such a concentrated display of blue. It is best planted in a mass where its spreading can be limited, or at least controlled. For instance, I have seen it effectively edging rose beds in a traditional formal rose garden where the bare beds of pruned roses look very stark and clinical in early spring. An edging of grape hyacinths not only adds colour and interest most effectively, but later their straggling leaves, so much a nuisance in other contexts, is actually an advantage in softening the edges of the bed. I have even seen them used in a very narrow bed between a hedge and the pavement where they have survived unscathed the vicissitudes of feet, dogs, and bicycles. During

their brief summer dormancy their place is taken by a pink oxalis which also copes very well with the unprepossessing location.

Chionodoxas and the small *Scilla sibirica* provide one of the most intense blues encountered in the garden. Having very neat shapes they are perfect for massing at the edge of a bed, although scillas in particular really need a lighter-coloured plant as a foil. The chionodoxas, on the other hand, provide their own contrast by having a pure white centre to the flower. Both of these are ideal for planting on top of late-emerging plants, such as peonies, or with shrubs such as roses or *Berberis* where they tone rather well with the often red stems and foliage. The addition of pink, possibly in the shape of a hyacinth, the purple of 'Bowles mauve' wallflower, or red, as in polyanthus, would enhance the picture still further, especially if a grey-toned plant was incorporated, such as *Geranium renardii* or one of the artemisias.

Peonies emerge from their winter sleep later than many other herbaceous plants, leaving a rather empty gap in the border, with just red buds showing. It is perfectly possible to overplant the peony crowns, provided that it is carried out with great care as they resent being damaged, with various small spring bulbs, not only to add interest, but also to contrast with the emerging red stems. The bulbs will be dormant by the time the peonies flower, and the peony foliage will help keep the bulbs dry during their summer dormancy. The pure white versatile *Anemone nemorosa* (wood anemone) can be used in this way, but as it can become rather invasive the double form is probably better. The blue flowers of *Anemone blanda* or the glistening form 'White Splendour' would provide a good contrast to the red, as would *Scilla sibirica* or any of the chionodoxas. At Sissinghurst Castle the peony beds are most effectively underplanted by clumps of the soft blue *Ipheion uniflorum* 'Wisley Blue', a beautiful South American bulb which produces masses of flowers throughout the spring. Herbaceous euphorbias such as *E. griffithii* 'Fireglow' can be treated in much the same way.

One of my favourite euphorbia and bulb associations is that of *E. myrsinites*, with its vivid lime-green bracts (they look like flowers), and *Muscari latifolium*, which is a really arresting combination suitable for a sunny, well-drained border. *M. latifolium* has flowers of deep blue, almost black, at the base, and a paler top.

Grape hyacinths and scillas need not be limited to blue, and, indeed, they are probably best when mixed with the white form as they give a lift to what can be a solid mass of blue. I particularly like the neat, pure white of *M. botryoides* 'Album' combined with the strong blue of *Scilla sibirica* 'Spring Beauty'. Coupled with primroses and cream or white polyanthus, they form a perfect edging for borders or for planting in front of evergreens. I make no apology for my continual recommendation of polyanthus and primroses as they are among the most reliable and undemanding of spring plants and are excellent for mixing with so many spring bulbs.

Although it flowers much later, the tall white Spanish relation of our bluebell can, if used with discretion and circumspection, be most effective in borders when used as a focal point, especially where shrubs and herbaceous plants are grown together. I have seen large drifts of *Scilla campanulata* 'La Grandesse' throughout a border where the main colour would be much later in the summer, but I prefer to see them in one tightly packed clump strategically placed, such as in front of *Paeonia mlokosewitchii* whose beautiful, cream, tissue-paper flowers supersede the scilla.

I find that delightful dwarf grape hyacinth, *Muscari azureum* (*Hyacinthus azureus*) really does live up to its name as it has flowers of the most intense turquoise. I use it liberally at the very edge of my border from whence it has rather generously spread its progeny into the neighbouring gravel path. However, the seedlings are easily transplanted to another location and the colour is so beautiful that I really forgive them their generosity. Mine have been rather overtaken by an enormous plant of *Daphne cneorum* 'Eximea', and the resulting combination of pink and turquoise is exquisite.

The true tall hyacinths are always difficult to place successfully in the garden without making it too formal as they are rather top heavy. However, if left in the garden for a few years their flower size deteriorates in a most welcome fashion, becoming much smaller and more graceful. I have found one of the blue-coloured hyacinths, 'Ostara' or 'Delft Blue' particu-

larly good following crocus, among *Lamium maculatum* 'Roseum' and *Geranium renardii* in front of my large clump of *Alstroemeria ligtu* hybrid, where the emerging leaves have a fine glaucous bloom. Blue polyanthus and the small turquoise *Muscari azureum* could be added to the group, with a touch of lightness provided by primroses or cream polyanthus as well as the white form of *M. azureum*. This grouping is an ideal mixture for the front of a border, with perhaps the cream being echoed in a clump of tall daffodils behind, such as 'Dove Wings' or 'Jenny' that flower at the same time. Although both these daffodils are yellow and white, fading to cream with age in the case of 'Jenny', from a distance their overall effect is of a creamy lemon.

Bowls of hyacinths that have been forced for the house can be used in this way. The big advantage of planting them after flowering is that they are added to the garden at the time they would normally be in flower and you can therefore see the contrasts or harmonies that could be created. I particularly like the combination of white hyacinths, 'Carnegie' is very good, followed by the late-flowering creamy 'City of Haarlem' mixed with the creamy white *Tulipa fosteriana* 'White Emperor'. Placed where they can be seen with the sun behind them the effect is truly eye-catching, even if you have to stand in the border to achieve it!

I have also seen hyacinths edging a bank of shrubs along a drive most attractively. They were planted in clumps backed by a wide variety of daffodils, which were also ex-house plants. In the summer months the border would be filled by annuals for a continual display of colour. Although most of the hyacinths were blue and white, the introduction of the occasional pink one almost destroyed the harmonious picture of blue, white, and yellow. Pink can be a very difficult colour to place in the garden in early spring when there is such a preponderance of strong yellow. This is unfortunate as the pink hyacinths are probably my favourite for indoors and there is always a recurring problem of where to plant them next. I would suggest mixing them, along with blue and white varieties, with other reddish-toned plants, such as bergenias, *Geranium macrorrhizum*, or the young growth of *Phlox*, perhaps under a plant of *Ceanothus impressus*.

Left: The double-flowered *Muscari* 'Blue Spike', mixed with the golden pansy 'King John' make a brilliant grouping for the front of a border

Right: An eye-catching planting in the white garden at Tintinhull House. *Tulipa* 'White Emperor', artemisias and *Helictotrichon sempervirens*

White daffodils could be added to provide a little extra height and brightness, and blue-toned foliage such as *Sedum spectabile* could be used to provide a contrast in texture.

No herbaceous border should be without its tulips, and this is especially true in the early spring when, long before the familiar tall varieties are ever in bud, there is a whole range of dwarf hybrids available based upon the species. Given suitable growing conditions (well-drained soil in a sunny position) these are excellent for the edge of the border, some of them being tall enough to be planted towards the back from where they will be followed by the more traditional varieties later in April and May.

The earliest are *T. tarda* and *T. urumiensis*, both of which produce two or three yellow and cream flowers on 3 in (8 cm) tall stems. They are best tucked in among low plants at the edge of the border where they will give many years of service. The *kaufmanniana* and *greigii* hybrids are slightly taller, at 6–10 in (15–25 cm), and these also flower a little later. Their colours are bold, frequently bi-coloured, and there is often a strong orange hue in their reds, which can make them a little difficult to place, although I have seen the white and red *T. k.* 'Hearts Delight' beautifully combined with a large clump of silver variegated grass *Carex trifida*. The *fosteriana* hybrids, on the other hand, can be much taller and contain some of the most reliable and useful of all early tulips, the Emperor range. 'White Emperor' ('Purissima'), with its huge flowers, is quite stunning in a mixture of silver and grey plants. 'Yellow Emperor' ('Candela') is a very bold colour and is superb with purple foliage such as berberis or peony leaves. I have it mixed with *Doronicum plantagineum*, where the two yellows mingle quite happily. 'Red Emperor' ('Mme Lefeber') could be added to the group for a really eye-catching effect of yellow and scarlet.

The crown imperials (*Fritillaria imperialis*) are such beautiful plants that they must be planted where their statuesque characteristics can be fully appreciated, in groups in a border where they can tower over their neighbours, otherwise much of their architectural beauty is lost. Each bulb produces a 3 ft (1 m) stem topped by a cluster of several large nodding flowers which may be clear yellow, 'Lutea Maxima', orange,

'Aurora', or bronze-red, 'Rubra'. The flower-head is topped by a tuft of leaves that gives it its name crown imperial. The individual flowers are well worth a close examination as they have very prominent white nectaries, each containing a glistening drop of nectar. There is a delightful story told that at the Crucifixion it failed to bow its head to Christ and that it has cried with shame ever since.

Crown imperials are not always easy to establish but, if you are successful, they are long lived. They will grow happily in full sun or semi-shade and can even be naturalized in grass but their prime requirement is for a deep soil, rich in humus and well-rotted manure, that does not become sun-baked in summer. They are greedy bulbs and must be mulched with more leaf mould, peat, and well-rotted manure every autumn, when a dusting of bone-meal is also beneficial. Their seed-heads, although very handsome and excellent for flower arranging, greatly weaken the bulbs, and it is better to forgo them and remove the seed pods once the flower has faded.

If you examine the large bulbs, you will find that the large scales clasp each other, leaving a gap in the middle where the previous season's stem was and from where the new one will emege. There is a danger that this will fill with water, causing the bulb to rot, so they should be planted on their sides at least 6 in (15 cm) deep and with 12 in (30 cm) between the bulbs.

When really happy they can form enormous clumps that should be left undisturbed unless they begin to deteriorate. It is best to divide the clumps as soon as the leaves have dried as the bulbs root very early in the year and they are easily damaged if you divide them in the autumn. Indeed, accidental damage, coupled with slugs, is my main problem. The dormant clumps must be labelled clearly as it is the gap left by their departure that attracts first the weeds and then the careless weeder.

Much is said about their scent, likened by some to foxes and others to cats, but I must admit that I am rather fond of it and do not find it at all objectionable, but then my family always says that I have strange tastes! The smell is only really apparent when the leaves first appear, and a clump in full flower is quite odourless.

Although crown imperials are probably at their best when seen above foliage, when their individual beauty can be really appreciated, they can be mixed with other flowers. The white-flowered honesty, especially the perennial one, *Lunaria rediviva* is a very good companion for the deep orange 'Rubra', and I have seen a most beautiful combination of 'Lutea Maxima' with the lemon *Narcissus* 'Binkie' underplanted by vivid blue chionodoxas. The background was a yellow ivy-covered wall with bold clumps of *Acanthus* leaves. This group was truly spectacular as so many bulbs are, when viewed with the sun behind it.

Having such a bold shape, it is only necessary to plant them in small groups of three or five. Indeed, it is a case where small (in number) is beautiful, and in massed plantings, as sometimes seen in public gardens, the bulbs loose their individuality which is their major strength and beauty.

The other fritillary that is suitable for the border is *F. persica* which is usually encountered in the form that is grown near the Turkish town of Adiyaman. Its tall stems of grey leaves are topped by a fine spike of purple–black bells, each with a plum bloom. E. A. Bowles describes them as 'bronze bells wrought by some Japanese artist' but sadly, although very beautiful, they rarely perform well in this country. They need a well-drained, rich soil in full sun and, if you can achieve it, they look spectacular above and through grey-leaved plants.

Late spring–early summer

As spring progresses so the first herbaceous plants flower, opening up a further range of exciting associations. This is coupled with the main flush of bulbs, and there is such an enormous range that I can only scratch at the tip of the iceberg of possible combinations.

The months of late April and May are dominated by the taller hybrid tulips, when it seems as though every garden disappears under a sea of brilliant red and yellow. They are the brightest of all spring bulbs and are available in a range of colours unsurpassed by almost any other. The early single tulips begin flowering in the second half of April and the varieties continue through until late May with the single late tulip (formerly known as Darwin tulips). As each type is available in a wide range of colours there are tulips suitable for virtually every colour scheme, from soft pastel to strong primary. Their shape is also variable, many having the traditional cup-shape, but there are beautiful lily-flowered varieties, and those with fringed petals, as well as double ones. A list of the divisions will be found in the tables at the end of the book.

These tulips require a deep, rather heavy soil that is limy, and the latter requirement is most important as on acid soils they rarely persist beyond one or two seasons at the most and where they should be regarded as annuals and new clumps added every year.

One of the secrets of successful tulip growing is to plant them really deeply, 6 in (15 cm) to 8 in (20 cm) is ideal, although in the wild in Central Asia they can be found up to 18 in (46 cm) deep. My soil is very dry and hungry and we find that tulips do not persist for much longer than three years, those, that is, that I do not 'spear' when cultivating the border. By planting a few new clumps of similar colours each year I thereby ensure their continuity, though I am sure that one of my reasons for failure is lack of persistence in excavating a sufficiently deep hole. However, by adding a new variety in a toning shade exciting new harmonies are always being created.

Ideally the soil, although fairly heavy, must be well drained, as waterlogged soils cause rotting in winter and poor ripening of the bulb in summer. In wet soils it is advisable to lift the bulbs once they have died down and then store them in a cool, well-aired place, until replanting them in the autumn. This ensures an adequate baking period that is necessary to promote next season's flowers. Storing can also be carried out where tulips form part of a bedding plan and the land is required for annuals during the summer. Only the large bulbs should be replanted as the smaller ones are unlikely to flower in their first season. However, I find this a tiresome chore and would rather leave the bulbs in the ground to take 'pot luck', especially as they look much more natural as they begin

Tulips dominate the late spring garden. *T. 'Preludium'* with lavender and rosemary

to clump up and loose their stiff, newly planted appearance and even spacing. Their flower size may not be as large but I feel it is more attractive that way, when combining tulips as part of an overall scheme. Like so many bulbs, the seed-heads should be removed as soon as the petals drop, in order to maximize the bulb size.

One of the main drawbacks of these taller tulips is their inherent stiff nature, standing up to attention like soldiers on parade. This can make their incorporation into a scheme with other plants difficult. Some of the older hybrids were much less stiff but sadly their 'at ease' tends to be total collapse within a few days. I am particularly fond of *Tulipa* 'Rosy Wings' which is a single late tulip with gently flaring flowers of a beautiful soft salmon, with just a hint of lavender shading. It is virtually indestructible and I know one garden where it has been increasing steadily for more than 25 years. However, within a few days of opening the stems contort and the tulips collapse to the ground in a heap. This is not so important if planted through a supporting plant such as *Brunnera macrophylla*, with its clusters of bright blue forget-me-not flowers, or the early flowering *Geranium malviflorum*, which has large, beautifully veined lilac flowers and the tangled combination of tulip and geranium is most attractive. 'Palestrina' is a similar shade to 'Rosy Wings' but is shorter and therefore less liable to recline in such an undignified, although utterly delightful manner.

Tulips need little attention beyond a light dressing of potash in early spring, before the leaves appear, which could be applied as a general fertilizer for the whole bed. They will also tolerate well-rotted manure or compost. However, the ubiquitous slug can cause much damage to the leaves, ultimately weakening the plant as well as leaving it unsightly, so precautions are advisable. In a true herbaceous border, tulips, like all bulbs, can cause cultivation problems when they are dormant, but if space is at a premium all borders must be made to work overtime. Even if you are a purist, it is possible to tuck a clump towards the back, or at one end, to make an impact. I even saw a narrow bed of tall bearded irises planted with clumps of the scarlet 'Apeldoorn'. They looked most spectacular with the light behind them

rising above spikes of light green iris leaves. I like to plant tulips liberally throughout the border, always planting in groups of five as a minimum, using toning colours, and I am very careful to ensure that I plant a few of the early varieties as well as the later ones to ensure a succession of colour. They can, of course, be mixed together so that the 'same' clump is in flower throughout April and May. For example, the pure-yellow, early 'Bellona' followed by the late, creamy 'Sweet Harmony', or the salmon-pink 'Elizabeth Arden' with the almost black 'Queen of the Night'. In each of these cases the two colours tone together so that it does not matter if it is an early spring and their flowering overlaps, but to avoid a messy transition period the dying heads should be removed as soon as they fade. In the same way, tulips and *Narcissus* can be planted in the same clump. Although they may not co-habit in a vase, they are quite content to in the garden. We have had one clump of multi-headed daffodil 'Geranium' mixed with the scarlet *T.* 'Apeldoorn' for the past 16 years. They are planted in a tiny bed by the back door which receives afternoon sunshine only. As the pure white narcissus, with its small orange cup, fades it is replaced by the scarlet tulip. This very harmonious picture is enhanced by the variegated *Euonymus* 'Emerald 'n' Gold' behind them, and the scent of the daffodil is an added bonus!

Traditionally, tulips are mixed with forget-me-nots or wallflowers, and fine displays are produced by parks departments in every town. Magnificent though they are, these are of limited value to the gardener for whom time, as well as space, is at a premium. Narrow beds bordering the front path could be treated in this way, with the purple 'Maytime' above creamy wallflowers, or the pink 'Clara Butt' and forget-me-nots, for example. As the bulbs fade so they are lifted and stored through the summer and the beds replanted with annuals. Although this involves much effort, the results are always colourful. However, simpler, time-saving schemes, can be just as effective, if in a quieter way. While driving through London I saw a small front garden pleasingly planted with small conifers and hebes – some carpeting, others low hummock forming, providing low-maintenance evergreen framework of varying shapes and shades of green. What drew my attention to the garden was the careful planting of clumps of scarlet tulips at irregular intervals along the beds, transforming a pleasing garden into an arresting one.

Scarlet can be a very difficult colour to integrate successfully into a garden, and this is especially true of the ubiquitous red tulips, usually 'Apeldoorn' or 'Kaiserkroom', which seem to be present in almost every garden – many, I suspect, like mine, the result of a successful coffee promotion! This strong colour demands bold handling otherwise the effects can be very muddled. I love to see scarlet tulips in big clumps rising up from the soft new foliage of the herbaceous borders – aquilegias are particularly good companions with their delicate ferny leaves – or planted boldly among golden doronicums, whose flattened heads and strong yellow are a very good foil for the globular tulips. The bright green of new foliage in the spring garden lends itself to the addition of scarlet tulips, and I think that it is as visual punctuation marks that they excel. I know one lovely garden where tulips are used in a breathtaking manner, none more so than a huge clump of a scarlet *T. fosteriana* hybrid at the end of a long path leading into a lightly shaded area. The tulips made a dramatic focal point for the garden, pulling the visitor towards them and along the path. Another good combination was a mixture of *T.* 'Couleur Cardinal', with its deep red flowers above dark foliage, mixed with 'Princess Irene' which is almost tan, veined deep red and, incidentally, repeats well. These were in a narrow bed at the foot of an enormous *Prunus serrula*, and the colour of the tulips echoed perfectly that of the polished bark of the tree.

The traditional herbaceous border with its neat, regimented mounds of emerging herbaceous plants can be dramatically altered by the addition of a few well-chosen tulips. Add a few of the early flowering plants and the whole border can be as colourful as later in the summer. Soft pink tulips, especially my favourite – the lily-flowered 'China Pink', can be planted to rise through a sea of *Dicentra eximea* 'Alba' with its grey ferny foliage and dangling white lockets. A plant of *D. spectabilis* 'Alba' in the background would add a little height by continuing the white theme up to the tulips. There are so many colours available that a tulip can be found to match almost any scheme. They should be planted in groups of five–30, depending upon the space available and the effect required. A few can be used to emphasize a colour grouping or to add a contrast. In one garden a path was edged with blue *Brunnera macrophylla* and the overall blueness was relieved by a small clump of deep plum coloured *Tulipa* 'Purple Star' that continued the deep red of the new growth of the peonies in the bed behind. A completely different effect would have been created by using a soft lemon tulip such as 'Sweet Harmony' and backing the brunnera by lime-green *Euphorbia robbiae*.

This effect of changing the overall appearance of a plant by adding differing contrasting plants was illustrated in one garden where a narrow path dissected a wide bed liberally planted with *E. robbiae*, herbaceous geraniums, and hostas. On one side of the patch the bed was backed by a large golden berberis and golden tulips were scattered through the bed, emphasizing the acid-green of the euphorbias and giving a general yellow cast to the whole bed. On the other side of the path the contrast could not have been greater. Here the same basic group of plants was backed by a group of dark camellias and the yellow tulips had been replaced by soft salmon-pink ones. The euphorbias suddenly became much greener, blending into the surrounding foliage.

Vibrant colours, especially those in the orange–yellow range, can be very useful to bring an interesting, but rather flat, planting alive. The extraordinary 'Queen of Sheba' is a lily-flowered tulip in an intense mixture of browny-red and yellow. When seen in isolation I am not certain that I like its gaudy colouring, but a few strategically placed in front of a rather ordinary *Berberis thunbergii* 'Aurea', become quite electrifying. In the same way, the single, yellow *Kerria japonica* charmingly underplanted by creamy 'Sweet Harmony' and purple ajuga comes alive with the addition of a clump of 'Gudoshnik' with its huge orange flowers flecked with red. Even on a dull, sunless day both make striking pictures but when the sun does shine the colours appear to vibrate.

The addition of pure white tulips, 'White Triumphator' is one of the most beautiful, to grey and silver plants creates a picture of cool, classic charm. The tulips can be followed by *Lilium regale* and white

Right: The tall creamy spikes of *Eremurus himalaicus*, dominate the early summer garden and are best seen against a dark background

Left: Late spring interest has been given to this attractive yellow border by the addition of *Tulipa* 'Queen of Sheba'

delphiniums to continue the picture. White tulips are also useful for adding a touch of lightness to an otherwise dull area of evergreens where the interest comes later in the year.

It is very important to look up as well as down when planning colour combinations, as this is the month when many trees and shrubs come into flower and their colours must also be taken into consideration. This is especially so as April progresses and the flowering cherries begin to dominate many gardens. The white or very pale pink cherry blossom blends well with most other colours but the strong sugar pink one needs very careful handling. It is probably best to keep to a similar pink shade coupled with blues and whites when underplanting them. Yellow should certainly be avoided if possible. This means, of course, that late yellow daffodils should not be included in one of these beds. However, I have observed over the years that our daffodil field displays a noticeable change of colour as spring advances. Early in the year, when the light is weak, the strong golds predominate with hardly any white present at all, but as spring progresses so the field becomes evenly split between white and yellow, until April when white becomes the predominant colour, at a time when increased sunlight and the presence of many other colours in the garden all serve to make the yellow daffodils seem rather faded.

I love the glistening purity of sunlight upon a well-placed clump of white daffodils, 'Tresamble' or 'Mount Hood', beside a narrow conifer for instance, or tucked in at the back of a border, to rise up above the lower plants in front of them.

One plant that has no problem in dominating any border in which it is planted is *Eremurus*, or foxtail lily. Although a member of the lily family, it is not really bulbous but its long period of dormancy and frequent inclusion in bulb catalogues warrants it a mention here. Foxtail lilies have an enormous growth of thick, fleshy roots that can be as much as 2 ft (61 cm) across when mature. They need a sunny, well-drained position and will not cope well with cold, waterlogged soils. As the crowns are planted just below the surface it is a good idea to mulch them with ashes to protect them against severe frost, although I do not find that necessary on my dry soil. Their height, 6–7 ft (1.8–2.1 m) means that only a few are needed for a really bold impact, and they should be planted towards the back of the border. Various colours are available, but in all cases they are best viewed against a dark background, as in a hedge, or towering above the border. I grow the creamy white *E. himalaicus* above the shorter lemon spikes of *Asphodeline lutea*, with a white, tall bearded iris to complete the picture. *E. robustus* has flowers of a clear pink, good for planting behind soft blue and deep purple iris, whereas the most commonly offered Shelford hybrids are available in a wide range of rich colours, varying from bronzy yellows to palest pink. They are excellent when seen rising up from the flat purple-hued leaves of *Ligularia dentata* 'Desdemona'. However, the sheer size of their crowns, coupled with their long dormant period, means that they should be planted with some other, more feathery, plant to flop over the large gap that will be left in the border from late June. My clump is immediately behind the 'Iceberg' roses which effectively hide the naked space, and in a mild winter the creeping white daisy, *Anthemis cupaniana*, which is a ground cover for the roses, frequently spreads round them as well, but avoid too heavy cover or the eremurus will fail to flower.

Towards the end of May and the middle of June there is a period when the garden seems to be dominated by blues and purple, with tall bearded irises in all shades, *Clematis*, *Ceanothus*, geraniums, and aquilegias. Among them are the blue spikes of the camassias, particularly *C. quamash* (previously known as *C. esculenta*, meaning edible, for these were eaten by the North American Indians). These graceful 3 ft (1 m) spikes of strong blue flowers are excellent for mixing with any of the many other blue flowers, or else they can be used as a contrast for golden day lilies.

Camassias prefer a moist position but we find that they are very tolerant, growing well in any good garden soil. We have had a clump in our very dry bed for years and they look superb with the blue *Clematis* 'Mrs P. B. Traux' mixed with a plant of *Eccremocarpus scaber* var. *rosea* on the wall behind and a cloud of blue aquilegias in front of them.

However, not all camassias are blue. *C. leichtlinii* is usually a pale, steely blue but there is a creamy white form, *C. leicht-*

linii 'Alba', and also a much bolder double *C. l.* 'Semi-plena', which has rather stiff spikes of creamy white flowers. It is most attractive when grown with one of the dwarf day lilies, such as *Hemerocallis dumortieri*, *H. minor*, or *H.* 'Golden Chimes' which are all early flowering with delicate gold flowers above neat clumps of narrow leaves, a good foil for the stiff camassias behind them.

However, this camassia has the unfortunate habit of virtually always aborting the flowers at the top of each spike, despite careful and regular watering. This small blemish apart, it is very striking and most desirable standing up ramrod straight like all camassias unless, like mine, they are grown against a wall – when they lean out and, being top heavy, collapse onto the plant in front, from which recumbent position the tips of the flower bend up again in an ungainly manner. I always try to remember to stake them, but as they are not visible when I add the plant supports to my border, they creep up on me unawares and collapse inevitably follows, leaving visitors very mystified as to what the plant is, as it seems to appear out of the day-lily foliage.

Summer

As with all attempts to divide the year seasonally, the actual dividing line is arbitrary and totally subjective, as plants do not readily fall into neat categories. I therefore propose to treat late-flowering members of genera such as *Tulipa* and *Narcissus* as spring items although they frequently accompany the first roses. Unfortunately, many of the true summer-flowering bulbous plants are not hardy and are therefore outside the scope of this book, but there are some notable exceptions.

The Dutch, or florists' irises, need no introduction with their stiff, rather uncompromising habit. They have been specifically bred for the cut-flower trade and are derived from crossing the Spanish *iris xiphium* with the Algerian *I. tingitana*. They require a rich soil in a warm, sunny border that is well drained and where the overwintering leaves will not be damaged. It is essential that the bulbs are planted firmly and, although some gardeners are successful in cultivating them, they are frequently a great disappointment, often failing to reappear. In this case it is probably best to lift the bulbs once the foliage has died back and leave them in a warm, dry place, which helps bud initiation. Fortunately, the bulbs are relatively cheap and it is always possible to add a few new groups each year. You must also remember that cutting the flowers for indoor use also removes most of the leaves and therefore drastically reduces the amount of nourishment available to replenish the bulb. For this reason irises for cutting are best grown in the vegetable garden.

These irises have rather stiff, solid flowers and they can be difficult to place in the garden so that they do not look like a row of soldiers on parade all standing stiffly to attention. Although most frequently available as mixed colours, it is best to buy groups of individual shades and plant them close together so that they look like a well-established clump. They are available in a wide range of colours, the most common being 'Wedgwood' (mid-blue), 'Imperator' (dark blue), 'Golden Harvest' (brilliant yellow), and 'White Perfection' (pure white).

Flowering as they do in late May and early June when the garden is bursting into colour, they are useful to create sudden patches of clear, bright colours. One of my favourites was a beautiful planting in a border on the top of a bank, now sadly hidden from view behind a fence. Every year it delighted me with its stunningly simple combination of deep blue irises among huge clumps of double white peonies. You can, of course, make a virtue out of a necessity and use their unbending character to great effect using bold clumps, to punctuate borders of low subjects, such as dwarf hebes or prostrate conifers, or by combining them with other spiky subjects like *Libertia formosa*. In the latter case the intermingled *I.* 'Wedgwood' and *Libertia* were behind the lime-green *Euphorbia robbiae*, with the grey leaves of *Sedum* 'Autumn Joy' to provide contrasting texture.

Their flowering also overlaps with the end of the tulip season and very good colour combinations are possible here as well. White irises can be used to follow

Left: The inherent stiffness of Dutch iris totally disguised in an exquisite way. Two 'Golden Harvest' hover like exotic butterflies among intense blue aquilegias

Right: Allium aflatunense with white honesty at Barnsley House

white tulips above grey foliage plants, or blue ones can be mixed with soft pink tulips to add a lovely soft colour to a border, perhaps where the majority of the plants flower much later in the year and are still only in leaf.

The superficially similar Spanish irises add another rather uncommon tone to the garden, at least at that time of the year (June), by providing us with bronze shades and lovely bi-colours, as well as the more usual blue, white, and yellow. They are also shorter, only 18 in (45 cm), and are useful for adding depth to yellow and orange plantings. However, they also must have a sunny, well-drained bed, protected from the worst of the winter weather or they, too, will fail to thrive.

The so called English iris (*I. latifolia*) is much more adapted to our wet climate and only produces its leaves once the worst of the weather is past. It is a much bolder plant altogether, with very wide spoon-shaped falls and standards, giving a slightly shaggy or dishevelled appearance. Frequently the second bud opens while the first is out and for a while they overlap. Although being rather muddled, this has a softening effect upon their overall appearance. As they prefer a moister soil in the summer they make excellent border plants, but their range of colours is limited to blues, deep purple, and pure white. Unfortunately they are usually sold as mixed bulbs so they would have to be planted in the vegetable garden first and the plants labelled according to colour if you want single-colour groups. Provided that you tie a label to the stem you can easily sort the bulbs immediately the leaves turn brown as the dry stems stay firmly attached for quite some time. All these irises need dead-heading as soon as the flower fades, to encourage them to produce a flowering-sized bulb for the next season.

For a purely architectural effect in a border it is difficult to beat the taller alliums. The name *Allium* elicits different responses from different people. For some, troubled by various wild garlics, they are pernicious weeds, while others avoid them, believing their smell to be off-putting. They are dismissed as being only suitable for planting among crocuses to discourage mice, although most are far too tall to plant in any bed where I have crocuses. However, the smell is not at all noticeable unless the leaves are bruised, and, in fact, the flowers have a sweet honey scent that is quite unexpectedly strong in some varieties. To dismiss the alliums is to lose a whole range of fascinating bulbs and possible associations.

Most of the taller ones come from the dry hillsides of the Middle East and Central Asia and prefer a dry, sunny border, although we find them remarkably tolerant. They are excellent for mixing with shorter similarly coloured plants or placing towards the back of the border to give extra height. *Allium aflatunense* has tight, spherical heads of pale purple flowers on 3 ft (1 m) stems and is most effective above *Geranium* 'Johnson's Blue' in front of an enormous delphinium whose soft purple 'eye' matches the alliums perfectly. The geranium not only provides a harmonious ground cover for the alliums it also hides effectively its very untidy, decaying leaves. The heads of *A. aflatunense* will remain on the plant, slowly fading from purple to beige as the whole plant dries. These heads make excellent dried flowers, or they can be left as a feature in the garden, but this can be a little dangerous because, if happy, they are very generous with their offspring. I am very fond of the new hybrid 'Purple Sensation' which looks exactly like *A. aflatunense* only in a deep, reddish-purple. Its strong colour can be used most effectively with other blue and purple shades. I once saw it in an interesting tonal mix with the double pink *Aquilegia* 'Nora Barlow'. Both plants were the same height and the resultant combination was most unusual. I must admit that I use it in a more traditional mixture of a deep blue camassia, *Aquilegia* 'Adelaide Addison' (double blue and white), and a deep, velvety-purple bearded iris, under the blue *Clematis* 'Mrs P. B. Traux'.

Another similar allium is *A. rosenbachianum* from Afghanistan. This has slightly larger heads but they are very distinctive, having white rather than purple stamens. They are also about 32 in (80 cm) tall, but the height of all these alliums varies a little according to the position. The giants of the genus are *A. giganteum* and *A. elatum*, the former reaching over 5 ft (1.5 m). However, *A. giganteum* is slightly tender, needing a sheltered position, but it does tend to contort unless it is grown in the open. This is not necessarily an unattractive habit. White, or rather off-white, forms of the last three alliums are available, and look good mixed with yellow plants, or on their own against a dark background.

The shorter 20 in (50 cm) *A. albopilosum* (*A. christophii*) has huge starry heads of pale, silvery-purple flowers that have a strange metallic sheen. It should be planted towards the front of the border otherwise it will be swamped by the taller herbaceous foliage and its beauty will be lost. Its larger heads mean that its colour is less intense and it can easily blend into the background and disappear, so it is better if it is able to rise above lower plants at the front of a border. It looks very good when used as an architectural feature beside a seat or at the edge of a pergola where they are excellent mixed with hostas. Its dried heads may be left in the garden for continuing summer interest, or removed and dried for the house.

The soft, almost metallic purple of these alliums is a good foil for grey foliage, and I know one most unusual garden where there is an entire grey border filled with artemisias, grasses, *Helictotrichon sempervirens*, and young *Eucalyptus*. Throughout the length of this very long border, groups of alliums, mostly *A. aflatunense*, had been planted to give both height and a unifying colour, which was echoed by a pale purple clematis covering the wall behind and scrambling through the shrubs.

The classic planting of *A. aflatunense* is at Barnsley House in Gloucestershire, where a tunnel of laburnums has been liberally underplanted with thousands of alliums. The resultant combination is quite beautiful, although I must admit that for me the colours are too pale to form a really striking contrast and I prefer the combination of white honesty and white foxgloves that is to be found with the alliums to either side of the tunnel. The clean white makes the colour of the alliums appear much deeper than it does when combined with the pale yellow laburnum.

A. siculum is not really an allium at all but a member of the related genus *Nectaroscordum*. It has unusual flowers that begin life as buds pointing upwards. As the flowers open so each brown and creamy bell descends until it is hanging. Once it is pollinated it fades and returns to its stiff, upright position. As this all happens over a period of two weeks or more they are continually changing shape. Like the other alliums, they need a sunny, well-drained position that does not become too dry. Their rather quiet colouring of purplish brown overlaying cream needs careful placing in the garden if they are not to be overlooked. As they will tolerate a certain amount of shade they can be planted among shrubs and they are good above blue hostas or mixed with *A. aflatunense*.

There are two other alliums that are much smaller than the previous ones but which also have their place in the summer border. The first of these should properly be in the spring section because, although it flowers in late May and June, it is primarily grown for its fine blue–green leaves that are reminiscent of those of a hosta. The leaves of *A. karataviense* appear early in April and, being only 6 in (15 cm) tall, are ideal for the front of dry, sunny borders. They make an excellent edging to a combination of 'Bowles Mauve' wallflower and cream tulips. Their flowers, which are a rather insignificant purple, more washed out than delicate, do not persist.

A. caeruleum (*A. azureum*) has tiny heads of soft blue flowers on wiry 18 in (45 cm) stems. These seem congenitally incapable of growing in a straight line and adopt the most amazing contortions. They need a very well-drained soil and are frequently rather short-lived, but they are relatively cheap and easily replaced. Their strong blue, and you will need many bulbs to make an impact, is excellent with clear yellows or mixed with grey foliage such as lavender, where they intermingle well with the blue lavender flowers.

The crowning glory of the summer must surely be lilies and there is perhaps no more beautiful and versatile a group of bulbs. There is also, probably, no other genus that is so difficult to satisfy really successfully. Their long season of flowering, May to September, with flowers from virtually the whole colour spectrum, coupled with their exotic shapes and widely differing cultural requirements, would lead you to expect them to be as popular as tulips and, like them, to be present in virtually every garden. However, lilies probably constitute the most frustrating of genera, thriving in one garden yet refusing to grow in the next. On my light sandy soil I am afraid that, loving lilies as I do, I tend to treat them as annuals or biennials at the most, and am pleasantly surprised by the few that wish to stay longer.

Left: Allium albopilosum with phlox, *astrantia maxima* and delphiniums

Right: Lilium (Citronella) an easy turk's cap lily for a sunny border

Many of the modern hybrids are highly bred, one is tempted to say highly strung, and like all thoroughbreds can be very temperamental. The main problem is to reconcile two very disparate requirements, that of perfect drainage, coupled with ample moisture. If, while they are growing, you provide the former adequately, the ground will quickly dry out and regular watering by hand will be necessary if their growth is not to be checked. Any sudden period of drought, as is frequently experienced in late spring, will check them and, if they become stressed, they will quickly go into early dormancy. The resulting bulb, which will be much weaker than one formed at the end of a long growing season, will then need two or more seasons of good growth to build up to flowering size again. It is also very important to keep the bulb growing for as long as possible after flowering, so the seed-heads must be removed as soon as the flowers fade and the plants copiously watered at regular intervals throughout the rest of the summer. If this after-care is neglected, the bulb will be weakened and probably not flower. If lilies fail to thrive, moving the clumps to a new site every two years may help.

The soil must be thoroughly prepared if the lilies are to have any chance at all. Dry, sandy soils naturally drain well, but peat and well-rotted manure must be added to aid water retention or the bulbs will be weak and spindly, with few, if any flowers. Heavy soils are naturally moisture retentive but their drainage must be improved if the bulbs are not to rot. The ideal method here is to dig a deep hole and refill it with a mixture of sand, leaf mould or peat, and soil or old potting compost. We have grown the white *L. regale* and 'Pink Perfection' magnificently in such a mixture. Making a virtue out of a necessity, we created a narrow pergola over my path where it runs between the wall and an enormous bay tree. I decided that if it was naturally a tunnel it might as well be a flowering one and my 'folly' has certainly proved to be a great success. When we built the pergola all the topsoil was removed and we replenished it with a mixture of old potting compost and peat with a liberal dose of slow-release fertilizer. The lilies love the jungle of *Dicentra eximea* var. *alba*, *Stachys lanata*, lavender, and *Rosa* 'Natalie Nypels' at their feet, and rise up magnificently to mingle both their scent and colours with roses and clematis festooning the pergola above them.

Most lilies prefer a soil that is either side of neutral, either slightly alkaline or slightly acid. However, some have very distinct likes and dislikes, details of which will be found in the tables. Many lilies also produce roots from the underground part of the stem and they will only thrive if there is sufficient depth of soil above the bulb. It is a good idea to mulch these lilies while they are growing to encourage the formation of these roots and keep them moist. As it is not always easy to know which are stem-rooting and which are not, although most catalogues will tell you, it is advisable to plant all varieties quite deeply with 4 in (10 cm) or more covering them. Most prefer to have their heads in the sun but their feet in the shade, which helps to keep their bulbs moist, and planting the bulbs on a layer of sand will also help with drainage.

Lily bulbs are available from late autumn through to spring, with the exception of the madonna lily which has a very short dormant season and should be planted in August. All lilies are without any protective tunic and the bulbs are very vulnerable to poor storage conditions, as they can easily become dehydrated or infected by mould. It is a good idea to soak the bulbs for one hour in clean water before planting them and to water them once they are in the ground. If conditions are not suitable for immediate planting when you obtain the bulbs, they should be potted up in a suitable compost and kept moist in a cold place until such time as you can put them out into the garden, when the whole pot can be planted without disturbing the roots. Keeping the lilies in pots and just plunging these into the garden when in flower is one way of overcoming adverse soil conditions, and it does give you the freedom to add a clump of bulbs to just the spot where it is needed. If the bulbs are not stem-rooting, then there must be sufficient depth of compost under the bulbs for good root formation.

Clumps of lilies are ideal for adding colour to borders that have finished flowering, such as those containing azaleas, or for mixing with the other flowering plants where the colours are complementary. It may be necessary to stake some of the taller varieties, and this is best done when you plant them as there is nothing more frustrating than to drive a cane right through the middle of the bulb just as it is coming into flower.

There are three main flower shapes available – the nodding, reflexed turk's cap, the long, narrow trumpet, and the more open cup-shaped ones that are frequently upward looking. All are available in a wide range of colours so it is possible to have a lily of virtually any shade or shape to match any groups of plants. I have *L*. 'Citronella' with its clear yellow turk's cap flowers, growing in front of a dwarf yellow day lily. By mistake I added the golden cup-flowered *L*. 'Connecticut King' instead of more 'Citronella' but the resultant mixture was very successful. *L. hansonii* is a magnificent lily, 4–5 ft (120–150 cm) when growing well, which produces 10–12 large, clear-orange, reflexed flowers in June and is one of the most reliable, having grown well in my hungry soil for many years. It should be placed at the back of the border, where it is useful for adding height, or for mixing with, the blue of delphiniums. It would also be very effective against a wall covered by a yellow rose such as 'Golden Showers', perhaps mixed with the clear blue *Clematis* 'Perle d'Azure'. In this case the lily would need careful staking or it will lean away from the wall, like mine which appears horizontally below the lime-green *Thalictrum flavum* var. *glaucum* (*T. speciosissimum*) rather than mixed with it. Another strong combination that relies upon colour harmonies is the deep pink lily 'Pink Perfection' mixed with the blood-red spikes of the annual *Chenopodium purpurescens* and the large, clear pink flowers of *Lavatera* 'Tanagra'. This occurred by accident in my garden where I let the dock seed at will. It frequently puts itself into just the right place and any unwanted seedlings are easily removed. In this instance it placed itself alongside a young *Lavatera* in the gap in front of my clump of 'Pink Perfection'. The result was rather a jumble but, none the less, very effective and certainly a very striking combination of pinks and deep reds.

The well-known *L. candidum* (madonna lily) with its spire of glistening white, sweetly scented flowers has been cultivated in Britain since at least the tenth century and was so common by the seventeenth century that Gerard reported: 'Our Eng-lish White Lily groweth in most gardens.' It differs from other lilies in that it should be planted in August, with the top of the bulb just below soil-level, in a limy soil in full sun. It needs excellent drainage and is probably best planted on its side to prevent water rotting the centre of the bulb. Once planted it almost immediately puts up a basal rosette of leaves which over-winters until the flower spike appears the next June, but it may well take some seasons before the clumps begin to flower. Traditionally madonna lilies are seen in cottage gardens where they are mixed up with other plants that give them protection from full sun. Given the right conditions they can form huge clumps, and I know of one sad, neglected garden that has one brief moment of glory when the madonna lilies and an enormous blue delphinium burst into flower, inextricably mixed. Such a grouping could be enhanced by the addition of the brilliant red *Lychnis chalcedonica*, flowering around the base of the taller plants.

These lilies are also very beautiful if grown as a feature and left to rise above the surrounding foliage; but they really need a dark background to do them justice, when viewed against a white house-wall they blend and rather disappear. One word of warning, however, *L. candidum* is a host for lily virus and, although it is not affected by it, it may infect other lilies if growing nearby.

There are so many lilies available that it would take the rest of the book to describe them. The tables at the end of the book list some of the more reliable species that may be considered for a sunny border. If they have proved difficult, then your soil must be checked and one of the more vigorous varieties chosen. One indication of vigour may be the cost of the bulb, the cheaper ones usually being the most vigorous, although this does not always follow. Occasionally you can find bargain packs but frequently these can contain small bulbs that will take many years to begin to flower, if they do at all.

However, even in gardens where lilies refuse to grow well it is still possible to enjoy their unsurpassed beauty, either by treating them as annuals or by potting them up and plunging them in the garden while in flower.

Earlier, I mentioned *Lychnis chalcedonica* as a good foil for *L. candidum* and it

The trumpet hybrid *Lilium* 'Pink Perfection' underplanting a pergola with *Clematis* 'Rouge Cardinal' and *Rosa* 'New Dawn'

also featured in a lovely planting of artemisia and a western American bulb, *Triteleia laxa*, often still erroneously called by the name of a closely related genus, *Brodiaea*. This infrequently encountered bulb flowers in midsummer and is ideal for the front of any sunny border in a well-drained soil. *T. laxa* is a mid-blue, good with whites or grey, and the variety 'Queen Fabiola' is probably the best, being a deeper blue. The flowers, which come after the leaves, form a rather lax umbel, and as each individual flower is rather small they make little impact unless tightly packed together; but a small clump at the edge of the border, poking out from low grey-leaved plants, such as helianthemums or artemisias, is quite charming. There is a yellow form, *T. ixioides*, which is less hardy and is best in a sunny, sheltered spot against a wall, where its delicate colouring demands sympathetic companions, if it is not to be overshadowed.

The summer, or Cape, hyacinths of South Africa bear little resemblance to the well-known spring hyacinths. Their leaves cluster in an untidy heap on the ground around the 4 ft (120 cm) stem, which is crowned in August by widely spread, large, pendulous, waxy bells. These are usually pure white (*Galtonia candicans*) but may be a rather delicate grey–green (*G. viridiflora*). There is a shorter form (*G. princeps*) which tends not to stand so stiffly upright as the other two, and is much more lime-green.

They are virtually hardy and should be planted at least 6 in (15 cm) deep in a sunny situation, in a deep, rich soil that is also free-draining. They will not tolerate heavy soils and neither will they give of their best on poor, sandy ones, so soil conditions may have to be modified. They need ample feeding with well-rotted manure and a winter mulch is beneficial in cold districts prone to hard frost, or the bulbs can be lifted and stored.

The pure white *G. candicans*, is an ideal companion for early flowering plants that take up so much space in the border once their brief time of glory is over. The bearded irises are just such a case where they are really spectacular for a few weeks in late May and then just sit rather sulkily for the rest of the summer. Their early leaves may be accompanied by daffodils or tulips and these can be followed in late summer by *G. candicans*. Although most

attractive, I must say that I find them a little difficult to use effectively as they are a very 'see-through' plant, each spike having a rather sparse appearance. I think that they are best when planted in a tightly packed group which goes some way towards compensating for their individual thinness. They are excellent with blue *Agapanthus*, and I have seen a whole sunken garden entirely planted with these and pure white galtonias, which had seeded to create a lovely blue and white picture in August.

The delicately coloured green forms need careful placing in the border if they are not to be overlooked. They could be planted in a group behind one of the deep purple michaelmas daisies or, perhaps more effectively, left on their own to rise up above the surrounding foliage. A dark background would help give them more definition.

Crinums could never be accused of being retiring plants. Not only do they have one of the largest bulbs, it is enormous, they also produce one of the largest clumps of untidy foliage that I know. My first introduction to them came many years ago when I was newly married. I could not understand why my elderly neighbour was so proud of this untidy mass in her garden until the huge heads of pink trumpet flowers, rather like a lily's, appeared. I still find them rather too untidy for all but the largest borders, but I have relented as far as *C.* × *powellii* 'Album' is concerned. It is planted at the back of my border where a large day lily and *Althaea rugosa*, a lovely soft lemon hollyhock from the Caucasus (which has a delightful branching habit), masks its untidy shape. Each year it rewards me with two or more clusters of the purest white flowers imaginable. Each individual flower is about 6 in (15 cm) long, shaped like a trumpet, and lasts for several weeks. *C.* × *powellii* is the usually encountered, free-flowering hybrid, but its scented flowers are a rather pale pink. *C. p.* 'Krelagei' has much deeper pink flowers with a better shape.

All crinums need a very deep soil, rich in organic matter. The bulbs should be planted with the long necks above the ground, and they benefit from an annual mulch of manure. In all but the warmest counties, where they can be grown in open borders, they are best under a sheltering wall. My *C. × p.* 'Album' has survived very severe frosts on a sheltered east wall. I must admit that it looked very unhappy, but the slimey outer covering of the bulbs was quickly replaced by strong new growths. It is a good idea not to remove any of the old leaves until the spring so that they can help protect the bulb from the worst of the weather. In cold districts a mulch of straw is a good idea.

Immediately summoning up images of large flower arrangements and harvest festivals, the plants that spring to mind when *Gladiolus* is mentioned, are the large-flowered florist's varieties. For me they also bring back happy memories of holidays in France where virtually every vegetable garden has its compulsory edging of gladioli. However, these tall varieties are not hardy, the corms needing to be lifted in October and stored in a frost-free place.

Once again, adequate drainage is their single most important requirement. They will tolerate heavy or light soils, provided that they are not waterlogged, but there must also be ample moisture during their growing period. Once the bud is formed they need regular watering to ensure a good spike with well-formed flowers, and liquid feeds are beneficial. They prefer a neutral soil and should be planted in full sun. Although they can be planted in March once the worst of the frosts are past, in cold districts it is advisable to wait until the soil is warm and damp, rather than cold and wet. They will flower approximately 90–100 days after planting, which is usually between July and September, depending upon variety and planting time (it is possible to stagger the planting times to give a succession of flowers).

Gladioli are available in an enormous range of colours and there must be one to suit every planting scheme. I must admit that I find their very regimented, unyielding appearance difficult to place in the border and prefer to keep them in the vegetable garden where both flowers and corms can be 'cropped' with relative ease.

There are basically four main types of large gladioli – the usual large-flowered florist's varieties, with their huge flowers and wide range of colours; the butterfly hybrids that are shorter, 2 ft (60 cm) and have smaller, tightly packed flowers with ruffled petals, the lower three petals having contrasting marks on them which give them their name; the primulinus, with their hooded top petal; and the miniatures, which have small, heavily ruffled flowers, rather triangular in outline, often bi-coloured.

All these non-hardy gladioli are inherently stiff and also rather untidy as the bottom flowers fade while the top ones open, therefore I feel that they are best mixed with other plants, and where they will provide a strong focal splash of colour, or give height. I once saw a very vivid group where brilliant pink gladioli were combined with an enormous clump of vibrant purple michaelmas daisies, the gladioli lightening the michaelmas daisies while they in turn disguised the stiffness of the gladioli. One word of warning, the gladioli will need staking securely or else they will lean out at strange angles, not in a relaxed 'at ease', but still ramrod stiff. The easiest way to cope with this is to dig out a hole about 1 ft (30 cm) across and 6 in (15 cm) deep, line it with sharp sand on heavy soils, or peat if the soil is light and dry, then plant six to eight bulbs before refilling the hole. It is then possible to support the whole group as they grow.

There are, of course, some relatively hardy gladioli, but these need the shelter of a warm wall if they are to be left in the ground all the year (they will be found in Ch. 5). However, there is one group of gladioli that are almost hardy, and these are dwarf hybrids. They have much smaller, more delicate flowers, on often thin, rather wiry, stems; and their colours are usually relatively soft, in the white, pink, salmon range, often with a contrasting flash on the lower petals. In milder districts it is possible to leave them in the ground where they should survive all but the worst winters but they should be planted 6–8 in (15–20 cm) deep to protect the bulb. However, they detest waterlogged soils and this is more likely to kill them than a frost.

Their corms are usually available from the late autumn and through to early spring. Those planted in the autumn should begin flowering in late June, while those delayed until March or April will not flower until August or even September. In colder districts it is possible to pot up the bulbs in the autumn and then plant out the pot, without disturbing the root ball, in their final position in the spring, so that an early display is obtained. Those gladioli will be found in catalogues under the

A single spike of *Lilium regale* coming through a white lavender provides an unusual contrast of textures

names *G. nanus*, *G. colvillei*, or *G. tuberge-nii*, and I find their more delicate appearance quite charming. They can be clustered at the base of shrubs, such as a ceanothus, or the dwarf pure white *G.* 'The Bride' can be tucked in at the front of the border, whilst any of the soft-pink varieties would look good behind and through a wide range of silver shrubs.

Probably the most unusual gladiolus is one that flowers in the autumn and always excites much interest and speculation. *G. papilio* (*G. purpureo–auratus*) is quite hardy and has strange flowers of greenish yellow, overlaid with purple, which are hooded and produced along a nodding stem. Unlike the others it is stoloniferous and produces masses of young corms, each with its grey sword-like leaf. These can cover quite a large area but, as it takes some two or three years for these young corms to reach maturity, even large patches may only produce a sprinkling of flowers. As flowers are produced in a succession over a two-month period from late summer into autumn, they are best planted in a herbaceous border or among shrubs, where they like a cool, rich, moist soil in which they can spread, their flowers often popping up in unexpected places. Unlike their stiff, large-flowered relations they tend to flop, achieving the most amazing contortions, and are best grown where other plants can support them, or in full sun where they can rise up above low surrounding plants. Their liking for a rich soil was amply illustrated in my parents' garden where the gladioli were removed from a bed and roses planted in their place. The few corms that were overlooked revelled in the rich, well-manured soil that was prepared for the roses and produced a truly magnificent display above the golden 'Arthur Bell' roses. *G. papilio* has a very quiet charm rather reminiscent of a fritillary, and it needs sympathetic planting if it is not to be lost. In the herbaceous garden at Knightshayes Court there are two groups of them. The first was planted on its own surrounded by sympathetically coloured plants – dwarf asters in the foreground and the tall blue *Echinops ritro* behind. Without a contrasting colour the gladioli blended into the border and were completely overshadowed by the surrounding flowers, to the extent of disappearing. Further along, however, they were planted behind, and had flopped through *Argyranthemum frutescens* 'Jamaica Primrose' (*Chrysanthemum frutescens*), whose soft lemon flowers formed the perfect foil for the dusky purple of the gladioli. A touch of grey from *Santolina pinnata* var. *neapolitana* below the chrysanthemum completed the picture.

If. *G. papilio* extends the gladiolus season into summer, then *G. callianthus* continues it into winter. It should really be in the next chapter but it seems better to finish the discussion of gladioli here.

G. callianthus is probably unknown to all but a few botanists, but under its common name *Acidanthera bicolor* 'Murielae' it is well known for its 3 ft (1 m) spike of sweetly scented flowers produced in late autumn. Each hooded flower, which is pure white with a deep purple blotch at the base of the petals, hangs down on a long perianth tube, giving the whole plant a graceful appearance. Sadly, the flowers are not frost hardy and the plant is frequently killed in the ground before it has finished flowering. In order to have flowers earlier in the autumn, or even in late summer, the bulbs must be planted early in the spring preferably in a warm situation, or in a pot which can be kept in a cool greenhouse until May when they can be planted out in their final position. They need a rich, free-draining soil in full sun and, like most summer-flowering bulbs, copious amounts of water while they are growing. White is an unusual colour to find in the garden late in the year and they are most welcome, providing a touch of lightness to borders dominated by heavy clumps of michaelmas daisies. Their strong scent makes them ideal subjects for planting near the house, or even in tubs on a patio. Sadly, they are not hardy in all but the warmest counties, and the corms should be lifted, but as they are frequently cut down by the frost before they have a chance to finish their natural cycle the corms are often too small to flower again the following year. However, they are very generous with their offspring, and bulbs are available very cheaply in the spring.

Autumn

Although not strictly autumn bulbs, as they commence flowering at the height of summer in August, crocosmias, with their burnt-orange flowers, are for me a sign that autumn is approaching. As they continue to flower throughout September, and the last flowers are usually still present in October, I will treat them as autumn bulbs, although there is an equally strong case for calling them the last of the summer bulbs. Although principally plants of semi-shaded woodland situations (q.v.), they also have a place in the sunnier borders, provided that these are not too dry. The strength of crocosmias, namely their strong colouring, is also their chief drawback. Their colours are predominantly orange and flame-reds, softened by a few cooler orangey yellows, and great caution must be exercised when introducing these shades to the garden, particularly so late in the year when the crowning glory of late summer, the intense purple michaelmas daisies, are at their peak. Orange is spectacular when mixed with blue, as with *Agapanthus*, or with deep purple michaelmas daisies, but it is not so compatible when planted among more pinkish-coloured ones.

It is well worth looking very carefully at the garden in late August and September and seeing just where they will fit in, either to add a touch of colour to an area where the plants are now in seed, as among day lilies for example, or where they will enhance the existing colour scheme.

Each individual spray of flowers is rather transparent, so clumps of crocosmias benefit from being framed by a deeper background, such as deep purple canna leaves or a purple-leaved shrub. The apricot 'Solfaterre' with its unusual, lightly bronzed foliage, is undoubtedly my favourite. Sadly, it is not very hardy, but in a sheltered spot it is most beautiful. It is excellent mixed with *Phygelius aequalis*, with its profusion of orangey scarlet tubular flowers, which also requires a warm situation. They can be mixed with golden daisies such as *Anthemis* or *Inula*, with perhaps a dark-leaved dahlia for a truly fiery combination. In colder districts, *C.* 'Solfaterre' can be replaced by another dwarf variety, such as the delicate bi-

coloured 'Jackanapes' whose enchanting flowers have alternate deep orange and yellow petals.

A softer tone could be introduced by using one of the yellow hybrids such as 'Canary Bird' or 'Citronella'. Grey and purple foliage, as in *Cotinus*, willows, or *Berberis*, is particularly pleasing with them. In one garden *Agapanthus* is followed by *C.* 'Citronella', the whole picture backed by an enormous plant of *Bupleurum fruticosum* whose flowers are the same acid-yellow as the crocosmia.

Although most are not very tall, being about 18 in (45 cm), there is one that should be at the back of every herbaceous border. 'Lucifer' is a scarlet hybrid between *Crocosmia* and a related genus, *Curtonis*. It has distinctive sword-like leaves that are held stiffly upright, and not only is it the tallest, it is also the earliest to flower, usually in July. It is excellent among golden achilleas and blue salvias or monkshood. There is a dwarf hybrid, 'Emberglow', from the same parentage that is once again much stiffer in habit and is excellent at the front of the border where its bold scarlet flowers are perfect with deep purple and blue.

Completely the opposite from these is the *Tritonia rosea* (*Montbretia rosea*) or *T. rubrolucens* as we must now call it. It has myriads of delicate, salmon-pink, lily-like flowers on very wiry stems that are capable of taking up incredible contortions. It needs a warm, sunny situation, and I grow it towards the front of my border where it flops delightfully out over the path. Its soft tone harmonizes well with a pale blue salvia and the pink-flushed flowers of *Abelia × grandiflora* behind it.

All crocosmias are heavy feeders and are among the few bulbs that thrive on well-rotted manure and are therefore well suited to the herbaceous border, provided that it is not too dry. Full cultural details will be found on page 96.

There are not many true autumn bulbs that can be grown in a herbaceous border, as they tend to be rather delicate and are easily swamped by the rather untidy end-of-season foliage left by the taller plants. However, I add a few colchicums to my border, judiciously tucking them in where their large leaves will not be an embarrassment the following summer. *Lobelia × vedrariensis* always flops in an untidy mass, but I love its clear purple colour so I have given it C. 'Lilac Wonder' to flop alongside it in a striking, if rather untidy, heap. Perhaps in a more open position, and not, as mine are, against a wall, they might both stand up, but, either way, the combination of the deep purple lobelia and the clear lilac of the colchicum is most attractive in late September. The ever-useful white-marked leaves of *Lamium maculatum* 'Roseum' coupled with *Stachys lanata* form a good underplanting to this group that cluster at the base of one of my pergola pillars. Further along the pergola, clumps of the small *C. cilicicum* poke out from between the stachys edging. In the summer the large leaves of the colchicums are swamped by the luxuriant growth of the clematis and roses smothering the pergola.

Although most colchicums require a deep, rich soil that is not too dry, and would not be happy in a sun-baked bor-der, *C. agrippinum*, with its tiny, che-quered, star-like flowers and small leaves prefers a drier, sunnier place. I know one rather neglected garden where it has formed an ever increasing clump, happily popping up through the weeds at the edge of the border early in September every year. It is also excellent with the spotted leaves of pulmonarias.

Where shrubs are mixed with herba-ceous plants there is greater scope to add more of the colchicums, and even one of the autumn crocuses such as *C. speciosus*. These can be tucked in under the shrubs to provide colour and interest as the shrubs' leaves fall, and where little else will grow in the deep shade cast by the shrub. *C. specio-sus* could be planted with spring bulbs like snowdrops, chionodoxas, or wood ane-mones, which also enjoy a similar situation and which would replace the crocuses in the spring, bringing us in a full circle back to the winter again.

A delightful grouping of *Gladiolus nanus* 'Good Luck' through *Caryopteris clandonensis*, looking as though the coryopteris had sprouted huge flowers

3 Shady borders

The heading of this chapter is rather a misnomer, as what I am going to discuss primarily is not bulbs for shade but the growing of bulbs in areas that are totally or partially shaded for much of the year, but receive sunshine during the winter and early spring. In other words, these are plants for growing under deciduous trees and shrubs where the leaf canopy, or rather lack of it at certain times, dominates the choice of bulbs. Other factors such as soil type certainly play an important role in determining the specific choice, but the control, by the trees, of moisture and temperature levels is of the greatest importance.

Moisture is vital for all growing plants, and bulbs are no exception. Some may be adapted to withstand long periods of drought during their dormancy, but all require a regular and adequate supply of water during their growing season. Deciduous trees allow any rainfall to be available from late autumn through to early spring, but by mid-spring the burgeoning leaf canopy acts as a very effective umbrella, reducing quite considerably the amount of water that reaches the ground directly under the tree. As anyone who has ever taken shelter under a large tree will know, it takes a long time before rain begins to percolate through the leaves and drip down your neck. Light summer showers make little impact upon these very effective natural umbrellas. Obviously, smaller trees, such as *Prunus* and *Acer*, and young trees have less of an effect than a mature oak, and the size of the tree should be remembered when considering bulbs for underplanting. The bulbs chosen for planting under a single mature horse chestnut or oak will be different from those chosen for planting under *Sorbus* or *Acer*. At the same time as the umbrella effect comes into operation, this ever increasing leaf canopy needs vast amounts of water to maintain itself and so the root system of the tree begins to draw moisture from the surrounding ground.

Flower beds under a single specimen tree of almost any size also receive quite surprising amounts of direct sunshine throughout the year, which increases their dryness in summer. They are therefore very suitable for planting with a wide range of early spring bulbs that can take advantage of the sun and moisture early in the year and flower before the umbrella effect of the tree takes effect. *Crocus, Chionodoxa, Scilla, Muscari*, and early daffodils are all suitable subjects, turning what could well be a problem area into a splash of bright colour throughout early spring. Later, when the tree is in full leaf, the area will become dry and any bulbs planted here should be able to withstand these very severe conditions that will prevail during the summer months. It is necessary, therefore, to avoid plants that resent this long, dry dormant period, such as erythroniums, snowdrops and certain cyclamen. There are many early spring bulbs (*Crocus tommasinianus*, aconites) that will positively enjoy these conditions, seeding around happily. It is therefore best to concentrate on them and to remove unhappy bulbs to cooler conditions elsewhere. Many suitable bulbs will be discussed in the chapter on bulbs for naturalizing in grass. Those suggested for growing under trees in grass are also suitable for flower beds in similar situations.

As the tree commences its growth so the overshadowed area becomes very dry, and late-flowering bulbs may well suffer from drought. This is almost certainly the cause of bulbs aborting their flower buds. Many late-flowering bulbs are especially prone to this, particularly the pheasant's eye narcissus *N. poeticus* 'Recurvus' and many lilies. I am frequently asked what is wrong with the bulbs. The answer is that nothing is wrong with the bulbs, only the area in which they are growing. Should this be a persistent problem, rather than caused by one particular season, then the only real answer is to move the affected bulbs to less dry situations. I always try to remember to throw a bucket of water over my late bulbs should the weather turn warm and dry in April. Not only does it maintain the active growth of bulbs that have still to flower, but it also encourages those that have finished flowering to prolong their growth and consequently strengthen their bulbs for the following year.

Evergreen trees, which cast a year-round shadow, create a very different problem to that of deciduous trees and shrubs. Not only do they provide a permanent umbrella against moisture, but they also have very shallow, questing roots, as anyone who has tried to garden under a yew tree will know to their cost. We have a venerable yew near our rose bed and every year fight a losing battle against its mat of fibrous roots that lie inches below the soil surface. Each year they seem to encroach even further into the bed, revelling in the manure mulches. However, some bulbs do thrive in these almost desert-like conditions, and I have found that it is the only place where the delicate autumn cyclamen, *C. cilicium*, and the similar *C. mirabile* really thrive. They produce a succession of tiny pale pink flowers above well-marked leaves during the autumn and, although not spectacular, they do have a very special charm of their own. Each individual flower bears close inspection as they are the most delicate shell-pink with deeper, thread-like veins. The tubers are perfectly hardy, having survived − 10°C, but they will not tolerate any excess moisture during the winter or summer and are very prone to rotting. However, on the sunny side of my large yew they have seeded into a large area.

Narrow conifers do not create such a problem, but as all have shallow, questing roots the soil will always be dry in the immediate neighbourhood and only the most tolerant bulbs will survive. Bluebells, especially the larger, more robust Spanish form (*Scilla hispanica*) will be happy here, and, indeed, can be safely banished to fulfil a useful function. The white form *S. h.* 'La Grandesse' is particularly fine against dark conifers and, if used to plant under a hedge, add a touch of lightness. Similarly, the ordinary blue grape hyacinth, *Muscari armenaicum*, can be massed at the bottom of a hedge, its high rate of increase and almost evergreen leaves being most welcome in this unrewarding situation. I have seen grape hyacinths, and once a mixture of them and white bluebells, forming a bright ribbon between a dark cypress hedge and a drive.

True woodland, rather than single trees, opens up the possibility of a much wider range of specially adapted bulbs. Where there is a large number of trees and shrubs the conditions are very different to those that prevail under a single tree. Although the trees control moisture in the same way, their numbers reduce the amount of sunshine received during the summer months, and there is a perceptible lowering of the mean temperature under them. A walk through woodland is always a pleasant escape from a hot summer day and it is in these relatively dry but cool conditions that many true woodland bulbs thrive.

In natural woodlands the sheer volume of leaves available for leaf mould means that the topsoil is light, with a very high humus content, a vitally important factor that must be remembered when attempting to grow woodland bulbs. If you examine the actual bulbs of bluebells, dog's tooth violets (erythroniums) or wood anemones (*Anemone nemorosa*), all of which grow naturally in woods, you will see that they do not possess the hard outer skin, or tunic, that is found on most other bulbs. On tulips and daffodils, for example, this tunic acts as an insulator, protecting the bulbs against total desiccation in the hot, dry conditions that often prevail in their wild homes in summer.

The acidity of the soil is of less importance than its structure and, particularly, its humus content, which is almost as important as the cool, shady conditions of summer. In most gardens such shady areas have been artificially created and the soil is therefore unlikely to be the virtual pure leaf mould encountered in a natural woodland. Therefore much leaf mould or peat must be added, both to lighten heavy soils and to aid water retention on dry, sandy ones. If the soil is heavy clay, then it is necessary to add coarse sand as well as peat, to create the humus-rich soil that is none the less moisture retentive, as required by woodland bulbs.

One possible method of creating small areas suitable for these bulbs is to build raised beds of specially prepared soil. These can be a very effective way of coping with heavy clay, or around trees where the soil is thin and root-dominated. The rough proportions should be one-third loam (ex-potting compost is ideal), one-third peat or rotted leaf mould, and one-third sharp sand. If loam is not available, the natural garden soil can be used instead, but the proportion of peat should be increased if this soil is clay.

Peat blocks make a most attractive edging to such beds, or you could use railway

sleepers for a stronger, if rather hard, edge. We have a narrow raised bed against a low north-facing wall where the soil is one-third moss peat, one-third sedge peat, and one-third light loam. We use this bed for growing small rhododendrons and other calcifuge plants which look most attractive with many woodland bulbs, particularly erythroniums. Low walls of peat blocks can be used to raise levels within the beds and thus create more interesting shapes. At Knightshayes Court in Devon a whole woodland garden was created using peat-block walls. *Cyclamen repandum* was planted between the blocks as the beds were built and has now seeded, forming a bright pink carpet in April.

Such beds can be planted with a full range of woodland bulbs, starting with *Cyclamen hederifolium* and colchicums in the autumn, through snowdrops and crocuses, to the true woodland bulbs in spring – *Narcissus cyclamineus*, wood anemones, and erythroniums. Mixed with violas, ferns, and other spring-flowering woodland plants – primulas, *Anemonella, Dentaria*, and hellebores – they can create a fascinating feature out of what may have

been a neglected corner.

Also at Knightshayes Court a whole bed under a chestnut tree has been given over to an extravagant mixture of bulbs and plants. It is a riot of colour and texture, completely random and unplanned, but very exciting. I think it is worth listing the plants to give an idea of the enormous range possible – crocuses, snowdrops, *Leucojum aestivum, Corydalis solida*, various celandines (*Ranunculus ficaria*), *Ipheion*, erythroniums, bluebells, snake's head fritillaries (*F. meleagris*), crown imperial fritillary, daffodils, primroses, *Viola labradorica, V. cornuta* var. *alba, V. pennsylvanica*, honesty (purple, white, and variegated), *Cyclamen*, wood anemones, *Geranium*, foxgloves, *Brunnera*, and *Euphorbia robbiae*. One or two of the perennials will continue the interest and are able to cope with the deep shade and relatively dry conditions later in the year, particularly *Brunnera macrophylla, Euphorbia robbiae*, and *Geranium macrorrhizum*.

Shade plants, such as quick-growing shrubs, may have to be planted on the south side of such a bed to keep conditions cool in the summer.

All woodland beds should be top-dressed annually with peat or leaf mould. In very dry summers, particularly in small, shady areas and raised beds, it will probably be necessary to water the bed once a week to maintain moisture levels. Those lucky enough to have large areas of natural or mature woodland need do little more than top-dress annually. Specially built beds also have the advantage of an artificially created soil, which means that a wider range of associations is made possible, for example by the creation of an acid soil for rhododendrons and camellias. However, do be warned that all such beds ought to carry a health warning! We made one, in an elliptical shape round a very large and very ancient hawthorn, to house my collection of trilliums and erythroniums. The bed has now grown into a woodland garden some 200 ft (60 m) long and is still expanding. All subsequent shade has been artificially created, but provided attention is paid to the nature of the soil and regular watering is carried out during the summer this form of gardening is fascinating and very rewarding.

There remains one other area of shade in the garden, and that is where the shade is artificially created and is more-or-less permanent. These are areas which are shaded by either buildings or walls and they can be amongst the most difficult to plant in an interesting manner. However, provided they receive at least some sunshine during the day and the soil is suitable, some of the less demanding woodland bulbs can be grown quite happily. We have a small area of our garden affectionately known as the Green Gloom. This has high walls to both the south and west, therefore light is only received from the north and east, while direct sunshine only falls during early morning in summer but is not received at all in winter. This could easily have been the Cinderella of the garden, but in fact it has, like the fairy tale, turned into a success story. In autumn *Cyclamen hederifolium* pushes up its tubby pink flowers in front of a back-drop of variegated grasses and a sweetly scented winter-flowering *Sarcococca* sp. By early spring large clumps of snowdrops, all special tall forms, such as *Galanthus* 'Ophelia', *G. elwesii* 'Maximus', and *G. plicatus* 'Warham' jostle for space beneath a large precocious specimen of *Helleborus*

orientalis that frequently produces its white flowers before Christmas. Other hellebores would also be attractive in a similar situation. Later the snowdrops are replaced by small, blue *tardiana* hybrid hostas, crowned in midsummer by the glorious blue willow gentian. I have, rather recklessly, allowed the golden-leaved raspberry to roam at will, adding, along with a self-sown *Alchemilla mollis*, a touch of lightness in this dark corner. Although the raspberry is rather rampant, and should never be planted in less jungle-like situations, it can be controlled by the regular pulling up of unwanted suckers. In the winter the old stems should be removed. The walls above my jungle are covered by early blue *Clematis alpina*, a golden hop which regularly attempts to scale the telegraph pole, and an unknown golden honeysuckle. The crowning glory is *Cornus capitata*, which, while rather contorted, has survived three very severe winters and now proudly spreads out its branches over my Cinderella area like a fairy godmother. In May and June it is smothered in large creamy bracts. The whole area is so densely planted that it needs very little attention other than tidying up in winter.

Small shaded patches of garden beside a front door can often be a dismal, rather neglected area, frequently planted with a few sad evergreens that only add to the depressing appearance of the shadowed front door. It is true that the lack of sun for much of the day precludes the successful growing of many brightly coloured herbaceous plants, but it is certainly possible to take advantage of the situation and make a virtue of necessity.

I know one garden where the entrance is alongside part of the house, leaving a relatively narrow, roughly triangular bed between it and the front gate. This part of the garden faces north-west and only receives sun during the late afternoon, but it is one of the most interesting patches of dense planting that I have ever seen. It makes waiting at the front door a joy rather than a chore.

Three native silver birches have been planted to give structure to the beds and privacy to the front door, and as their canopy is light they only add a little extra shading to the beds. In winter the naked branches of the birches and their gnarled white trunks are a feature in themselves, and as February approaches so clumps of snowdrops, both common single and double, and one fine clump of *Galanthus* 'Atkinsii' pop up around the bases of the trees through a blanket of small-leaved variegated ivy. From then until the end of April the area is a sea of shifting colours and textures. The silvery *Crocus tommasinianus* and various of its deeper relatives have seeded throughout the bed, as has the gentian-blue *Chionodoxa sardensis*, with its sparkling white eye. *Muscari armenaicum*, banished from the rock garden, pokes up through clumps of primroses. At one side a clump of blue hyacinths, long since banished from the house, flowers beside the fading purple flowers of *Helleborus orientalis* (that always remind me of Victorian dowagers in their faded mourning purple). The scent from the hyacinths is an added bonus.

A more sophisticated, but shorter lasting, planting in a similar shady situation is that using only massed bulbs of one variety. The sky-blue *Scilla sibirica* 'Spring Beauty' looks magnificent when planted in this way, but it requires some sunshine for at least part of the day. The softer blue *Scilla messenaica* (or the very similar *Scilla bithynca*) seems to tolerate a higher amount of shade. At Great Dixter they are massed under a deciduous magnolia growing against a wall. The young red stems of peonies and the beautifully marbled leaves of *Arum italicum* 'Pictum' add an interesting contrast to this sea of pale blue.

Terraces are normally built where they receive sun for much of the day, but occasionally houses have a paved area on the primarily shady side. These need not be left to become areas of gently greening paving but can be planted up with suitable small bulbs. In one such garden, quite surprisingly, the useful, almost evergreen, *Ipheion uniflorum* had colonized the cracks between the paving stones, despite its normal preference for sunshine. It produces a succession of small star-shaped flowers of an exquisite shade of the palest blue, above narrow, apple-green leaves. *Ipheion* 'Wisley Blue' is just as easy and has deeper blue flowers. Both look enchanting when mixed with that other weed, the blue grape hyacinth (*Muscari armenaicum*). The soft yellow of primroses and the lovely blue and white of *Anemone apennina*, with its ferny foliage, completed this picture. They had filled all the available cracks in the paving

and had overflowed, or may be vice versa, into the narrow bed against the house wall, which was brimming with *Helleborus foetidus* and a small-leaved variegated ivy, and all jostled under a quince, and *Euonymus fortunei* 'Emerald 'n' Green' trained up the wall above.

In the same garden a dark hedge of pencil-thin junipers was lightened by clever use of blue and white. White arabis and *Pulmonaria saccharata* 'Alba' with primroses for contrast, formed the background to drifts of *Scilla messenaica* and the wonderful grape hyacinth, *Muscari latifolium*.

Shady areas, whether they are under a single tree, beside a house, or are true woodland need not be dull, neglected areas, filled with easy-care ground cover and evergreens. These, indeed, have their place, but, given the right kind of soil, these often problem areas can be planted with many fascinating bulbs and thus become places of interest to be visited, rather than ignored. Colours and shapes may not be bright, but they have a cool charm of their own. In the rest of this chapter I propose to take a more detailed seasonal look at woodland bulbs. Other bulbs can be mixed with them but, in the main, these are the true woodland bulbs that need shade and a humus-rich, moisture-retentive soil in order for them to thrive.

Autumn

The shade garden comes alive in autumn. It is, after all, when the rapidly disintegrating leaf canopy exposes the beds to light and moisture, and woodland bulbs first come into their element.

For me it is the hardy cyclamen *C. hederifolium* that is the herald of autumn. The wonderfully scented *C. purpurascens* (*C. europaeum*) can start its sporadic flowering in early July, but its sparse deep carmine flowers do not disturb the pattern of midsummer green that is prevalent in the cool shade under trees. Indeed, it is their scent rather than their colour that usually draws one's attention to them. I well remember walking through pine woods in Austria and smelling the well-loved and evocative scent drifting on the cool air, but it took us some considerable time to track the plants down.

On the other hand, *C. hederifolium* (often still known by its former name, *C. neapolitanum*) is only slightly, if at all, scented but its pale pink, or white flowers, each with their dark knobbly noses, are produced in tremendous profusion, making a very noticeable impact on the garden. Although the weather may still be warm and sunny, and autumn colour barely noticeable, they are one of the first signs that summer is ending and autumn is on the way. The pink-flowered form has a rather blue tint and this can be a difficult colour to place successfully, so they are perhaps best planted on their own or with interesting foliage plants to complete the picture. The white forms are more versatile and look especially well under shrubs with early autumn colour, such as witch hazel (*Hamamelis mollis*) or *Cercidiphyllum*. They can, of course, be used among the pink-flowered ones to add a touch of lightness, as their pure white reflects the smallest amount of sunshine.

Cyclamen hederifolium does not begin to flower until three or four years old, but once it starts it can live to a very venerable age. That doyen of gardeners E. A. Bowles recorded one tuber with a verifiable age of 60 years. As the years pass so the tuber expands, becoming increasingly wrinkled and cracked but still capable of producing hundreds of flowers in one mad spurt in late August and September. When the flowers first appear the leaves are no more than tiny coiled threads on top of the tuber, but as the season progresses so they quickly expand into heart-shaped leaves, each with its own distinctive silver patterning. Many enthusiasts spend much time searching for clearly distinct patterns but I have yet to find a dull one. These leaves form neat mounds that persist throughout the winter and are of almost more value than the flowers, brightening otherwise dull areas left naked by departed herbaceous plants. This is especially noticeable when the winter sunlight catches the silver markings. As E. A. Bowles says, 'I know of no other plant that will turn patches of dust under thick trees into stretches of beauty so permanently and so thoroughly'.

These cyclamen also make ideal companions for other small bulbs, especially the winter and early spring ones. Snow-drops, aconites, and clumps of crocuses will quite happily shelter under their leaves, poking up their flowers in due season. They are particularly fine when, echoing their native habitat, they are planted under pines (as at Knightshayes Court in Devon) where their leaves look wonderful against the carpet of fallen needles.

Although the beautiful domes of leaves formed by *C. hederifolium* are probably best appreciated when planted on their own, great care should be taken to avoid an extraordinary sight I once saw. A lovely woodland path was lined with a narrow bed of enormous plants of *C. hederifolium*. In the interests of obsessive neatness the ground between the tubers had been carefully raked, leaving each stranded like a green tortoise. Nothing could have looked more uncomfortable and artificial in that wonderful wild setting.

The other hardy autumn-flowering cyclamen is the delicate, pink *C. cilicium*. This has the reputation of being temperamental and is inclined to dwindle unless really happy. We find that it needs really dry conditions whereas *C. hederifolium* does not really like such a dry position and is happier in moister soil. *C. cilicium* makes a charming picture in October, continuing after *C. hederifolium* has finished flowering. It begins to flower when very young but produces only sporadic pale pink flowers during a two-month period from September to November. Once the tubers are fully established and mature they can give a surprisingly bold display considering the small size ($\frac{3}{4}$ in, 1.5 cm) of the individual flowers. It does well in a rock garden where, provided it is given good drainage, it will cope with a remarkable amount of sun, but in these circumstances, however, it can be vulnerable to damage by severe frost. Its small size, and the fact that its beautifully marked leaves appear with the flowers, make it ideal for trough gardens. *C. mirabile* is similar but we have found it to be less hardy.

An even smaller cyclamen is *C. intaminatum*, which may have plain or strongly marked leaves. The white, grey-veined flowers are only $\frac{3}{8}$ in (1 cm) long. It can survive in sheltered, well-drained sites but its size makes it best suited to an alpine house.

Cyclamen are to be found round the Mediterranean, and this climate of cool,

Cyclamen hederifolium, the mainstay for autumn flowering

wet winters and long, hot, dry summers should be remembered when planting them in more temperate gardens, especially in Britain where summers are, unfortunately, frequently wet. Good drainage is the single most important requirement both in winter, when cold, waterlogged soil can lead to rotting, and also in summer, when the dormant tubers can easily die if they become too wet. The ground, therefore, must be prepared thoroughly, but given suitable conditions and good preparation many species will thrive. One of the best situations is under large deciduous trees, not for the shade they provide but for the leaf canopy during summer, which keeps off much of the rain. Heavy soils should have a generous amount of sand or grit added and all soils benefit from the addition of leaf mould or peat – acidity is not important. Too much moisture is the single most common cause of failure, but once favourable conditions have been established cyclamen should prove trouble-free and, in time, spread to form large colonies, even seeding out of the bed into surrounding grass and paths. They have few problems, but slugs and wireworm can cause much damage, especially in newly established gardens, so protection such as slug bait may be necessary.

All cyclamen are heavy feeders and an annual top-dressing of well-rotted leaf mould and bone-meal should be given in late summer or early autumn – just before the appearance of leaves and flowers. Although shallow planting is often recommended, many cyclamen are top rooting, so sufficient compost must cover the corms – 1–1½ in (2–3 cm) is ideal. Care must also be taken that they are not allowed to push themselves out of the ground, or flowering will be greatly impaired.

One of the most common problems when confronted with a cyclamen tuber is knowing which way up to plant it, especially if the shoots are not present. This is especially true of *C. hederifolium* which looks like an inverted saucer with both the roots and shoots coming from the convex upper surface. However, the little nodules indicating the buds should be visible on the upper surface but, if in complete desperation, plant them on their side and they will quickly sort themselves out.

Cyclamen are frequently encountered as dry tubers lurking on shop shelves throughout the autumn and winter. Many of these may have been dug up in Turkey in the wild and, moral considerations apart, can be very difficult to resuscitate. The Lybian cyclamen, *C. rohlfsianum*, is reputedly able to withstand drought for 10 years, but for most cyclamen removal in growth, followed by a long period of exposure to the air leads to death. Many nurseries today offer cyclamen as young, growing tubers. Although these will not have the impressive size of the imported wild ones, they will be much more vigorous plants and will soon form good-sized tubers. However, all cyclamen resent disturbance and newly planted tubers may take a season or two to settle down and flower happily. If, after a couple of seasons, they are still not performing well, it is without doubt the fault of their situation and they should be moved. Should it be necessary to move tubers, this can be done successfully at any time, provided they spend the minimum of time out of the ground. As their leaf stalks are very fragile, often continuing for quite some distance underground before emerging, it is probably best to move them just before or after flowering. Incidentally, it is this amount of 'white' stem that often deceives people into planting the tubers too deeply.

Unlike many bulbs, cyclamen tubers do not produce offsets, and the only method of increase is by seed. However, as a tuber will take five years to reach full flowering size this is inevitably a slow process, especially since the seedlings are minute and easily lost. Your chances of success will be greatly increased if the seed is collected as soon as it is ripe and is sown in seed boxes or trays. No matter when they flower, all cyclamen seed ripens at roughly the same time in late June or July. Each seed pod is pulled down to ground-level by a spring-like stalk which relaxes its tension once the seed is ripe. Mice and ants are particularly partial to the seed, which has a hint of sweetness, so one must be quick. On one memorable occasion visiting children also sampled them! However, they suffered no ill effects, but we were short of cyclamen seedlings for a season or two. The seed should be sown thinly in deep seed trays as soon as it is collected, and these should then be kept in a cool, shaded place and not allowed to dry out. Damping off can be a serious problem with young seedlings (especially for *C. repandum*) so good ventilation is advisable if they are being kept in a greenhouse. Once the young corms begin flowering and are large enough to handle they can be planted out in their permanent position.

Cyclamen do not compete well with grass, unless it is very thin, and are best planted in specially prepared beds under trees. Most are dormant for 3–4 months in the summer and, as there is no sign of them above ground, there is a real danger of damaging them. It is best, therefore, to overplant with a low, sprawling ground cover that needs little attention, thus minimizing the risk of spearing the tubers with a fork. Violas are ideal for this as they enjoy similar conditions – shade and humus-rich, free-draining soil. We find *V. labradorica* is especially useful as the purple leaves contrast well with the silverwashed cyclamen foliage and they also provide an attractive background for the flowers. *V. labradorica* is evergreen and in time forms large clumps that can easily swamp the smaller species. In these circumstances it is better to choose a herbaceous viola that is dormant in winter, such as *V. cornuta*. Accompanying plants can be valuable for the more tender species and those that produce scattered leaves and flowers over a period, such as *C. purpurescens* and *C. trochopteranthum* (formerly called *C. alpinum*), which has wonderful propeller-like flowers in spring. Ivy, especially the smaller-leaved forms, is another good partner for the more vigorous species such as *C. hederifolium*.

There is another rather special bulb that

can be mixed with *C. hederifolium*, and that is the rarely seen autumn snowdrop, *Galanthus reginae-olgae*. It is very similar to, and is possibly a form of, the common snowdrop, except that it flowers in September and October without its leaves. It is a rather weak flower and, to my mind, looks a little uncomfortable on its own, rather like a guest who has arrived too early for a party. Although it is recommended for full sun, we find it does best in a well-drained humus-rich soil in semi-shade. It is excellent with the leaves of *C. hederifolium* or, as we grow it, among the bright yellow fallen leaves of a horse chestnut tree.

Making their first appearance at much the same time as the autumn cyclamen are the colchicums. Erroneously called autumn crocuses because of their superficial similarity to crocuses, they are in fact members of the lily family, having six anthers, unlike crocus which have three and are members of the iris family.

These 'naked ladies', or meadow saffron, are very evocative of autumn, with clusters of small, pale-lilac flowers suddenly appearing in the close-mown turf. They were originally named after Colchis in Armenia where many species grow, and are in fact highly poisonous. Gerard, in his herbal of 1633, recommends that the 'stamped roots ... mixed with the whites of eggs, barley meale and crums of bread' should be applied to the swollen foot to 'ease the paine of the Gout, swellings and aches about the joynts'. He also suggests that it is taken as a purge by those that have gout, but fortunately he does warn that death 'presently ensueth' as it is 'hurtfull to the stomacke'. Remarkably, the drug colchicine, which is obtained from colchicum, is still an effective cure for gout.

The leaves, which follow the flowers, emerge around Christmas and expand during the spring, only reaching their full stature during May and June when the seed-heads appear above the ground. This gave colchicums their old name of *Filius ante Patrem* – the son before the father – as it was believed that the seeds preceded the flowers (rather than vice versa), whereas the seed-head is kept below the ground after flowering to protect it from inclement winter weather, and only emerges and elongates during the summer months. These seed pods have also been mistaken

for flower buds and one gardener was mystified as to what went wrong every year – why did the buds die and not open?

Unfortunately the leaves, often 12 in (30 cm) or more long and 4 in (10 cm) broad do not wither and collapse until July when there is only a short dormant season before the new roots are formed in August and flowering begins shortly afterwards. However, although the presence of large leaves for much of the summer must be taken into account when placing colchicums, they add such interest and colour to dull, faded corners that some should be present in every garden. Planted with care and discretion they can enliven the autumn garden and add a further dimension to autumn colours.

Most colchicums need a rich, deep, moist soil in semi-shade in order to do well. In light, sandy soils they can dwindle, and humus should be added to the soil to help moisture retention. Some can tolerate growing in grass (*C. autumnale* and *C. byzantinum* in particular) but they increase best in well-cultivated soil, where they are quite trouble-free, only requiring dividing every three years or so as the clumps become congested. However, care should be taken to avoid waterlogged positions as the bulbs can suffer from the fungal infection basal rot. Fungus (Botrytis) can occasionally attack the bulbs through the dying flowers, and later the decaying leaves, so their removal is both visually and hygienically useful, especially as the flowers look very sad and bedraggled after the inevitable autumn rain. It also helps discourage slugs, which can attack both flowers and corms. Indeed, we find that in some years slugs are a major pest, and lifting corms for sale can turn into an archaeological dig where only the skin remains outlining the shape of the corm, like the remains of a Saxon wooden bowl, often with a fat slug nestling at the base. Provided the damage is not too extensive and there is no trace of rot, these corms can be replanted and protected against further slug damage. A new, undamaged corm will be produced at the end of the season. However, it is advisable to dip such corms into a fungicide first as the damaged tissue is open to attack by Botrytis.

Colchicums are best planted in an informal setting, tucked in among low herbaceous plants in a semi-shaded position where their flowers are supported both visually and physically, as they do have a tendency to collapse in the wind or rain. In such a position their large leaves will blend in later and, provided their neighbouring plants are of sufficient stature not to be swamped, they can even form an added feature in summer by providing a change of texture. Good companions are the large rich purple flowers of *C. speciosum* and *C. bornmuelleri* with pulmonarias, *Viola cornuta*, or *Viola labradorica*, where the purple leaves add a further dimension, and the herbaceous peonies with their rosy autumn tints. Here colchicums can add a point of interest to what can easily be a rather sad picture at the end of the year. At Sissinghurst Castle the peony beds have a large clump of colchicums as a centre piece. In the spring their leaves provide a bold background for the emerging red-stemmed peonies.

Plant combinations such as this are ideal for use under large, spreading shrubs or small trees such as *Magnolia* and *Hamamelis* or where the usual lilac shades of the colchicums are echoed by the autumn colouring of the tree or shrub. *Hydrangea villosa* and *H. arborescens* or *Callicarpa bodinieri* var. *giraldii*, for example, have soft lilac autumn tints, while *Euonymus europaeus* (spindle), with its pink–scarlet berries, or *Viburnum opulus* var. *sterile* are other good shrub associations, where the reddish tints of the leaves blend well with the purple shades of the colchicums. I have a clump of *C. byzantinum* which produces masses of soft pinky-lilac flowers from each bulb, tucked under a purple form of *Cotinus coggygria*, where it tones in beautifully with the deeper-shaded leaves of the cotinus.

A striking contrast can be created by underplanting the graceful arching stems of *Rubus cockburnianus*, with its fine white sheen, with a soft lilac colchicum such as *C. byzantinum* or the larger hybrid 'Lilac Wonder'. The colchicums have the added bonus of disguising the rather unattractive lower stems and crowns of the rubus. An associated planting of pulmonarias, especially the vivid blue *Pulmonaria angustifolia* var. *azurea* not only hides and supports the naked stems of the colchicums but also creates a pleasing contrast with the rubus during spring.

In the case of colchicums with double flowers extra care must be taken with their location as they are naturally top-heavy

and collapse very quickly, often disappearing from sight under the surrounding foliage. The best known, and earliest-flowering double is the aptly named hybrid 'Water Lily' – a fine pink–lilac offspring surprisingly of two pure white parents, *C. speciosum* var. *album* and *C. autumnale* var. *album* 'Plenum'. Its huge heads, often six to a bulb, appear from mid-September to early October and are best at the front of a woodland or shrub bed and in association with low herbaceous plants such as primroses, or perhaps backed by the blue-grey leaves of *Helleborus foetidus*, *Euphorbia characias* subsp. *wulfenii*, or the blue-leaved *Hosta tardiana*. The primroses and violas will flower before the colchicum leaves elongate, and the hellebores, etc. will provide interest later in the year. I also

Above: The naked flowers of colchicums can easily be damaged by inclement autumn weather and are best supported by other plants. *C.* 'Rosy Dawn' is planted beside an epimedium

find epimediums very useful planted alongside colchicums, as their neat foliage is stiff and well able to withstand the large leaves later.

There is one other beautiful double colchicum that is not as well known as it deserves to be. This is *C. autumnale* var. *pleniflorum* which has small, perfect flowers of deep lilac, rather like a little double rose. Its neat size and shape is its main attraction, but it is also useful to extend the season into November as it is one of the last to flower. Any plant that flowers so late in the year is vulnerable to damage from inclement weather, but given a sheltered spot at the base of a tree, or tucked in among epimediums or similar stout plants, it is a delightful addition to any woodland garden.

There are many hybrid colchicums available. All are basically very similar, having goblet-shaped darker or lighter lilac flowers, which may be plain or chequered (tesselated), and a greater or lesser amount of white, and all can be planted most effectively in clumps throughout a shrub border. Some particularly fine forms are 'Conquest' (good deep red–purple with a good shape), 'Violet Queen' (strong red–purple, well chequered but poor shape), and The Giant (huge flowers of mid pink–lilac produced in great profusion).

Colchicums, however, do not only come in shades of lilac, there are also white ones, the most common being the small-flowered *C. autumnale* var. *album* and the beautiful, large, goblet-shaped *C. speciosum* var. *album*. These look best among

Above: Colchicum speciosum with the fern Blechnum penna-marina

dark foliaged herbaceous plants such as *Helleborus foetidus*, or even coming through the fallen brown leaves, especially under a tree which loses its leaves early. They are useful for lightening a dark corner, or perhaps a shady border beside the house. They can equally look stunning in association with grey-leaved plants in a border.

Once colchicums are planted they need not be disturbed until overcrowding occurs. This is useful for items planted under trees or shrubs where regular cultivation can damage the roots, and so careful advanced planning of planting can be doubly advantageous. Bulbs in these situations need not be limited to autumn-flowering varieties. *Eranthis hyemalis* (winter aconite) and *Galanthus nivalis* (snowdrop), followed by *Crocus tommasinianus* and *Erythronium*, perhaps, will extend the season of interest. Small violas, such as *V. labradorica*, and wood anemones (*A. nemorosa*) can be planted amongst the bulbs along with the larger herbaceous plants such as pulmonarias, hellebores, small geraniums, and epimediums to maintain the interest by providing an evergreen carpet under the trees during the summer months. Other combinations will be discussed in greater detail in the sections on winter and spring.

Although primarily bulbs of open, sunny places, some true autumn crocuses are also quite happy in a shady situation, provided that it receives sun for at least part of the day. They are especially useful under small trees or large shrubs where their intense colours and unexpected appearance adds a touch of cheerfulness to sombre autumn colours. *C. speciosus* is probably the best crocus for this purpose. Not only does it have bold flowers of an intense blue–purple, it is also virtually indestructible and increases rapidly, which is a very important consideration when planting-up large areas. I love to see drifts of it between shrubs that have long since finished flowering. It is rather tall (6 in, 15 cm) and, flowering as it does before its leaves, tends to have a rather straggly, naked appearance, and to be prone to collapse following heavy wind and rain. The useful prostrate *Hebe pinguifolia* var. *pagei*, with its tiny grey leaves, provides excellent ground cover for it, as does the completely prostrate *Cotoneaster dammeri*.

The intense purple *C. medius* and the superficially similar *C. serotinus* subsp. *salzmannii* are excellent around the base of small trees. We grow them in a bed below our specimen of *Ginkgo biloba* and hope that each year will be the one in five that sees the coincidence of the bright yellow ginkgo leaves and the purple crocus. It is pure magic when it does occur and is well worth waiting for. A yellow-tinted *Acer* or the golden *Robinia pseudoacacia* 'Frisia' would be good alternatives. *Cyclamen hederifolium* var. *album* planted in the same bed would extend the flowering season and increase the odds on achieving the coincidence of leaf and flower colour, but it is best to avoid the pink cyclamen as it does not tone well with the purple crocus.

One crocus that delights in and needs a cool, peaty soil in partial shade is *C. banaticus*. It originates in Rumania and is a most unusual and distinctive crocus, having relatively wide leaves and soft lilac-blue flowers where the three inner petals are much smaller that the deeper outer ones, giving it a definite iris-like appearance, which was echoed in its original name of *Crocus iridiflorus*. Sadly, the flowers are very fleeting, being rather prone to damage by inclement weather, but it is a very choice subject for a special corner. I grow it in a raised peat bed with dwarf rhododendrons.

We find that the tiny white *C. ochroleucus* requires a dry position, but in a sunny bed under a tree it can be used to extend the flowering season well into November. As each individual flower is so small they are best planted in quite tightly packed clumps for maximum effect.

Winter

In mild winters it is possible to have crocuses in flower virtually every day, or at least every week from September until Spring. The linking crocuses are *C. laevigatus* 'Fontenayi' and *C. imperati*. In colder districts than ours there is a definite gap between the two, the former being the last of the autumn crocuses and the latter the first of the spring ones, but in mild areas their flowering virtually overlaps and I have known them to flower together. Both require a sunny, well-drained position, and we find that they thrive under our large lime tree.

Crocus laevigatus 'Fontenayi' has delightful purple flowers with deeper veining on the outer petals. It flowers with its leaves at any time from late November until January. Our clump is tucked away from the wind that at that season can do so much damage to the flowers, and we are rarely without one in flower around New Year. Indeed, it is one of my traditions to look for this crocus on New Year's Day and, at the same time, see if *C. imperati* is showing as well.

On a bright, sunny day *C. imperati* is quite spectacular, revealing its intense purple inner petals but when it is dull and overcast it retreats behind its biscuit-coloured outer petals which effectively camouflage it. It often surprises me by its sudden appearance, overnight as it were, although its buds must have been present for some days.

All crocuses require sun, both at flowering time to persuade them to open and reveal their full glory, and again during the summer in order to ripen the bulbs for the following season's display, but provided that the canopy is not too dense or the soil too moist, beds under trees can be filled with *Crocus tommasinianus* and its various deeper-hued cultivars, 'Whitewell Purple' and 'Ruby Giant'. They all seed themselves around, sometimes a little too vigorously, but provided the spot is not a choice one this can be a positive advantage. Nothing is more attractive than dappled winter sunlight falling on mixed clumps of deep purple *Crocus tommasinianus* 'Whitewell Purple' interspersed with snowdrops. Variegated periwinkle and domes of leaves of *Cyclamen hederifolium* complete this picture, which is simple but very effective. I would also include the strikingly mottled leaves of *Arum italicum* 'Pictum' that first appear in early autumn and remain fresh and green all winter. The scarlet berries (which are highly poisonous) are produced in the summer.

The snowdrops chosen for this planting could be the ordinary common single *Galanthus nivalis*, but there is an enormous range of hybrids available to choose from. Snowdrops must surely be present in every garden, making, as they do, such an optimistic statement about the approaching end to winter. Their small stature demands that they be planted in closely packed clumps and not scattered singly, or their effect is quite lost.

Although basically similar, having three large, white outer petals clasping three smaller ones (except, of course, the doubles), snowdrops can be divided by flower, leaf, height, and flowering time. It really doesn't matter which you choose, all fulfil the same functions equally well. However, this is not to disregard the wide choice available. One disadvantage of most photographs of snowdrops is that they are taken in close-up at eye-level, which tends to give a false impression as this is not the usual position adopted to view snowdrops on an icy day in February. The normal view is that from some 5 ft (1.5 m) immediately above, when all but the most obvious differences are not at all noticeable. At East Lambrook Manor, Margery Fish overcame this by lining a dry ditch with snowdrops so that the characteristics that distinguish them can be clearly viewed and fully appreciated comfortably at eye-level.

However, this is not a practical solution for most of us, but there are some forms which are sufficiently distinctive to add an extra dimension to any planting. All snowdrops have green markings and it is the shape, size, and location of these marks that are one of the most obvious distinguishing features between plants. Those with very obviously different markings are much sought after, and 100 or so hybrids have been named, but many of these are very similar and are best left to the enthusiastic collector. However, some are sufficiently distinct to warrant a place in every garden.

I would not be without 'Atkinsii', which has large flowers on 9 in (23 cm) stems. It flowers two weeks before the common snowdrop and even a small clump makes a bold display. We have massed them under two shrubs of the variegated *Elaeagnus pungens* at the end of a path, making a bright and attractive feature out of what would otherwise be a rather dull corner.

'Magnet' would be my second choice for charm and enchantment. It has very large flowers suspended upon improbably long pedicels (the little flower stalks that are found at the end of the stems). In the sun they open their petals wide, and with the slightest breath of wind nod and dance enchantingly.

For sheer size and availability 'S. Arnott' must be included in every collection. The flowers are really huge, having beauti-

fully rounded petals and the added bonus of an almond scent. I have seen them coming through the prostrate mats of *Polygonum vacciniifolium*, where they contrasted well with its winter-bronzed leaves. They also look most attractive with ivy, or in association with ferns that will spread in the spring to fill the area left bare by their departure. However, care must be taken to match the stature of the neighbouring plants to the snowdrop. I once planted a fine clump of 'S. Arnott' beside a prostrate hebe (an unnamed hybrid, but possibly 'Glengariff'). For a couple of seasons the grey-leaved hebe was a perfect foil for the tall snowdrops, but one year the snowdrops failed to appear. I thought that I had lost them but they were discovered struggling under the hebe which had become so dense as to smother them.

Although the green marks normally occur on the inner petals, in some instances they are also found on the outer ones. *G. nivalis* 'Viridapicis' was discovered in the northern Netherlands at the beginning of this century, and has relatively large flowers quite strongly marked with green. It is a very robust snowdrop, flowering a

little later than the common snowdrop, and quickly makes a handsome clump. *G. n.* 'Scharlokii', on the other hand, is more of a curiosity. It is shorter than 'Viridapicis' but is equally well marked with green. Its individuality lies in the manner in which the spathe is split into two, just like asses' ears. I must admit that it is among my favourites. Some double snowdrops also have green markings on the outer petals. The best known of these is 'Pusey Green Tip'. This was discovered growing wild on the banks of the Thames, and is a delightful plant, best planted where its individuality can easily be appreciated.

The 'yellow' snowdrops cause much interest but are not really reliable garden plants. By some quirk of nature the occasional yellow-marked common snowdrop (*G. n.* 'Lutescens') occurs in Northumberland, but the yellow markings tend to vary from year to year. This variability is especially noticeable in the double 'Lady Elphinstone', where some years the flowers are almost indistinguishable from ordinary ones. They also tend to be much weaker plants and shy flowerers.

The double snowdrop is, by nature, a much bolder plant than the single, and this is especially true of the tall double hybrids. One of the boldest and most vigorous is 'Ophelia'. The flowers are not always very perfect but they are 9 in (23 cm) tall and long lasting. Other tall doubles, some with very perfect flowers, as though cut off with a knife, are 'Desdemona', 'Jaquenta', and 'Hippolyta', which are occasionally available from specialist nurseries.

Under the autumn section I mentioned *G. reginae-olgae*, which flowers in September or October. There are two other true winter-flowering snowdrops that frequently produce their first flowers around New Year. These are *G. caucasicus* var. *hiemale* and *G. corcyrensis*. The latter is probably no more than an early flowering form of *G. nivalis*, but is none the less welcome.

Whereas all have basically similar flowers, the leaves of snowdrops vary greatly according to the species and are one of the most obvious differences between them. *G. nivalis*, the common English snowdrop, has narrow, blue-green leaves, whereas *G. elwesii*, the giant Turkish snowdrop, has broad, grey leaves. In *G. plicatus*, as the name suggests, the leaves are folded at the edges, and *G. caucasicus* has wide, grey leaves that are recurved at the top. Clumps of the large-leaved snowdrops can be quite a feature, and are interesting even when out of flower. We have a fine clump of the beautifully marked *G. plicatus* 'Warham' underneath a cornus in a north-facing bed, where it is most attractive even when out of flower. It is planted just in front of a large hosta which covers the bare area left by the snowdrops later in the year. Thus, it can be seen that by careful choice a succession of obviously distinct snowdrops can be achieved throughout the winter months. Full cultural details will be found on page 102, but it is worth mentioning when to plant snowdrops.

Many theories abound regarding the correct time to plant them. The only area of agreement is that snowdrops that are lifted in early summer (June) and stored for sale during the autumn, like most other bulbs, tend to have a high proportion of dead bulbs when they finally come to be planted in September or October. The reason for this high failure rate is that, as we have already seen, snowdrops are naturally plants of light woodland and resent drying out for long periods at any stage. Another factor that has led to the wide distrust of dry bulbs is that many of the ones offered for sale on garden centre and supermarket shelves are, in fact, dug up in the wild while still in growth. Quite apart from the conservation issues, this inexperienced and rough handling does nothing to improve the bulbs' chance of life.

Various answers have been suggested – and moving plants in full growth, after flowering, has become popular. Provided the bulbs are lifted daily, for immediate despatch, and not left to dehydrate on some packing shed shelf, this is a very successful way of moving them. It also has the advantage of allowing you to 'fill the gaps' when all herbaceous foliage is dormant.

All newly planted snowdrops will take a couple of seasons to settle down, but once established they should flower each year with no problem. However, if after trying different methods of buying and transplanting snowdrops they still do not succeed in your garden, it is almost certainly not the quality of the bulbs, but the prevailing conditions that need attention.

In the depths of winter a woodland garden can be a very dismal place of bare stems and dripping evergreens, but the planting of a few clumps of snowdrops throughout can instantly brighten it. The taller and bolder varieties are particularly good when planted with evergreen subjects, such as the purple-leaved wood spurge (*Euphorbia amygdaloides* var. *purpurea*), yellow archangel (*Lamium galeobdolon* 'Variegatum'), or the variegated form of *Vinca minor*, whose overall grey appearance blends well with the stately *G.* 'Atkinsii'. We have a fine clump of *G.* 'Magnet' that has been covered by an encroaching *Geranium macrorrhizum*. These beautiful snowdrops look especially effective dancing above the red hues assumed by the geranium leaves in winter.

However, it is important that the geranium or other plants are not allowed to completely smother the snowdrops. It is advisable to check the clumps once they first appear above the ground. Any excessive ground cover can then be easily removed without damaging the bulbs. Removing the plants at a late stage often leads to the untimely decapitation of the snowdrops.

One of the most surprising sights in the depths of winter is to see in full flower a patch of that most valuable of all winter plants *Cyclamen coum*. This delightful plant has dark-nosed flowers in all shades, from carmine through to white, and its round leaves may be plain glossy green, more or less marked with silver. Few plants that are quite so small have had so many names given to them in the past, some of which may still be encountered today. This plethora of names is due partly to its widespread natural distribution – from the Balkans in the west through Turkey to the Caucasus – and the associated variability. Some synonyms are geographic in nature – '*C. ibericum*' and '*C. caucasicum*' – while others are more descriptive, such as '*C. orbiculatum*' which refers to the circular leaves. The name '*C. coum* var. *atkinsii*' is also frequently encountered, and refers to the form with well-patterned leaves.

C. coum is completely hardy and has remarkably weather-proof flowers considering the time of year it flowers, January in mild districts and February in colder ones. In really severe winters, however, strong winds coupled with intense frost can completely desiccate the leaves, so it is best to choose a location that is protected from the worst weather. It will tolerate a certain amount of sun but is happiest in a peaty soil in a semi-shaded situation. It also prefers a moister position than most other hardy cyclamen, particularly during the summer months, and is not really happy right in under the canopy of a very large tree unless the soil is well-prepared. It seems to thrive especially well on acid soils and is ideal for planting in front of rhododendrons, but I am certain that it is the high humus content that it requires and not the acidity. (Full cultural details for cyclamen will be found on p. 70.)

If sufficient quantities can be obtained (and it does not seed so freely as some other species) it is very effective massed on its own, making a vivid splash of colour on the dullest day. I have seen it edging some steps in a bed under large trees, or under spreading shrubs such as *Magnolia stellata* or even hydrangeas, which have such an untidy and uninteresting winter skeleton.

For most gardeners massed *C. coum* is not a practical proposition, but it is equally attractive when mixed with other early flowering bulbs and plants, such as snowdrops, violas, crocuses, or even with one of the larger mosses that are often found under trees.

Another perfect bulb for the shrub bed in winter is the winter aconite, *Eranthis hyemalis*, with its brilliant gold cup-shaped flowers that suddenly appear in February. It is discussed in detail on page 106 but, being a native of deciduous woodlands, it is ideal for relatively dry beds under trees or shrubs. It is most attractive planted in clumps at the edge of a bed, poking up through primrose leaves, or jostling with snowdrops. Large drifts of it can be used to carpet the ground left bare by the departure of herbaceous plants such as hostas. As very little other than snowdrops are in flower, the main function of aconites in the winter garden is to provide a welcome splash, or in favourable circumstances a veritable sheet, of colour. In the latter case it must be remembered that, as with many bulbs, their leaves enlarge quite considerably after flowering and may well swamp any later-flowering bulbs. However, they do form a most attractive carpet for the taller daffodils such as 'February Gold' or 'Peeping Tom'.

Anemone blanda, although primarily a spring bulb, can begin to flower in February and is, again, ideal for carpeting large areas under shrubs. I have a clump of blue ones that have happily settled on top of my very large *Euphorbia griffithii* 'Fireglow', where they look most attractive around the emerging red shoots. I love to see them mixed with primroses, tucked in at the base of a tree, or in large sheets under the pink-flowered *Viburnum* × *bodnantense*, provided that they receive as much sunshine as possible, otherwise they do not flower well and the flowers will refuse to open fully.

Spring

Spring is the highpoint in the life of a wood, when all plants rush into flower before the expanding leaf canopy becomes complete, dramatically reducing both light and moisture. Although woodland plants are not always striking, often having very subdued colours, they have a special charm of their own and are well worth close examination. Our native woods are

relatively poor in bulbous subjects: wood anemones and bluebells spring to mind, but woodland areas throughout the temperate world have yielded a harvest of bulbs that can turn a wood, be it only a small bed under trees and shrubs, into a veritable treasure house of fascinating plants. Dog's tooth violets and wood lilies from America jostle with lilies from China and Japan.

I will begin an excursion into this fascinating area with the wood anemones. *Anemone nemorosa* epitomizes English woodlands, but, unless you are fortunate and have a relatively large garden, it is probably best left there as it is very vigorous and can quickly spread to form a complete carpet under shrubs. It is ideal massed under hazel, as in a loose hedge, or used to lighten other more permanent ground-cover plants such as golden archangel (*Lamium galeobdolon*) 'Variegatum' or *Pachysandra terminalis*, which frequently look terminally ill by the end of winter. One of the most striking groups I have ever seen was nestling between the stems of *Berberis thunbergii* 'Rose Glow', whose emerging pinkish-purple leaves echoed the pink backs of the anemones, especially on

a cloudy day when they hang their heads. As soon as the sun shines they quickly turn their faces to the warmth and display the glistening, white, inner surface of their petals.

There are various double forms available, which make an ever bolder impact as they tend to form tighter clumps than the single one. We use them effectively under a dark holly, while the tiny semi-double 'Hilda' is exquisite in front of *Viola labradorica*, and both are used later as a ground cover for trilliums.

E. A. Bowles recommended planting them with the autumn-flowering *Saxifraga fortunei*, as each flowers while the other is dormant and both like a peaty soil in the shade. Wood anemones are not really happy unless planted in a light, humus-rich soil that remains cool in summer. They have strange rhizomes which look more like twigs than roots. These are very vulnerable to dehydration and should never be allowed to dry out, especially when available for sale, when they should be packed in peat or damp sand and never left dry in a bag. They need immediate planting horizontally into a well-prepared bed, and should be well watered. It is quite

Above: Here winter flowering *Cyclamen coum* has seeded itself extensively through this woodland rock garden at Forde Abbey

Right: Anemone nemorosa 'Allenii' with *Helleborus argutifolius*. This blue wood anemone is excellent for growing under shrubs

likely that little will happen in the first year other than the brief appearance of a few straggly leaves, as they always take some time to re-establish themselves following disturbance. However, once they have settled in they will quickly spread to form quite large patches. This was graphically illustrated a few years ago when I spread, among my dwarf rhododendrons, what I believed was just peat left from the anemone trays. The first year nothing untoward happened, but in the second and subsequent years a great and increasing mass of *A. nemorosa* 'Allenii' appeared from the few overlooked rhizomes. *A. n.* 'Allenii' has enormous, pale-blue flowers and is very beautiful in the right place, with *Helleborus argutifolius* (*H. corsicus*) for example, but not swamping my poor azaleas. There are various named clones of *A. nemorosa* available, most with blue flowers of variable intensity and vigour. Some of the best are 'Robinsoniana' (pale blue with silver backs), 'Royal Blue' (clear blue with purple backs), and 'Bowles' Purple' (light purple).

Closely related to the *A. nemorosa*, but having much smaller flowers of brilliant yellow, is *A. ranunculoides* from the mountains of SE Europe. Although preferring similar cool conditions, it is much more tolerant of the sun and will thrive on a limy soil. It seems to be a variable plant, with at least two distinct clones available: one being 6 in (15 cm) tall with apple-green foliage, the other being much more compact with dark stems. Both are quite delightful and are particularly attractive mixed with primroses and dwarf daffodils such as 'Jumblie' or 'Tête a Tête'. There is also a delightful semi-double form available which we grow under a large fern, mixed with *Ourisia* 'Snowflake'.

Hybrids have occurred between *A. nemorosa* and *A. ranunculoides* and, as one would imagine, they have inherited characteristics from both parents, although *A.* × *seemannii* (*A.* × *intermedia*) has slightly larger flowers than *A. ranunculoides*. However, their colouring, a soft, creamy, sulphur yellow, is delicate and they need sympathetic placing in the garden if they are not to be overlooked. I grow mine mixed with a clump of dwarf Solomon's seal, *Polygonatum roseum*, that does not make its appearance until late May well after the anemones have died back. This combined clump is in front of a camellia whose dark leaves form an ideal back-drop for the pale anemones.

Another anemone that likes shade is *A. apennina*, which looks very similar to *A. blanda* but has much taller flowers and an elongated rhizome. It can be a little difficult to establish initially but well worth persevering as, once happy, it will readily colonize relatively dry areas beneath large trees. I have seen *A. apennina* plants in their thousands mixed with snowdrops and primroses under an oak tree. They are also most attractive when planted with hellebores under apple trees or among *Euphorbia robbiae*, whose lime-green bracts are a good foil for the delicate blue and white anemones.

All these woodland anemones are extremely useful to underplant shrubs that perform late in the year, like the deciduous azaleas. They can be massed with a whole range of other shade-loving plants – primroses, *Veratrum nigrum*, *Euphorbia robbiae*, epimediums, bluebells, lilies for the summer, and colchicums for autumn colour – to provide a wealth of interest while the azaleas are not in flower.

Blue is also encountered in various other woodland bulbs, the bluebell being the classic example. It will be discussed at great length in Chapter 4 and, as its promiscuity renders it unsuitable for beds in all but the largest gardens, it it best left to colonize wild areas. Having said that, I once saw a narrow bed between two trees beautifully arranged with golden plants – euphorbias, grasses, *Valeriana phu* 'Aurea', and epimediums. Scattered through this rather acid-yellow bed were a few bluebells mixed with white tulips. The whole picture was simple but quite stunning.

The Spanish bluebell, *Scilla hispanica*, is much bolder and forms quite large clumps compared to the isolated plants of the native bluebell. The white ones, *S. h.* 'La Grandesse', are particularly useful to mass through a shrub border for early interest. Being practically indestructible they will cope with any subsequent cultivation, and are especially pleasing when viewed against the dark background of conifers and mixed with white foxgloves or purple honesty, for example. If the heads are pulled up as soon as they have faded, it will prevent them seeding. The bold blue scilla is magnificent when massed on its own under a large shrub or a small tree such as *Magnolia × soulangiana* 'Alba', where the blue is a perfect foil for the luxurious pure white flowers of the magnolia. All these scillas are ideal for planting in island beds where their progeny can be kept under control by mowing. The beds could be planted with a ground-cover plant, such as *Ajuga*, to provide interest once the scillas have faded.

Similar plantings are possible earlier in the spring, using some of the early, blue-flowered bulbs, such as grape hyacinth or *Scilla sibirica*, whose strong, almost electric, blue is very effective when massed on its own in a bed around a small tree, especially when the tree flowers too.

I have seen a fine specimen of *Magnolia stellata* rising out of a sea of *Scilla sibirica* 'Spring Beauty'. A more subtle planting of scillas would be under the deep pink *Magnolia* 'Leonard Messel', where pink primroses such as *Primula* 'Buckland Wine' and 'Wanda' could be added to create a subtle, overall purple effect.

Although only occasionally offered, *Scilla messenaica* and the similar *S. bithynica* are excellent for naturalizing in large drifts under trees and shrubs. They both have 4 in (10 cm) soft blue flowers with relatively wide leaves, and can quickly spread to form dense drifts, as at the Cambridge Botanic Garden where they are intermingled with hellebores and wood anemones. *S. lilio-hyacinthus* is very similar, only with smaller flowers, and is also best used to colonize unimportant areas of the garden, as it can be rather a thug and swamp more choice subjects. I have seen it used in a narrow shady bed beside a wall where it looked attractive with the red stems of peonies poking through the soft-blue carpet that it makes. Similarly, it would form a good back-drop to the creamy *Corylopsis pauciflora* that flowers at much the same time.

As we have seen, shady beds need not be limited to true woodland plants. Many bulbs are suitable for planting under specimen trees where the conditions are relatively dry during the summer months, but some varieties more traditionally associated with sunny borders will tolerate damper conditions, and in some cases require them in order to thrive. One of the earliest daffodils to flower, *Narcissus cyclamineus*, and its hybrids are just such a case. *N. cyclamineus*, with its delightful flowers, having narrow, deep yellow cups

and completely swept back petals, prefers a moist, acid, peaty soil. It will grow very happily by the banks of a stream or pond in full sun, but we find that on our dry soil it needs the coolness of a shaded peat bed, where it seeds itself very happily. In similar, but slightly drier, conditions the lovely creamy *N. triandrus* 'Albus' (commonly called angel's tears) will grow well. One of the most natural groupings of these that I have seen is on a steep bank under deciduous trees, where the soil remains cool in summer but is never waterlogged. The bank is now weed-free after years of spraying with weedkiller during the summer months, when it is deeply shaded by overhanging beech trees. The resultant carpet of moss forms a pleasing background to a wide range of bulbs, many of them the more unusual varieties. The soil is naturally acid so the range of bulbs is extensive. It starts in the autumn with the naked, purple flowers of *Crocus nudiflorus*, and is followed in the New Year by snowdrops, *Crocus tommasinianus*, *N. cyclamineus*, *N. triandrus* 'Albus', with the blue *Iris histriodes* 'Major' and, later, *Fritillaria meleagris* and *Cyclamen repandum*. The season finishes with a few ghostly spikes of white foxgloves in the deep shade of summer.

A shady border or woodland during the early spring months can often be a rather dull area of dripping branches, brown earth, and sad evergreens. Clumps of early flowering bulbs are ideal to add highlights and interest before the main flush of spring bulbs appears.

One of the most useful is the *N. cyclamineus* hybrid 'February Gold'. Although it rarely flowers in February in most of the country (it was bred and named in Cornwall) and 'Early March Gold' would be a more apt name, it is one of the very first to appear and enjoys a similar cool, moist position to its parent. It has substantial golden petals which sweep back gracefully from the trumpet. As it forms quite large clumps, and each flower is carried on 12 in (30 cm) stems, I find it invaluable, and place large clumps at strategic points to punctuate my woodland path and draw the eye, and the observer, further along. 'Peeping Tom', which is a little taller and with an even more pronounced snout-like appearance, can be used in a similar semi-shaded position, as could any of the cyclamineus hybrids. We have small groups of the dwarf 'Tête a Tête' and 'Jumblie'

among our primroses which grow alongside a large hosta whose leaves, in summer, cover the resting bulbs. 'February Silver' is among my favourites. Although it never flowers until mid-March and lacks the delicacy of 'February Gold', its sturdy white and lemon flowers last for many weeks and are particularly useful when planted in front of a dark evergreen background, such as holly or conifer. We grow onc clump mixed with Solomon's seal and the giant summer snowflake, *Leucojum aestivum* 'Gravetye', for a succession of interest that begins in February with a small patch of self-sown snowdrops and continues into late summer, as the Solomon's seal fades, with a fine clump of *Crocosmia* ('Montbretia').

Early daffodils are not only useful as isolated clumps to cheer up otherwise uninteresting areas, they can, of course, be mixed with other early flowering plants. I once saw a very arresting planting of 'Peeping Tom' behind an edging of *Bergenia purpurascens* (*B. delavayi*) whose deep, blood-red winter leaves become transluscent with the low winter sun behind them. I found the colour combination, although very striking, a little harsh, and would

prefer to use a softer-coloured daffodil, such as 'Dove Wings', in a similar situation, but you would need to choose an early flowering variety.

The blue and yellow combination is a common one in spring and many sympathetic groupings are possible using these tones. One of my favourites is clumps of 'February Gold' rising through a sea of intense-blue *Pulmonaria angustifolia* var. *azurea*. The introduction of primroses, and perhaps the soft cream of *Ribes laurifolium*, would soften the effect without destroying the harmony. Another useful blue-flowered plant for mixing with bulbs in shady beds is another pulmonaria, *P. longifolia*, which maintains its narrow, beautifully marked leaves all year, unlike *P. angustifolia* var. *azurea*.

The snowflakes, or leucojums, are related to the snowdrops, but their superficially similar flowers have six white petals, each green tipped, rather like fat snowdrops' skirts without the inner petticoat. Culturally, they resemble snowdrops as well in their need of a cool soil that remains moist in summer. In the wild they are frequently found in damp meadows or on river banks, and they thrive in similar

Above: The delightful daffodil species *N. cyclamineus* needs a moist, acid, peaty soil

Right: Narcissus 'February Gold' rising above a carpet of *Pulmonaria angustifolia* 'Azurea'

conditions in the garden, but they are also ideal for cool, dappled shade among trees and shrubs, provided it is not too dry in summer.

The spring snowflake, *Leucojum vernum*, with its broad strap-like leaves, produces its relatively large flowers on a 9 in (23 cm) stem during February and March. It is a native of Central Europe, where it grows by streams, and moisture is its single most important requirement. If grown in a dry soil, it can be one of the saddest sights in the garden, with flowers barely above the soil, but when growing well it is magnificent. It is ideal for mixing with *Helleborus orientalis*, snowdrops, and early crocuses for a rich display under large shrubs or small trees. *L. v.* var. *carpathicum* has yellowish markings rather than green ones, whereas *L.v.* var. *vagneri* is very robust and produces two flowers per stem.

The misnamed summer snowflake, *L. aestivum*, is a British native and is found throughout Europe and the Middle East. It is very prolific and has become almost a weed in our garden, being far more tolerant of drier conditions than *L. vernum*. We even have a precocious clump in one of the driest beds in the garden, under the office window. It is often in flower by the end of February, but April is the usual flowering time. Instead of the one or two flowers of *L. vernum*, *L. aestivum* has six more on 18 in (46 cm) stems. However, the accompanying leaves, rather like those of daffodils, can tend to swamp the flowers. The form originally found in Sussex, *L. a.* 'Gravetye', has much larger, more robust flowers that are carried well above the leaves, making a bolder impact. It is also much taller overall and ideal for clumps at the back of a shady border. We have one enormous clump behind my giant Solomon's seal. They have now become inextricably mixed but, as the *Leucojum* is over long before the Solomon's seal appears, it does not matter – indeed the graceful arching stems of the Solomon's seal hide the dying leaves of the *Leucojum* very successfully.

L. aestivum forms large clumps and is excellent massed amongst shrubs and mixed with daffodils, but not in complete shade. Its rather lax habit makes it ideal for planting beside water and it is one of the few bulbs that really revels in clay soil.

Another moisture-loving bulb is the snake's head fritillary, *Fritillaria melea-gris*. Although primarily a plant of damp water-meadows, it also thrives in a cool, semi-shaded bed where it is an ideal companion for many other spring bulbs. The extraordinary black sarana lily, *Fritillaria camschatcensis*, is another moisture-loving fritillary, which is probably not surprising considering that it originates from the area stretching between Alaska and Japan. It does not like hot, dry soils and we grow it in almost total shade against a north wall. It is not a boldly striking plant when seen in the garden but it is certainly one of the most unusual, normally having up to six deep purple and brown, almost black, flowers on 12 in (30 cm) stems clad in whorls of glossy green leaves. It needs to be placed in a choice position where it can dominate the surrounding foliage and not be swamped by it. The black leaved *Ophiopogon planiscapus* var. *nigrescens* or *Viola labradorica* would provide a sympathetic carpet for it, maybe with a clump of the pure-white *Trillium grandiflorum* for company and contrast.

The less dramatic, but none the less beautiful snake's head fritillaries, with their chequered soft purple, occasionally white, flowers are ideal companions for erythroniums in a semi-shaded bed. The common name of erythroniums, dog's tooth violet, conjures up such a splendid contradictory vision. Nothing could be less assertive than the traditional 'shrinking violet' or more aggressive than a dog's tooth. The name, in fact, refers to the distinctive shape of their bulbs, which in the European species, *Erythronium denscanis*, are very tiny, little bigger than a dachshund's tooth. Most of the North American erythroniums are much more robust and have bulbs up to 2 in (5 cm) long. The name 'violet', in the sixteenth century, was applied to all small purple-flowered plants, but in America erythroniums are given names, such as trout lily, which are much more descriptive of their lovely turk's cap flowers and mottled leaves.

Erythroniums are extremely variable in height and colour, varying from white, through cream, and yellow, to purplish pinks. However, all require a leafy soil in partial or even full shade, that is not too dry but enjoys free drainage. The main secret for successful cultivation is to prepare the ground thoroughly, adding leaf mould or peat, and also sand on heavy soils, and then to plant the bulbs 4–6 in (10–15 cm) deep. They should be planted vertically and then left undisturbed. Many refuse to flower the first year and it may be some seasons before their contractile roots pull the bulbs down to a level at which they will perform well. Planting bulbs under the edge of a large stone is a useful method of creating a cooler environment for them in, for example, an area of young shrubs where the shade is limited.

Erythronium bulbs are usually bought in the autumn, but like so many shade lovers they resent drying out, having no protective tunic, and thus they should be bought packed in peat. Some nurseries lift the bulbs just prior to despatch and this is the ideal method to ensure a fine vigorous bulb.

The European *E. dens canis* is shy to flower unless really happy but it is very beautiful when it does. The flowers, which may be white, pink, or purple, all with a dark blotch in the centre, are produced above clumps of dark green leaves that are heavily marbled with purple and are almost as attractive a feature as the flowers. Once planted they should be left alone to form large clumps, as at Great Dixter where they are planted in grass with snake's head fritillaries, wood anemones, Lent lily daffodils, and crocuses. I grow them with snowdrops, the large, purple flowers of *Viola bertolonii*, and trilliums under rhododendrons.

Most of the North American erythroniums are ideal in association with rhododendrons and camellias, none more so than *E. revolutum*, which is arguably the most attractive of all, with its graceful deep pink flowers on 9 in (23 cm) stems. Sadly it is rarely available, but occasionally hybrids of a paler shade are offered and these are well worth growing. Given almost pure peat, shade, and ample moisture, they are very vigorous and, if happy, will seed themselves around. The seedlings are slow to mature, taking some 5–6 years, but are well worth the wait. I have seen fine drifts of them mixed with snake's head fritillaries and the clear pink of *Cyclamen repandum*, or with the soft, ferny, grey leaves of *Dicentra formosa*, whose nodding locket-like flowers are a complimentary shade of purple. Sadly, the impact of this particular grouping was spoiled by its background of a large clump of the grass *Hakonechloa macra* 'Aureola', whose strong golden colouring made the delicate pink of the erythroniums appear dingy and washed out.

Others of the North American species and hybrids are freely available, and most are undemanding and rewarding woodland plants. All should be planted in small clumps and then left undisturbed to create a feature around the base of a tree or between shrubs. The dark leaves of *Viola labradorica* are a good foil for the apple-green leaves of *E. tuolumnense*, with its relatively small but beautiful, clear golden flowers. The hybrids 'Pagoda' and 'Citronella' have much larger, paler flowers and fine, softly marbled leaves, which are most attractive in themselves. The flowers of 'Citronella' are slightly lemon in colour; it flowers about a week later than 'Pagoda' and is therefore useful to continue the succession.

E. 'White Beauty' is outstanding, with its beautiful creamy-white flowers with golden centres, above finely marked leaves. At Knightshayes it is spectacular massed below a scarlet rhododendron, or in large drifts with the tiny yellow violet *V. pennsylvanica*, intermingled with the purple *V. labradorica*. I even saw one fine clump tucked in under the shady side of a trough where it had grown into a fine and most unusual feature. Some of the smaller ferns, *Polystichum setiferum* for instance, could be planted with it to provide interest later in the year and cover the bare patches left while it is dormant. The fern will also keep the soil moist, but care must be taken to remove its decaying leaves in the autumn or else the erythroniums will fail to appear.

As with most bulbs the flowers are relatively fleeting, but with erythroniums it is possible to take advantage of their fine, often marbled leaves and to use them as foliage plants once the flowers have faded. I saw one narrow, shady bed in April that relied solely upon foliage for its continuing interest. Groups of *E.* 'White Beauty', with its finely marbled leaves just like a trout's scales, were mixed with clumps of the silver-washed *Cyclamen hederifolium*, the white-spotted *Arum italicum* 'Pictum', and the lovely maidenhair fern *Adiantum venustum*, with its bronze-tinted young growth. The delicate, creamy, turk's cap flowers of the erythroniums were an added bonus when they appeared.

Another genus where the foliage is

almost as important as the flowers is *Corydalis*. It has clusters of snapdragon flowers above delicate, fern-like foliage and is found throughout the Northern Hemisphere.

Although most of them are not tuberous rooted, among those that are there are some excellent garden plants that deserve to be more widely known. They all require a well-drained, humus-rich soil in semi-shade where they will not become completely sun-baked in summer. They are ideal companions for other woodland bulbs. The scarce species, such as the electric blue *C. ambigua* and the pure white *C. caucasica* var. *alba*, are better placed in specialist peat beds or in a shady pocket on the rock garden, as their flowers, although very beautiful, are fleeting, the whole plant only being above ground for a few weeks. Arguably the most beautiful of all, *C. cashmiriana*, has almost turquoise flowers but is only really happy in Scotland where it revels in the cool, continually moist climate.

C. solida, on the other hand, is much less demanding and more vigorous, seeding itself freely when happy, and is useful as a ground cover for taller bulbs such as daf-fodils, or with hellebores and pulmonarias. At Kew Gardens it is used extensively under deciduous azaleas to provide early interest. There it is mixed with epimediums, but the rather acid-green of their young leaves is not a good foil for the soft purple corydalis, and makes them appear rather muddy. They are much better when seen with dark green foliage such as *Helleborus foetidus* or the silver-washed leaves of *Pulmonaria officinalis*.

Strictly speaking, the North American wood lilies or trilliums are not bulbs at all, but tuberous roots that must be kept moist even when dormant as the bud overwinters on the outside of the tuber. They number among them some of the most beautiful of woodland plants, as nothing is more attractive than a large clump of trilliums in a woodland setting. Acidity is irrelevant but soil type is of vital importance. They require a semi-shady position in a soil with a very high humus content, preferably well-rotted leaf mould but peat can be used instead. They actively dislike cold, water-logged soils, so sand as well as humus should be added to heavy soils.

Their name is indicative of their prime characteristic: all their parts are in threes.

Above: A charming informal group under a cherry tree of snake's head fritillaries and *Erythronium* 'Pagoda'

Right: Erythronium 'White Beauty', a plant for a cool humus-rich soil in semi-shade, with *Viola labradorica*

The stem, which may be from 4–18 in (10–46 cm) long gives rise to a whorl of three leaves supporting the flower which has three petals. They are very variable plants, and there seems much confusion about their naming, but among the species most likely to be encountered are *T. grandiflorum*, with large, white, recurved petals, and *T. erectum*, with similar-shaped flowers in deep purple or white. *T. sessile* (*T. cuneatum*) has beautifully marbled leaves and large, deep red, upright flowers, and is similar to *T. chloropetalum*, whose flowers are white or pink-flushed. *T. luteum*, with its pale, yellowish-green flowers is possibly a variant of *T. sessile*. It is a robust plant but needs careful placing in the garden if its delicate beauty is not to be overlooked. The other trilliums, though, make much bolder clumps.

Trilliums should be left undisturbed and will take three or four years to settle down and begin to clump up, but they are well worth the wait. The ultimate size of the clumps should be taken into account when planting them, so that they have space into which to grow and are not crowded by other tall subjects which would spoil their overall appearance. They look best when viewed in isolation and are excellent rising above lower-growing plants such as violets, *Cyclamen*, *Anemone nemorosa* 'Alba Plena', or the coloured forms of celandine.

Another group of woodland plants with relatively insignificant flowers and more normally grown for their foliage are members of the *Arum* family. *Arum maculatum*, the lords and ladies of the hedgerows, is almost indestructible, a weed in our garden, but the similar *A. italicum* 'Pictum' is invaluable for its cream-veined leaves. These are produced early in the autumn, often while the scarlet berries are still present, and remain all through the winter, providing beautiful immaculate clumps in even the worst weather. They are an excellent foil for snowdrops, hellebores, and scillas. The flowers are insignificant but should be left if you want the spectacular berries, although this does not guarantee their appearance.

Arisarum proboscidium, on the other hand, is more of a curiosity but is useful as ground cover for larger plants and bulbs in a cool peaty soil. The strange flowers are just like little, brown-tailed mice disappearing down their holes but, unfortunately, they are as shy as the real thing and

hide among the leaves, so they are only apparent if you search for them.

One does not think of tulips as bulbs for shady places, but there is one European species that is at home in cool woodland conditions. This is *T. sylvestris*, which has yellow flowers with pointed tips. It flowers in late April or May on wiry stems which seem to contort into the most amazing shapes. There seem to be two forms in cultivation. We have had one bulb that has produced two large flowers for 15 years but has never increased. The other form has smaller, slightly greener flowers, but spreads well by stolons and can form quite large patches. However, it seems to be fairly shy to flower and only produces a few flowers each year. We grow it among primroses and *Viola labradorica*, and one clump is mixed with *Anemone nemorosa* 'Allenii' – the anemones forming a mat of fern-like leaves below the golden tulip. It does need a certain amount of sunshine and will not flower in complete shade.

Ordinary tulips would not normally be planted in a shady garden, but in areas of dappled sunlight it is possible to use clumps to define the end of a path, to draw the eye along and relieve the monotony of overall greenness. The early flowering scarlet *T. fosteriana* hybrids are useful for this – 'Red Emperor' ('Mme Lefeber') for instance.

Summer

As the trees and shrubs complete their leaf canopy so many of the woodland bulbs become dormant, but there are a few that can be planted in more open situations to continue the interest through the summer months.

All lilies require some sunshine in order to perform well but given dappled sun and a good, deep soil with plenty of moisture available there are some that will thrive in cool woodland conditions, adding their distinctive charm and colours to what are often otherwise rather dull borders (cultural details will be found on p. 49.)

Perhaps we should begin by reluctantly dismissing the giant Himalayan lily *Cardiocrinum giganteum*. It is in fact not a true lily but its beauty seduces everyone and, indeed, I think it must be one of the most spectacular of all sights when in full flower. Its stem towers up to 8 ft (2.5 m) and is crowned by up to a dozen enormous, waxy, white bells. Unfortunately, it is monocarpic and its flowering signifies its death, but with any luck the flowering bulb will produce a number of offsets around it, although these can take up to seven years to flower. It requires a deep acid soil of virtually pure leaf mould, mixed with rotted manure, perfect drainage, and a plentiful supply of moisture. I have a friend in Scotland who grows it on her compost heap. It must have cool, moist conditions and therefore grows best in true woodland gardens in the north and west. Mercifully for the rest of us there are quite a number of other beautiful, reliable, and relatively easy lilies to choose from.

Drainage is the single most important requirement of lilies, coupled with a regular water supply. These two facts cannot be stressed enough and are probably the main reason for poor performance. Lilies are easily affected by drought, quickly aborting their flowers and becoming prematurely dormant, thereby weakening the bulbs which may take a few years to build up their strength again. Although many lilies are not fussy about soil acidity, there are some for whom high acidity is a prerequisite, so care must be taken when choosing varieties. There are many beautiful hybrids available but, sadly, most of them seem short-lived. The lilies listed below are mainly species that have proved reliably perennial in many gardens.

The earliest lily to flower is one of the oldest in cultivation, having been described by the herbalists of the sixteenth century. *L. pyrenaicum* originated in scattered localities in the Pyrenees and the Tarn Department of France, but it has so adapted to the British climate that it is now naturalized in many areas. Indeed, many argue that it is probably best planted in the wilder areas of the garden as it is not particularly striking, having a few rather small, bright yellow reflexed flowers on rather stout stems. However, I must admit to a fondness for it, as much for its virtually indestructible nature and early flowering, as for its overall apperance. It is ideal to tuck in among shrubs, especially dark-leaved ones such as holly, to bring a touch of colour in May and June. Some people find its scent rather fetid and overpowering and I must admit that my plants are odourless so I am unable to judge on this matter.

Following on from *L. pyrenaicum* is the classic turk's cap lily, *L. martagon*, with its stately spires of purple or white reflexed flowers, up to 50 on each plant. It must be one of the most adaptable of all lilies, having a natural spread over two continents. It is always found in association with woodland, and, indeed, one of my outstanding memories of the Pyrenees will be of finding a fine stand of these plants catching the sun in a glade among pine trees. Although it will grow happily in quite dense shade, the flowers really need some sun upon them to appear at their best. The leaves, arranged in symmetrical whorls, are very architectural and are most attractive in their own right. I have seen *L. martagon* mixed very successfully with epimediums, the latter shading the roots of the lily in the summer. Its colour is very variable, ranging from rather washed-out pink, through deep purple, to pure white. Despite its widespread distribution it is not always easy to establish, and it may take a couple of seasons for newly planted bulbs to flourish, but once happy it is very long-lived. We had one bulb that survived years of neglect. Every year it pushed its way through a jungle of epimediums and Japanese anemones, its 3 ft (90 cm) stem crowned by a glistening spire of pure white flowers. It has since been rescued and now gives its annual display among a fine, variegated Solomon's seal. A large clump of *Hosta sieboldiana* 'Frances Williams' in front of it completes the picture.

L. martagon has been used extensively for hybridizing, probably the best result being the Backhouse hybrids which need similar light-woodland conditions.

Midsummer is the peak time for lilies, with new ones coming into flower almost daily. Two of the easiest are *L. szovitzianum* and the similar, possibly synonymous, *L. monadelphum*. They are extremely beautiful, having fine, pendant, golden flowers, strongly recurved at the tips, and will tolerate a wide range of soils, from acid to alkaline and from heavy clay to light sand. Sadly, they are rarely available but can be grown from seed, although an enormous amount of patience is required as they are phenomenally slow to mature and the seedlings must be kept weed-free and pest-free at all times, and not be allowed to dry out.

One of my favourites is the rarely seen

L. duchartrei. It is lime-tolerant but requires a soil that is very rich is humus and with an ample supply of moisture. It produces one to five delicate, white flowers, each more or less spotted with purple. I grow it in my raised peat bed where its feet never see the sun, although it always raises its head well above the dwarf rhododendrons under which it is planted. Its main disadvantage is that it is stoloniferous and the stem continues underground for some distance, so it is difficult to know where it will make its next appearance. As it is never in quite the same place every year labelling does not really help, and I had to move it under the rhododendron from its previous home as I was always damaging it when weeding. It grows freely and quite quickly from seed and, provided it can be kept undisturbed, can spread into quite large areas, as at the Savill Gardens. Sadly, it is prone to attack from virus so the plants must be watched carefully and any diseased ones removed immediately. As the virus is spread by aphids these must be scrupulously controlled.

Lilium tigrinum is the tiger lily which flowers in July and on into September. It needs a slightly acid soil, and must have some sun or it will dwindle. Sadly, it seems to be relatively short-lived, possibly as a result of viral infection, but it is easily raised from the numerous bulbils that are found in the axils between the leaves and the stems. It is aptly named, having large, deep-orange flowers spotted with black, and I have a fine clump in a gap among my rhododendrons where it never fails to please, towering over the sad remains of the spring display. *L.t.* var. *splendens* flowers later, from mid-August to late September. Its flowers are of a deeper orange and the plant is more vigorous. *L. tigrinum* is also available in yellow (*L.t.* var. *flaviflorum*), white (*L.t.* 'White Lady'), pink ('Pink Beauty'), and red ('Red Fox').

Another late-flowering species that requires an acid soil is the beautiful *L. speciosum*, with its large, waxy, heavily scented flowers. It is among the last to flower and could almost be considered an autumn bulb as it is frequently a companion to the first colchicums. The large reflexed flowers, on gracefully arching stems, are very variable, being more or less flushed and spotted in shades of pink except for 'Album' which is a pure, glistening white. It is slightly tender and needs a

sunnier position than many lilies in order to ripen the bulbs after flowering, but in the milder counties it is delightful among rhododendrons and camellias, where their dark leaves form the perfect back-drop for this graceful lily. It is excellent in pots, being frequently more long-lived in these conditions. Pot culture is also the easiest way in which this acid-loving lily can be grown by gardeners on chalky soils. Not only are the pots attractive subjects in themselves, they can, of course, be plunged into the garden for instant effect. No apology need be made for growing lilies in this way as it is often the most satisfactory given poor or unsuitable soil conditions.

All the lilies mentioned so far, while needing ample moisture, must have excellent drainage if they are to thrive. The

Above: Lilium martagon 'Album' is a reliable lily for a shady bed under shrubs

well-named panther lily, *L. pardalinum*, on the other hand, actively requires a moist soil, coming as it does from the stream sides of western America. It needs a wet soil that slopes, or else, as in a friend's garden, a soil with a high water-table that never completely dries out. In my free-draining soil it only manages to produce a few leaves each year but in good conditions like my friend's it is a really magnificent sight in July. The deep orange–red turk's cap flowers, heavily spotted, can be as much as 7 ft (2 m) tall and, consequently, are vulnerable to wind damage, but in a sheltered position, under the light canopy of trees, its rhizomatous bulbs spread readily and form extensive patches. I once saw a magnificent planting of them beside a woodland lake where they towered above a bed of hostas and the beautiful bronzed-yellow *Ligularia* 'Desdemona'. A touch of soft lemon was provided by a large clump of *Primula florindae* at the water's edge.

Hybrids based upon *L. pardalinum* are known as the Bellingham hybrids and require similar conditions to their parent. However, they are not as long-lived and must be moved to a new position every two years. 'Shuksan' is probably the finest, with soft orange flowers heavily spotted with maroon.

Once you have chosen the appropriate lily for your soil and situation, the site must be well prepared and the bulbs kept well watered during any dry spells. A watch should also be kept for aphids as they spread the virus diseases that are so devastating to lilies. Lilies are best planted an isolated clumps and it is better to buy a large number of one variety rather than one bulb of many varieties. New groups can be added annually as required. Dappled sunlight is needed to bring out the full beauty of flowers, and by mixing the early, mid-, and late-flowering varieties it is possible to have groups of lilies to provide colour and interest throughout the summer months when shady borders are primarily composed of shades of green.

Unlike lilies, with their spectacularly coloured flowers, the summer-flowering relatives of the arums, arisaemas, have rather retiring flowers but they have a cool charm of their own. They are related to our wild lords and ladies and have similar 'flowers' which are, in fact, the flower spathes, the flower being inside it. Their

leaves, which are composed of three or more leaflets, form attractive clumps and are a useful addition to any cool, moist soil in semi-shade. *A. candidissimum* is probably the most attractive, having large, white spathes broadly striped with pink. As it only comes through the soil in May or June its position must be clearly marked to avoid damaging the emerging shoot. This species seems able to tolerate much drier, sunnier positions than the others.

A. triphyllum from N. America is a smaller plant with neat trifoliate leaves and a green spathe with striking deep brown stripes. *A. consanguineum* from China, on the other hand, has leaves reminiscent of those of lupins, with 15–21 leaflets arranged in a circle like the spokes of a wheel. The deep purple spathe, striped

Above: Mixed crocosmias with variegated grasses, echo the bronze tints of autumn at Knightshayes Court

white, is produced from the side of the stem and is followed by a nodding seed-head.

Late summer sees the advent of the small gladiolus-like flowers of the crocosmias. With their predominantly burnt-orange colouring they are a foretaste of autumn, although most of them commence flowering in August. The ubiquitous montbretia, described by Graham Stuart Thomas as a 'weed proof coloniser', is an invasive weed in my warm, damp climate and other members of the family have been tarred with the same brush and are often banished to nether regions of the garden, if they are allowed in at all. This is sad because there are many beautiful hybrids which are completely trouble-free, increasing well and flowering profusely at a time when the bulk of summer-flowering plants are past their prime and are beginning to look rather bedraggled and forlorn.

Their rather lax habit and often untidy foliage, which is present for much of the year, means that they are not really suitable for prime sites in the garden, but they are excellent massed among shrubs where they receive a certain amount of sunlight. Both deep shade and overcrowding can result in a reduction in the number of flowers. Should this be a problem, established clumps can be lifted and divided in early spring, which is also the correct time to plant new corms. Like crocuses, new corms build up onto the preceeding one, but in the case of crocosmias the old corm does not wither but remains as a continuing food source. There can be as many as six corms in a cluster, looking rather like a horticultural Tower of Pisa. It is not advisable to separate these as only the youngest is capable of producing leaves so the rest may as well be left to increase the vigour of the new corm. Newly planted single corms take a couple of years before they begin to flower.

Crocosmias require a moist position that does not become baked in summer, but they detest really heavy clay and cold, damp soils, therefore they tend to thrive best in the warmer parts of the country. Relatively large groups of corms should be planted 4 in (10 cm) deep, but deeper in colder districts where a covering of bracken may be beneficial in winter.

When viewed *en masse*, crocosmias can easily be dismissed as being very similar, but they are worthy of closer examination as the flowers are often bi-coloured, as in 'Jackanapes', or have strong markings, such as 'Emily McKenzie' which also has very large flowers almost 2 in (5 cm) across. Bowls of crocosmias, where the flower can be clearly seen, always excite much comment and interest at flower shows, and they make excellent cut flowers, lasting well in water.

I find crocosmias extremely useful to add a touch of colour to otherwise rather dull shrub beds, but discretion must be exercised when introducing such a strong, almost vibrant, colour. Many gardens in late summer are dominated by hydrangeas, and their often rather delicate colours, particularly the soft pinks, are not enhanced by the strident crocosmias. The effect of adding a strong orange is to diminish the pink still further until it appears dingy rather than delicate.

Whole beds can be devoted to clumps of the variously hued crocosmias intermingled with one of the golden or silver variegated grasses, such as *Molinia caerulea* 'Variegata', *Miscanthus sinensis* 'Variegata', or *Hakonechloa macra* to form a jungle of spikes. Such a planting in a shady bed, under spring-flowering shrubs at the end of a lawn perhaps, or in a narrow, partially shaded bed beside the house, would provide an unusual focal point for late summer, with a good contrast of textures, especially when the sun catches the flowers. Their leaves are an added bonus, being present for much of the year, making the bed virtually weed-free. Groupings like this are especially effective if the associated trees or shrubs change colour early in the autumn to continue the autumn effect started by crocosmias, especially as some of the varieties of *Crocosmia* will continue to produce flowers right into October.

4 Bulbs in grass

Whenever naturalized bulbs are mentioned, April, with drifts of daffodils under venerable apple trees, or beech woods in May turned to a sea of blue by bluebells, spring to mind. However desirable and enhancing such a sight may be, it is sadly impracticable for most of us, limited as we are by space and the conflicting demands upon such space as we may have. However, most gardens have a small area of grass where the addition of a few carefully chosen bulbs can add immeasurably more colour than their relatively modest number might at first indicate. When these bulbs are planted under a tree chosen for its flower, fruit, bark, or autumn colour, then the whole picture is considerably more than the sum of its parts – the striking sight of a drift of the blue autumn crocus, *C. speciosus*, under the yellow leaves of an *Acer*, or white daffodils under sugar-pink cherry blossom, for example. In country districts the boundary hedge often drops neglected to the road and is an ideal place for snowdrops and daffodils; and orchards, whether they contain a couple of gnarled, neglected apple trees or spruce, well-placed modern ones, can equally be well planted to give a complete succession of bulbs or, indeed, bulbs and plants to create a flowering meadow.

Obviously these two situations, the more formal lawn, and the 'wild' area, are not mutually exclusive, but they do make different demands and it is this that ultimately affects the choice of bulbs. Quite apart from personal preference, the length of time you are prepared to leave the grass uncut is the main limiting factor. If you have a small corner of the garden where grass can be left to grow, then experiments can be made to establish a traditional hay meadow, albeit in a modified and exotic form, including as it could crocuses from Turkish hillsides, daffodils from European mountains, and anemones from Greek islands. It is, of course, possible to create a meadow based on our own native flora but this would include few bulbs – the wild Lent lily (*Narcissus pseudonarcissus*), the snake's head fritillary (*Fritillaria meleagris*), with bluebells in shaded areas. Our native orchids, the prima donnas of the meadow, display an appropriate temperament, and are totally untameable. Their appearance, irregular and uncontrollable, should be welcomed and respected, but we can and should do little to introduce them. Therefore I propose that we draw on the wider range of bulbs available and create an exotic and exciting corner of the garden, by the judicious mix of 'wild' and cultivated bulbs and perennials.

The inclusion of perennial plants, even in a limited way, such as primroses and violets mixed with early spring bulbs under a tree, precludes the later production of a close-shaven weed-free sward. (The grass in this area will have to be kept long until midsummer and then only a high cut is possible.) If rolling, close-cut swards of green are your ultimate aim, then perforce you are limited to bulbous subjects, so that, once their leaves have faded and the grass mown short, a broad-leaf weedkiller can be applied, if required.

Bright crocuses followed by daffodils are the most usual concept of naturalized bulbs, but give an erroneous idea of the enormous range that is possible, from autumn crocuses in September through to camassias and lilies in early summer. Therefore the extent of the flowering season is very personal, and to a large extent dependent upon the length of time that you are prepared to wait until the grass can be cut – normally some six weeks after flowering in the case of spring bulbs. Thus, the inclusion of the delightful May-flowering pheasant's eye narcissus (*N. poeticus* 'Recurvus') would preclude the cutting of the lawn until late June, whereas a planting limited to autumn and early spring bulbs – crocuses, snowdrops, and early hybrid daffodils could be cut a month earlier.

I cannot stress the importance of this growing-on period too strongly. If you have ever examined a bulb when in full growth, you will see that it has a very pinched look, all its reserves being in the leaves. In order to create a mature bulb to flower the following season all bulbs need a period of unchecked growth so that the nourishment can be returned from the leaves. Once planted in grass, bulbs need

Above: Purple and white Dutch crocus with Lent lily daffodils have seeded over the years to carpet the lawns at Forde Abbey

little further attention other than to ensure that the grass is kept short for some time during the summer to enable the sun to warm the soil and help 'ripen' the bulb and initiate flower buds. A dusting of a potash-rich fertilizer in early spring is beneficial, and bone-meal can also be applied in the autumn, but only once every three years or so, as toxicity can result from too frequent application.

The acidity or alkalinity of the soil plays little part in the choice of bulb, with a few notable exceptions – *Narcissus cyclami-neus* and certain lilies, for example, require an acid soil – such specific requirements will be found in the tables. Moisture, drainage, and shade are of much greater significance. Certain bulbs, such as *Fritil-laria meleagris*, are naturally associated with water-meadows and will not thrive on dry, sandy soils unless the rainfall is high. This moisture requirement can, to a certain extent, be overcome by planting the bulbs in the shade of trees where the soil does not become so baked; but here, however, you can run the risk of drought, through competition for moisture from the tree itself, and the umbrella effect of its canopy.

Some woodland bulbs require shade during the summer months both for the drier conditions and a cool soil – bluebells are a classic example of this. They commence their growth during early spring, when there are no leaves on the trees and the ground receives ample moisture, and flower as the leaves appear on the trees, their seed ripening very shortly after. The larger Spanish bluebell is more tolerant of open, sunny positions and is often found as a weed in many gardens.

Many bulbs that are widely grown today originated in the warmer climate of the Mediterranean. These bulbs require a dry, sunny dormancy and should be planted in full sun where the bulbs can be ripened, otherwise they may fail to flower. Crocuses are a classic case, and non-flowering clumps may well need a sunnier, drier situation.

The actual physical planting of bulbs in grass can be a daunting prospect, and for large numbers a bulb planter is probably the best method. This tool removes a plug of turf and soil enabling the bulbs to be dropped into the hole – the long-handled form with a lever for removing the soil plug is the most efficient. The main disadvantage of this method is that 5–6 in (12–15 cm) is the smallest gap possible between bulbs, and although this is suitable for large bulbs, for many smaller ones, *Crocus*, *Chionodoxa*, and *Scilla*, the distance is rather excessive, at least for the first few years until the bulbs clump up. However, it is possible to plant more than one variety per hole – for example, early and late crocuses can be mixed for a succession of flowers.

Another, more time-consuming method, is to remove a layer of turf, and lightly fork the soil over, then the bulbs can be scattered in a natural manner before being planted and the turf replaced. This has a double advantage of creating a more natural, close planting of small bulbs and also allowing for the addition of sand to heavy, clay soils. It is, of course, not necessary to plant just one variety during this exercise, either snowdrops mixed with winter aconites and late-flowering crocus, or chionodoxas with scillas and daffodils are possible combinations.

These methods are suitable for planting in grass that has been cultivated, such as lawns, but planting direct into unimproved meadow may not be so successful as the grass may well be too coarse and may swamp the bulbs. In such problem areas the best remedy is to remove the turf completely, either physically or by spraying, and to plant the bulb in the exposed soil. The grass will quickly recolonize the bare patches but much less densely, giving the bulbs a chance to establish themselves. Careful management of the grass, with regular cutting once the leaves of the bulbs have died away, will encourage the finer grasses and in time improve it, but if the large, coarse grass persists it may be necessary to kill the entire area and re-sow, thinly, with a suitable grass mix. When bulbs are planted in a lawn or orchard and the grass is then mown regularly once they have died back, the actual type of grass is not important. However, if you wish to experiment with wild flowers and bulbs, particularly if you extend the season into early summer, then the type of grass becomes of paramount importance or the plants will be swamped. The Royal Horticultural Society have recently recommended a low-maintenance mixture of 60 per cent Lorina perennial ryegrass, 35 per cent Logro slender creeping red fescue, and 5 per cent highland brown top bent.

This need only be cut twice a year and may well provide a good base for a wild flower and bulb mix. The secret is – sow thinly, to give the bulbs and plants a chance to compete. However, I do not propose to go into details about how to achieve a true meadow or even an alpine meadow as there are excellent books available on the subject.

For planting small quantities, such as a few crocuses or one clump of daffodils at the base of a tree, I favour the simple expedient of inserting a long, narrow trowel into the grass, just dropping the bulb in the hole, removing the trowel and firming with my foot. Whatever planting method is your choice, this firming of the turf after planting is very important, but especially so when planting crocuses. One

Above: The meadow of Great Dixter with snake's head fritillaries, *Narcissus pseudonarcissus*, primroses and dog's tooth violets

large institution planted 1000 crocuses one day using a bulb planter, and the mice (or squirrels) followed them that night and removed the turf plug and the crocuses!

In an attempt to defeat mice I always make sure that I plant my crocuses very deeply and firmly and remove all loose bulb tunics from the soil surface, as I am certain that the mice locate the bulbs by smell. Autumn-flowering crocuses, however, seem not to be so vulnerable to attack from mice, possibly because they are planted earlier in the year, in August, when there are ample food sources available. Later, when the mice are looking for alternative food, crocuses are in full growth and the bulb has shrivelled.

As a general rule, bulbs in grass should be planted well below the depth of grass roots. Although there may be optimum times for planting bulbs, in my experience of running a bulb nursery, where there are always 'left overs' to be planted, often far outside the recommended time, I have found that many bulbs, which after all are designed by nature for a long dormancy, are very tolerant. This tolerance with certain types of bulbs, extends to moving them in growth. Snowdrops are well known for this, but I have seen an entire planting of daffodils, under a wall due for demolition, transplanted to the other side of the road and continue growing and flowering without a check. Therefore it is possible, with care, to move bulbs around the garden at the beginning of the growing season, or at the very end when you can see just where they would look most attractive.

Autumn

Autumn is an important, and beautiful, season in the bulb year. As the garden gradually prepares for winter it is alive with the changing colours of leaf and berry. For the majority of bulbs this is the equivalent of spring, when they break the dormancy of the dry summer months and growth begins. In most cases this early growth is confined to root production, but in some it begins with the production of flowers – often long before the appearance of leaves. Careful planting of these autumn-flowering bulbs can be extremely effective, glowing amidst the brown of the fallen leaves, or complimenting the bright autumn colours. A clump of blue *Crocus speciosus*, for example, planted under the deep-red *Quercus rubra* or *Acer* 'Crimson King' will enhance the colour of each.

Autumn-flowering bulbs are usually sold in August for immediate planting, followed by flowers a few weeks later, or in the case of colchicums even a few days later. When planting in grass, it is best to mow immediately before planting and perhaps again two or three weeks later, just before the flowers appear. As most autumn crocuses flower well before their leaves appear, there should also be time, if necessary, to make a final cut of the grass immediately after flowering, in late October or early November, just before the emergence of leaves. Nor, in fact, will it really harm the bulbs if the tips of the new leaves are cut, as they do not grow fully until the New Year. Colchicums, though, are a different matter and care must be taken not to damage the leaves as the damaged tissues are susceptible to fungal attack.

The earliest of the true autumn-flowering bulbs, normally in September but occasionally in August, is the hardy *Cyclamen hederifolium*. This produces masses of small pink or white flowers which are followed by beautifully marked leaves (full cultural details for cyclamen will be found on p. 70). *C. hederifolium* is at its best in beds under trees, although it occasionally naturalizes itself in thin grass. We have even had a mysterious straight line of seedlings appear in the lawn – presumably ants, using the mouse tunnels as underground motorways, dropped the seeds. However, flower production from plants in grass is sparse compared to those planted in beds, and such plantings also necessitate a long period (September–April) during which it is unwise to cut the grass.

Colchicums, often erroneously called autumn crocus, or naked ladies, also begin flowering in September. Primarily plants of rich soil and semi-shade, one or two species are suitable for naturalizing in grass, although they do not increase so readily when used in this way. Their attractive goblet-shaped flowers are followed by large leaves which persist until late July, therefore care must be exercised over their placing, and clumps positioned around the base of a tree are perhaps the best solution. The delicate *C. autumnale*, with a succession of small, soft-lilac flowers, and the larger *C. byzantinum*, sometimes found in catalogues as *C. autumnale* 'Major', are suitable for this treatment, as are some of the more vigorous hybrids, such as 'The Giant'.

Many of the true autumn crocuses are, on the other hand, eminently suited to naturalizing and are probably best used in that manner. Most are rather tall, 6 in (15 cm), and flower before their leaves, which give them a rather naked appearance and, in addition, makes the flowers vulnerable to wind and rain, so they are ideal for planting in the grass which gives them support, both visual as well as actual. Once planted they should need no further attention as the clumps will extend both vegetatively and by seed.

We have found *Crocus speciosus*, with its tall, blue-veined flowers and prodigious rate of increase, a plant of outstanding garden value. All forms have a strong scent of honey and last relatively well in water. They naturalize well in grass under trees, tolerate the damp English summer, and withstand the vagaries of the autumn weather. There always seems to be a bonus of a second crop of flowers to replace those damaged by rain. E. A. Bowles in *My garden in winter* describes how, a few years after planting a dozen bulbs he tried to move them. Despite collecting many hundreds of bulbs by sieving he still had masses of blue flowers among his cabbages where he had spread the old soil. We have a large patch among trees in a wild garden that begin to flower in late September just as the leaves begin to turn on the trees. Even at the end of November the last flowers are still vigorously pushing up through a carpet of fallen maple leaves. It is particularly good among yellow leaves, and, even when tightly closed, it has a rather cheeky appearance, with its bright-orange stigma appearing over the top of the tightly closed flowers. At the slightest rise in temperature or hint of sun the flowers open wide, attracting butterflies and many other insects.

Various named forms are available and it is well worth having a few of each as, although basically of similar colour and shape, they do flower at slightly different times, thus extending the display. Some of the most widely available cultivars are *C. s.* 'Artabir', with white inner petals and darker outer ones, *C. s.* 'Conqueror', with good, deep blue flowers, and *C. s.* 'Aitchisonii', a late-flowering variety with huge, pale lavender flowers. We have planted this around the white trunk of *Betula jacquemontii*, which turns into a spire of gold in late October or early November just as this crocus is at its best. One of my favourites is the cobalt blue *C. s.* 'Oxonian', with its dark flower-stem which looks good when planted to contrast with the pale-flowered varieties, as does the dazzling white *C. s.* 'Album', which is as sturdy as the blue forms and is a good foil for them.

Although *Crocus speciosus* is probably best for naturalizing, there are other suitable varieties. *C. pulchellus* resembles it but has soft lavender flowers with white anthers, and it has been known to hybridize with *C. speciosus* so intermediate flowers may occur. *C. pulchellus* thrives in full sun or semi-shade and is, in fact, almost indestructible. When we were excavating a pond some 18 in (45 cm) of topsoil was put on a clump; nothing daunted, they continued to flower magnificently every year. With a few notable exceptions (for example, cyclamen and bulbs that must have their necks at ground level), it is almost impossible to plant a bulb too deeply. For many varieties, and especially on light soils, really deep planting is one way of encouraging long life, and it is an added protection against frost damage. Most crocus bulbs are quite hardy but in really severe winters the leaves can be so damaged that the bulbs are weakened for a season or two, or even killed outright, and in areas that experience regular severe winters it is perhaps best to grow varieties that flower before the leaves are produced, such as *C. pulchellus* and *C. speciosus* where leaf production is delayed until mild weather. Those that have leaves while flowering (e.g. *C. ochroleucus* and *C. medius*) will always be vulnerable to damage during really severe frosts.

One of the most pleasurable sights of a sunny day in November is the sudden opening, from their very narrow, insignificant buds, of the pure white flowers of *C. ochroleucus*. They are produced with such gay abandon that one can forgive them their small stature 2 in (4–5 cm). In light soils they increase prodigiously and, if planted in the wrong place, can become a weed, as we have discovered by experience. We find them coming up all over the nursery as it is impossible to remove every one of the pin-head sized cormlets. The flowers, which may come just before the leaves, or with them just showing, are very effective coming through fallen leaves, provided the latter are not too large. However, the flowers can be vulnerable to attack from birds or slugs, and this, coupled with their small size, makes them especially suited to a sunny corner of the rock garden or at the edge of a sunny border, where perhaps their delicate beauty can be best appreciated.

There are other crocuses suitable for naturalizing, but their performance is more dependent upon the conditions of the preceding summer. *C. kotschyanus* originates in Turkey and needs a good summer in order to flower really well. It has small, lilac flowers with either a yellow throat (often called *C. zonatus*), or white (*C. k.* var. *leucopharynx* – often wrongly given as *C. karduchorum*). The small flowers are rather sparsely produced and do not stand the English weather well. E. A. Bowles describes them as the 'mad crocus' as they have a habit of producing their shoots horizontally underground so that they fail to reach the light and flower.

A striking and unusual variety for naturalizing in thin grass or among rhododendrons in a moist peaty soil is the stoloniferous *C. nudiflorus*. This can be temperamental and will take at least a couple of seasons to settle down, and it should then be left undisturbed. However, if it is happy it will eventually form widespread patches, as at Knightshayes Court in Devon where it tumbles down a mossy bank and is a delightful sight with the sun behind it.

Winter–early spring

There are no really true winter bulbs that will brave the severest weather, they all sensibly keep their heads well down, but there are some that are so early or late as to be considered winter-flowering, popping up whenever there is a mild spell in the weather. I am uncertain whether

C. laevigatus 'Fontenayi' is a delayed autumn crocus or an enterprising early spring one but it usually flowers around New Year.

One year we had a surplus of these bulbs (incidentally they are a most distinctive and strange-shaped corm – rather like the polished brown pointed dome that is seen on some Eastern churches) so we decided to try them in grass under a tree at the bottom of the garden where other autumn crocuses do so well. They have survived but that is all that can really be said for them. Their tiny flowers are sensibly tucked well down in the leaves, close to the ground, so unless you actually go looking for them they are lost among the grass and, like most crocuses, they stay tightly shut until the sun persuades them to open and reveal their true beauty. They are much better in a sunny pocket on the rock garden where they can be easily seen.

The other non-winter 'winter' bulb is the snowdrop. Everybody must surely love them, even if the many different varieties are dismissed with a 'those green and white things – they all look alike to me'.

One of my favourite sights on a dismal February day are the snowdrops that appear in the roadside hedges. Deeply bedded in the tangled undergrowth, the clumps tumble down the bank to the road, bringing a breath of spring to an otherwise bleak landscape. As they fade so they are replaced by primroses, violets, and later by bluebells. Although not advocating the planting of all hedge bottoms with snowdrops, it does serve to illustrate the fact that they are remarkably tolerant and useful bulbs provided that a few simple rules are observed.

They are found wild throughout much of Europe and are plants of woodland in the north and damp upland meadows in the south and east. They are the epitome of hardiness, or perhaps foolhardiness, flowering as they do throughout the coldest late-winter weather. Frost and snow only check their flowering, which continues unabated once the temperature rises a few degrees. Their leaf tips are even especially hardened to push through frozen ground. They can tolerate a wide range of conditions and are suitable for both acid and alkaline soils, but they prefer a semi-shaded site and moisture-retaining soil. Their main dislike is that of drought, and on dry, sandy, or chalky soils either peat,

Crocus speciosus is an autumn crocus for naturalising in grass

leaf mould, or well-rotted compost must be added to improve the moisture retention.

Once established, snowdrops need little attention other than the division of overgrown clumps. Unlike most bulbs, clumps of snowdrops are best divided while in growth. This can be done just as the leaves emerge, or they can be moved at any time after flowering. In both cases there is an added advantage of being able to see exactly where the gaps are, and being able to plant accordingly. The only vital fact to be remembered at all times is that snowdrops must not dry out. The new site must be carefully prepared in advance and care taken to see the bulbs spend the minimum time out of the ground. It is worth remembering that in some years spring can be remarkably and unexpectedly dry. Newly transplanted snowdrops should be watered while they still have their leaves, thus encouraging the formation of good-sized bulbs for next season, although those moved after flowering may well take a season to settle in their new location.

Apart from drought and the persistent problem of slugs damaging the bulbs snowdrops are remarkably free of problems. However, they are members of the daffodil family and can therefore suffer from the same pests, especially eel worm. Little can be done to control this pest, other than to remove and burn all infected bulbs and avoid replanting in the same area for five years. It is therefore a sensible precaution not to plant snowdrops in an area where daffodils have failed to thrive.

The common snowdrop G. nivalis and its sturdier double form G. nivalis var. plenus, deserve to be planted in as large quantities as there is space for in the garden. They are ideal for neglected areas where little else will grow, and most striking effects can be achieved by massing them in clumps under deciduous trees and shrubs where shade later in the year will be too dense for much else to grow. In such circumstances they bring a lightening of shade and add interest to what is often a dull area. I have seen beautiful drifts of double snowdrops under huge beech trees in a place which in summer will be densely shaded and devoid of all other plants. They are also particularly good mixed with ivy, especially the small-leaved variegated forms.

For the smaller garden where there is no space for large drifts, smaller clumps could be carefully placed under single specimen trees, such as Prunus subhirtella 'Autumnalis'. Clumps of snowdrops are particularly effective around trees with attractive bark, such as Acer griseum or Prunus serrula. However, common snowdrops are not very tall and in a mild winter they may be swamped by the grass. It is therefore a good idea to make a last cut as late in the autumn as practicable, and in extreme cases of mild weather and continued grass growth I have been known to hand cut round the clumps. Their leaves, like those of all bulbs, must not be removed until they have completely faded.

If large areas are to be covered then the common single and double snowdrops are ideal, especially in areas of rough grass, or neglected corners, such as drives, roadside banks, or the hedge at the bottom of the garden. Here they can be allowed to spread naturally, mixing with such wild flowers as may be naturally available – violets, primroses, red campion, etc. Where space is limited and a few snowdrops are required to add interest early in the year, under a single tree in the lawn for example, then some of the larger varieties could be considered. Full descriptions of them will be found on p. 77, but good, reliable varieties include Galanthus 'Atkinsii', G. elwesii, G. 'Magnet', and G. 'S. Arnott'. Quite apart from their larger size they also extend the flowering season by a few weeks. Snowdrops should never be planted singly but always in clumps randomly spaced to increase the natural appearance. Small, evenly spaced clumps tend to give an artificial 'lace edging' effect to a hedge or bank. If only a few bulbs are available, of a special variety for example, then it is much better to plant them together, leaving only 2 in (5 cm) between the bulbs, and then to divide them as the clump increases.

All snowdrops are excellent mixed with other early spring bulbs, such as aconites (Eranthis) and crocuses, especially C. tommasinianus. Much as I like the delicate lilac of this species, with its silver-washed sheen to the outer petals, it is less effective at a distance than its hybrids. I have also found that it is less tolerant of competition from grass, seeming to prefer the freedom of a bed, where the first hint that the hard winter is relaxing its grip is sufficient to trigger its appearance. However, its rate of increase, both by seed and by offsets is prodigious, and I would be wary of allowing it into more formal areas, especially as I observed my parents-in-law fight a losing battle against it for 30 years. In the spring its delicate flowers are most welcome and appear quite harmless, but by the time the leaves appear the border takes on the appearance of a shaggy overgrown lawn. This could be quite acceptable under shrubs, where the shade is so dense that little else will grow later in the year, or where shrubs almost touch the ground, as under certain viburnums, but in mixed borders it is usually disastrous. I always banish *C. tommasinianus* to the grass or wild areas where they look most charming among snowdrops. However, the other disadvantage they have is their sheer delicacy and soft colouring. On dull overcast days that seem so often to be the norm in late winter they stay steadfastly closed tight, refusing to display their lovely lilac petals. They therefore blend in to their background and I have been surprised on more than one occasion not even to know that they were there until the sun revealed their presence. The hybrid forms, on the other hand, have a much stronger colouring and so the contrast of purple crocuses with white snowdrops occurs even if it is overcast and the crocuses remain tight shut. I would choose a mixture of the small, deeper flowered *C. t.* 'Whitewell Purple' and the more robust *C. t.* 'Ruby Giant'. The deeper purple shades enhance the white snowdrops, especially when the sun shines and each glistens as though varnished. *C. t.* 'Ruby Giant' looks like a small form of the large Dutch crocus and is almost certianly a hybrid between it and *C. tommasinianus*. It is most attractive when planted under a grey-leaved *Buddleia davidii* hybrid, and has the added advantage of flowering a little later than *C. t.* 'Whitewell Purple' and thus extending the display into March, when it will associate well with *C. chrysanthus* hybrids.

The humble winter aconite (*Eranthis hyemalis*) has always held a special place in my affections. I find their first appearance one of the most exciting moments of the gardening year. One day all is brown earth and the next a sheet of yellow. I always watch avidly for the first uncurling stems, each with their golden flowers nestling among the leaves.

However, my special affection for them comes not so much from their welcome appearance but more for the manner in which I first made their acquaintance. When we first moved to Taunton our apology for a garden contained a triangular shrub bed screening the back drive from the front. This was a typical Edwardian monstrosity of measled laurel and pampas grass on a foundation of what could only be described as a rock tip. During one mad winter week we grubbed, dug, and burnt out the shrubs and created a rock garden, using the stones and tons of antique chicken compost that was lurking in the back of the barn. I must admit that it is an eccentric place for a rock garden as it faces due east and is entirely overshadowed by an enormous lime tree. It therefore only receives rain during the winter months, and even then its elevated construction means that it is very free-draining. However, it is ideal for bulbs and we use it as a showcase during spring, when it is full of colour and interest from February to early May, by which time there is little left but the untidy, decaying foliage. It then sinks into obscurity again until a sudden burst in the autumn, and no one much minds if the lime tree exudes its revolting sticky mess all over it all summer. Incidentally, it has proved an excellent testing ground for the perenniality of bulbs, but more of that later.

What we had not realized when we constructed this display bed was that there were many clumps of aconites lurking under the laurels. Once exposed to sunlight they took on a new lease of life and now totally cover the bed with their bright-yellow cups in January and February. In fact, they have become somewhat of a nuisance, and I now have to try to collect their seed before it ripens as they are threatening to swamp the later bulbs. The point of this story is, of course, that aconites revel in a dry situation, especially in summer. Like most bulbs, they will not swim, and indeed would rather not paddle either. The clumps in my border, although flowering well each year, have not increased in the same way as those on the rock garden, probably because the soil is regularly disturbed as well as being much wetter.

Aconites will not compete with coarse grass, but planted under trees with a spreading canopy, especially horse chestnut, they can colonize huge areas in a quite

Having grown both species for many years from many different sources, I am certain that there is a far wider variation from clone to clone than the botanists would have us believe. We have stock of *E. cilicica* that sets quite as much seed as *E. hyemalis*, despite the fact that most books say they will not do so in this country. Incidentally, the two species are quite distinct in seed, *E. hyemalis* having only four pods whereas *E. cilicica* has at least four times that number. The winter aconites have earned themselves a bad reputation as being almost impossible to grow. As with all woodland plants they do not tolerate a long period of drying out. Nurserymen, however, will insist on treating them like daffodils, leaving them to get drier and drier in a box on a shelf, and it is the conditions under which they are stored that is at fault. Provided that they are stored in peat and replanted quickly, they are quite trouble-free. Incidentally, many of the bulbs offered for sale, often incorrectly labelled 'Eranthis hyemalis', are, in fact, wild collected bulbs of *E. cilicica*, which can be very difficult to start back into growth and to re-establish. Some firms now offer *Eranthis* as bulbs in growth during spring. In this way it is possible to check not only the viability of the bulbs but also its naming. Dry bulbs can be soaked overnight in water to encourage them to break their dormancy.

Another bulb more normally associated with rock gardens and sun, but also excellent for naturalizing under small trees, is the lovely *Anemone blanda*, of which there are many named forms. The easiest is the blue, which will quite freely seed itself, in various shades, and can become a weed, as in our gravel drive. However, it is useful for filling the odd difficult corner. I find that the beautiful 'White Splendour' needs more sunshine and seems not so happy under trees or in grass. The same is true of the striking magenta 'Radar'. We have a fine chance clump of *Anemone blanda* that has tucked itself against the trunk of a young *Nothofagus obliqua*. Flowers in the clump are in all shades, from those so pale as to be almost white, through to a quite intense blue. It is mixed with primroses and forms a very cheerful patch throughout February, and much of March, when they are joined by the striking scarlet flowers of *A. hortensis* (I know this better as *A. fulgens* 'Annulata Grandiflora'). In

spectacular manner. The main entrance to Angelsea Abbey in Cambridgeshire has two huge sentinel horse chestnuts closely carpeted with aconites, and at Tintinhull, in Somerset, they encircle a knoll surrounding an ancient cedar.

Eranthis hyemalis is a native of European woodlands and tends to be much easier to establish than the Turkish *E. cilicica*. The latter flowers a little later and has bronze stems and very finely dissected leaves. Some botanists consider them synonymous, but for the gardener they are not only of distinct appearance but also have different cultural requirements. *E. cilicica* seems to prefer a dry, limy soil and requires more sunshine. However, we have a clump that has definitely not read the textbooks as they flower and set seed each year on the edge of my acid hellebore bed.

time *A. blanda* can spread to cover quite extensive areas provided the grass is thin. If mixed with the later-flowering *Anemone apennina*, the season is prolonged well into March. *A. apennina* is superficially similar to *Anemone blanda* but has a different tuber and taller, slightly hairy leaves. It is usually offered in either blue or white but all intermediate shades can be found, some even verging on the purple. Unlike *A. blanda*, however, it does require a cool, semi-shaded situation and is thus ideal for succeeding snowdrops and aconites under trees.

Mid-spring

Mid-spring sees the main flush of bulbs in the garden and the range is enormous, each genus having a huge number of hybrids, giving a bewildering choice. Rather than produce an almost endless list I will outline the main species that are suitable for naturalizing and only give one or two of my own favourite hybrids. A more extensive table will be found at the end of the book and many others will be found in bulb catalogues.

As winter recedes so the predominance of white gives way to a much wider range of colours before settling down to the dominance of one colour once more – this time yellow, as the daffodils truly come into their own, supported by the ubiquitous forsythia. However, for one brief period in early spring a much wider range of colours is available. This is when the crocuses are at their height of flowering. With the exception of the scarlet shades, crocuses cover virtually all the colour spectrum, from pure white, through creams and yellows, to purple and blue.

Many *Crocus* species are not suitable for naturalizing, requiring good drainage and sun, and are therefore better in beds or on the rock garden but, apart from *C. tommasinianus* which has already been discussed, there is still a wide range of crocuses which are suitable for naturalizing. All the hybrids between *C. chrysanthus* and *C. biflorus* are ideal for dry, sunny positions, especially under large deciduous trees. Originating as they do in Greece, they seem to require a relatively dry summer period to encourage flowering, and in

Above: Anemone blanda, with primroses provide an informal grouping at the base of a tree

some gardens they may be best in a dry border (q.v.).

Although they are selections and hybrids from and between *C. chrysanthus* and *C. biflorus*, in most catalogues they will be found listed under *C. chrysanthus*. Particularly good varieties are 'Cream Beauty' (rounded flowers of true clotted cream colour; I once saw a startling planting of these with the intense blue *Iris histriodes* 'Major' in Hyde Park), 'Gipsy Girl' (dramatically striped outsides reveal golden insides), 'Blue Pearl' (palest silvery blue), 'Skyline' (clear blue, veined purple on the outside), 'Snow Bunting' (pure white).

Crocus sieberi also originated in Greece, but the mainland form, *C. s. atticus*, and the hybrids 'Firefly' and 'Violet Queen' are remarkably tolerant of most conditions. We have one clump that was left behind long ago when a path was widened and they have never failed to flower, pushing up their tubby blue–purple flowers through the path every spring despite early and regular mowing of the grass.

The larger, so-called Dutch crocuses, have descended from *C. vernus* of the European Alps and are extremely tough, almost indestructible bulbs. They are more tolerant of our often wet summers than the Greek crocuses and therefore are ideal for large plantings, but I must admit that they are not amongst my favourites. Their stiff habit and rather gross flowers are indelibly associated in my mind with unsympathetic large-scale parks department plantings, their large, bright blue goblets standing erect and stiff, in regimental ranks round trees on roundabouts. However, if left to their own devices they eventually lose this rather blowsy appearance, and two of my favourite *Crocus* plantings involve Dutch crocuses. One is in a country churchyard where they have been thinly planted along the edge of a gravel path and over the years have seeded both in the grass and gravel, so that they now provide a soft blue edge to the path that most attractively wanders through the narcissus that have been naturalized in the churchyard.

The other planting is at Forde Abbey in Dorset where the garden is transformed in early March into a veritable sea of blue by hundreds of thousands of crocuses that over the past 60 years have seeded themselves in ever increasing numbers. They are so prolific that in order to maintain some crocus-free grass, mowing has to be very regular to discourage the seedlings. A policy of removing all yellow crocuses is followed, and the wide range is from deep purple and pure white blend to a uniform pale blue when viewed from a distance. The crocuses have also lost their overbred size. Mixed with them are various forms of Lent lily (*Narcissus pseudonarcissus*) which is another chameleon in regard to colour. It is in fact a bi-colour, having a yellow trumpet and creamy petals, but from a distance it assumes a soft lemon hue, which contrasts well with the blue–mauve of the crocuses. In some areas this blue hue is intensified by the vivid blue of *Chionodoxa luciliae* which also freely seeds itself.

Spring is traditionally associated with drifts of daffodils under the swelling buds of apple trees, and, indeed, massed daffodils are probably most effective when planted in this manner. There are many varieties suitable for planting in grass, so rather than give a long list of names I will discuss some of the groups of daffodils that are most likely to succeed. (Many other suitable varieties will be found listed in bulb catalogues.)

Daffodils are undemanding bulbs, most flowering well in their first year of planting. However certain varieties, especially the wild European daffodil (*Narcissus pseudonarcissus*) and its close relatives, are meadow or woodland plants and resent the disturbance and drying out that are inevitable when the bulbs are lifted for sale. They must also be grown in a damp position if they are to flourish. In total contrast, many other varieties, especially the jonquils (*N. jonquilla* and its hybrids), the multi-headed *N. tazetta*, and the *N. poetaz* hybrids (crosses between *N. poeticus* and *N. tazetta*) revel in the drying-off period following lifting and storing. They are best grown in a sunny, well-drained position, and are therefore not so suitable for naturalizing in our damp climate, which, as their home is in southern Europe, is not surprising.

It can be seen from the above examples that daffodils have disparate requirements, depending upon the variety. Daffodils that are commonly seen in gardens are hybrid varieties that have descended from wild species, and they are classified by experts according to their species parentage or, where they are many generations removed from the species, by their most obvious characteristics. The division of daffodils into 'narcissi' and 'daffodils' is also often encountered. However, this is a misunderstanding, as *Narcissus* is the botanical name for all members of the daffodil genus. Thus, *all* daffodils are *Narcissus*.

With few exceptions, the species daffodils are not really suitable for general garden cultivation as most of them originate from southern Europe and have very specific cultural requirements. The prime exception is Wordsworth's 'Host of Golden Daffodils' or Lent lily (the wild, bicoloured northern European daffodil, *N. pseudonarcissus*) and some of its more vigorous forms, such as the perfect golden miniature Tenby daffodil (*N. pseudonarcissus* subsp. *obvallaris*) and the large-flowered *N. pseudonarcissus* subsp. *nobilis* (sometimes listed as *N. pseudonarcissus* 'Gayi'). There is also a delicate, pale cream variety (*N. pseudonarcissus* subsp. *moschatus*) that comes from northern Spain and has lovely drooping flowers. This is one of my favourites, but it is not very freely available and is therefore probably best planted in a bed where its delicacy can be appreciated. The hybrid 'W. P. Milner' is very similar to it and is more freely available. These are all only 9–12 in (23–30 cm) tall and flower early in March. Other similar varieties can be found listed in catalogues under such names as 'Bambi', *N. lobularis*, *N. nanus*, etc.

For early effect on a large scale the Lent lily or its near relatives must surely be the main choice. They require soil that is not too dry, and it is very noticeable that they do not flower well after a dry summer the preceding year. These dry conditions are, of course, induced artificially when the bulbs are lifted and stored before sale and it is therefore unlikely that they will flower well in the first year after planting. However, after a couple of seasons in a not-too-dry situation they should begin to flower well.

Unlike most daffodils found in our gardens, which are hybrids, *N. pseudonarcissus* is a species and its prime method of increase is by seed. Naturalized plantings are composed of scattered individuals, not large clumps. It is therefore very important that the grass is not cut until not only the leaves are brown, but the seed is ripe and ready for dispersal. If the grass mowings are removed as the grass is cut, then the grass should not be cut until the seed is dispersed, but if the grass is cut, and then left before being raked up, this will aid the dispersal of the seed. The overall effect of massed Lent lilies, therefore, will differ from a mass planting of hybrid daffodils, which form large clumps. In the former case, the bulbs are scattered randomly in ones and twos, and this pattern of growing looks particularly good with Dutch crocuses, which flower at about the same time. Large areas can be planted with both of these (avoid the bright orange–yellow crocuses as they spoil the overall lemon tone of the daffodils), and they can then be left to seed and spread. Both grow well under the light canopy of mature trees.

The Tenby daffodil (*N. pseudonarcissus* subsp. *obvallaris*), on the other hand, is sterile and the bulbs increase vegetatively by division, so the spread of these must be by hand-lifting and dividing the clumps in the autumn. However, it may be difficult to find the clumps then, so they could be divided as the leaves turn brown in late spring or, alternatively, they can be divided just as the leaves emerge in February. Provided that this is done quickly and during a mild spell the bulbs should suffer no lasting damage, and I must admit it is far easier to cope with the job when the grass is short, than trying to find them in what amounts to a hayfield.

The old-fashioned 'Van Sion', with its strange, almost malformed double flowers, can be used among Lent lilies to create a patch of more intense colour and a bolder shape, as they are much sturdier. But they have considerably more foliage and form quite dense clumps. However, its iron constitution renders it virtually indestructible, and I find it invaluable for early flowering around trees.

Many colours change their hues with changing light intensities and this is particularly noticeable at twilight when certain primrose-yellows appear luminous. This quality is apparent in *N. pseudonarcissus* subsp. *nobilis* ('Gayi') which, although a creamy white and yellow bicolour, takes on an overall lemon appearance from a distance and, in the twilight, this colour seems almost to glow. I have seen an orchard densely planted with these, which in the soft evening light became quite magical. It was a simple and yet totally effective planting.

The mis-named summer snowflake (*Leucojum aestivum*) could also be planted in clumps between these daffodils to extend the season, as they both like damp situations. *Fritillaria meleagris* (snake's head fritillary) would also thrive in similar conditions, provided that the grass is not too vigorous. However, mowing could not take place until late June, when the fritillaries would have seeded, whereas it could be much earlier if the daffodil only or daffodil–crocus pattern was followed.

The *pseudonarcissus* group is also probably the best choice for those wishing to establish a true meadow and mix bulbs with flowering wild plants, such as cowslips or lady's smock (*Cardamine pratense*), or they could follow snowdrops, crocuses, or *Scilla bifolia*. They are among the earliest to flower and their sturdy sta-

Above: Massed daffodils in a Kent garden

ture stands up well to the often inclement weather experienced in early spring.

As spring progresses and the grass grows, taller hybrids are perhaps more suitable. Among the most reliable are the *cyclamineus* hybrids. Their parent requires moist conditions and so they thrive in our damp climate, doing best on heavy soils or in semi-shaded, not-too-dry situations. Especially recommended hybrids are 'Dove Wings', 'February Gold', 'Peeping Tom', 'Jack Snipe', and 'Little Witch'. These are widely used, being early flowering and thus ideal for more formal areas where untidy foliage can be removed relatively early. They look particularly fine at the base of specimen trees in a formal lawn, but they are equally good for naturalizing in the wild garden. They have small, neat flowers and all display to a greater or lesser degree the reflexed petals of their parent. The sturdy, deep-golden flowers of 'Little Witch' provide a good foil for the bright china-blue of *Chionodoxa* species, especially *C. luciliae* and *C. sardensis*, the blue greatly enhancing the gold and adding depth to the planting. Both flower at the same time and make an especially attractive combination for a small area at the base of a specimen tree, such as one of the flowering cherries, and as the daffodils flower in late March they do not clash with the cherry blossom so my *bête noire*, the unfortunate yellow and pink combination, can be avoided. We use this grouping to extend a planting that begins with snow-

Above: An orchard in early spring planted with daffodils, *Leucojum aestivum* and snake's head fritillaries

drops and crocuses and continues after the daffodils with *Anemone fulgens* and *Fritillaria meleagris*.

Not all *N. cyclamineus* hybrids have long trumpets like 'Little Witch'. 'Beryl' has a neat, orange cup and swept-back, creamy petals. It is only 12 in (30 cm) high and has a very 'relaxed' habit, not stiff like some daffodils, making lovely arching clumps. It is therefore ideal for planting in small groups in short grass. At Tintinhull in Somerset the garden is dominated by an ancient cedar and the thin grass around its base is planted with a ring of winter aconites with irregular clumps of 'Beryl' behind them. With the low spring sun shining through them they are most attractive.

These hybrids are very tolerant but their species parent, *N. cyclamineus* itself, with its 'asses' ears' petals, is much more temperamental. It originated in a small area of northern Portugal and Spain, and for 250 years was believed to be 'an absurdity which will never be found to exist'. The bulbs resent disturbance and will not transplant very successfully, each being relatively short-lived. They require a moist, acid soil and are best grown from seed as they do not propagate vegetatively easily. Indeed, the large numbers that are so striking at the Royal Horticultural Society's garden at Wisley originated from seed sown in 1892. However, patience is certainly a necessary virtue when growing any daffodil from seed as it will be about six years before the first flowers appear.

Sadly, not many of us have the rather specialized conditions of acid, well-drained soil with water running through it. I have seen *N. cyclamineus* growing successfully alongside a lake and stream, but for many gardeners their only real hope of success is to grow them as I do, in a shady peat-bed.

Another delightful species best grown from seed and requiring similar conditions is *N. bulbocodium*, or the hoop-petticoat daffodil. There are many forms of this in the trade, sadly many of them removed from the wild. They are often poor, shrivelled bulbs that rarely settle-in well, and it is worth searching for named clones (not hybrids which are often unsuitable for general cultivation but best grown in troughs or under glass). This name indicates the selection of a particularly vigorous plant and its artificial propagation. Once again, I have seen it in thin grass beside a lake, but unless you have similar conditions to either the Royal Horticultural Society's garden at Wisley or the Savill Gardens at Windsor then it is best kept to shady pockets on the rock garden. At Wisley *N. bulbocodium* bulbs are naturalized in their millions on a slope, above a stream, where there is almost a constant movement of water just below the surface, except for a short time in midsummer.

The other species daffodil that is occasionally successfully naturalized is *N. triandrus albus*. This also requires an acid soil but a drier situation than either *N. bulbocodium* or *N. cyclamineus*. I have seen it growing in thin grass under a hazel hedge in a delightful mixture with *Erythronium dens canis* (dog's tooth violet) and the dwarf *N. cyclamineus* hybrid daffodils 'Tête a Tête' and 'Jack Snipe'. Purple and white martagon lilies followed to add interest in June. Although *N. triandrus* is not a good plant for naturalizing, it has been used to produce a wide range of hybrids. These are mostly much taller than their parent but all share the nodding flowers, with usually two or more to a stem, and they flower after the *N. cyclamineus* hybrids, preferring a drier situation. Many of these are very good for growing in grass, especially the white hybrids such as 'Thalia' and 'Rippling Waters'. There are also some beautiful clear lemon hybrids which are especially fine for planting in small clumps around specimen trees in a lawn, or for putting in borders. 'Liberty

Bells' and 'Thoughtful' are both clear lemon and among my favourites.

I have discussed some of the more distinct varieties that you may consider planting in grass, but there are many hundreds of other hybrids, ranging from old favourites like 'King Alfred' (yellow) and 'Mount Hood' (white) through to more sophisticated varieties for planting in small clumps in prominent positions.

When planting in grass, whether in an orchard or more formally, it is best to follow nature and plant clumps of one variety rather than mixed bulbs. Over large areas quite big patches of each variety can be used to create a bold effect. Alternatively, smaller clumps can be randomly spread around, provided that each contains the same variety. Thus early and late varieties can be mixed together. In small areas, under a tree for instance, the earliest varieties should be in the middle of the clump, so that the dying leaves are masked by clumps of later varieties around it.

When planning small areas in grass, even greater care should be exercised to avoid the rather coarse solid-lump effect. The shape of the final planting should be soft in outline – boomerang shapes or gentle curves are good. Too regular shapes or sharp corners look clumsy and heavy-handed, and one way around this is to taper the shape out towards the edges, which gives a more natural feel to beds of the most modern hybrids. When planting around trees, the lens-shape is particularly good as it allows the grass to be mown up to the edge of the bulbs with ease, a very important point, as nothing is more frustrating than trying to mow round intricate patterns. A slightly more sophisticated shape is the flattened 's', with a wide middle round the tree. This could be planted entirely with one bulb, or a mixture could be used to disguise the shape – snowdrops round the base of the tree, crocuses at the points, and clumps of daffodils behind them. Thus the overall outline only becomes apparent when mowing. When daffodils are planted in an orchard or mixed with other plants it is more attractive and less time-consuming to leave the whole area until it is ready for mowing, only keeping a few paths cut, both to enable access and to break up the area into interesting shapes.

Once again, if you can face the back-breaking chore, the fading heads of daffodils, including the papery sheath, should be removed. Not only do the remaining leaves then blend in with the surroundings without drawing attention to the fact that they are over, but research has shown that the removal of the seed heads results in a measurable increase in bulb size and, as most daffodils are hybrids, the seeds are of little value. Vegetative splitting of the bulbs is much faster and results in identical plants, whereas seed takes up to seven years to flower, and even then the resulting offspring may not be very good. Exceptions to this rule are the species daffodils – our own Lent lily, *N. cyclamineus, N. bulbocodium*, etc. These bulbs increase slowly, if at all, by division and seed is the main method of propagation. Therefore with these bulbs care must be taken not to cut the grass until the seed is ripe. It can then be left to fall around the parents (mowing without removing the clippings is a good method of distribution) or collected. This collected seed can then be scattered in a new part of the garden or sown in seed boxes, where it may receive better attention. It can be left in deep seed trays for up to three or four years, when the small bulbs can be planted out in the early autumn, or as they begin to die down in the spring. If the seed is scattered or left to fall naturally, you must remember to leave that area of grass unmown for as long as you leave the part containing the parents, otherwise the seedlings will not be able to develop. One gardener once asked me why they had no seedlings of *Fritillaria meleagris* in the grass, only in the border. I pointed to the culprit – the lawn mower. The lawn was beautifully manicured up to and around the clumps of fritillaries, leaving no time or space for the seedlings to develop. The neighbouring border, on the other hand, was left undisturbed and there seedlings had begun to appear.

If left undisturbed until June or July, seedlings should begin to flower about seven years later. This sounds a long time but with many species it is the only practical method of obtaining a large quantity. Bulbs of these species, *N. cyclamineus, N. bulbocodium*, and *N. triandrus albus* in particular, do not take kindly to nursery cultivation. Vegetative propagation, if it takes place at all, is very slow and the bulbs do not really adapt to wholesale production methods. Very few of these have ever been grown commercially, the bulk of the bulbs offered for sale having been dug up in Spain or Portugal. These 'wild' bulbs rarely adapt well to our climate. It is therefore better to obtain only a few bulbs, commercially propagated if possible, and grow your own stock from seed. Most other bulbs suitable for naturalizing (snake's head fritillary, etc.) are freely cultivated commercially. Thus the numbers of these can be increased both by seed and by adding new bulbs from time to time.

The perennial question is always when can one safely mow. The Royal Horticultural Society carried out an interesting ten-year trial to assess the effects of early removal of foliage, and the results clearly demonstrated that the 'early cutting down of foliage and stems is a dangerous and debilitating practice'. Where the foliage had been removed two weeks after flowering the clump almost completely disappeared, and those removed after four weeks were very poor. Interestingly, however, there was no difference between those removed six weeks after flowering and those where the foliage was not removed at all. Thus the removal of yellowing foliage should not adversely affect the performance of the bulbs, provided an adequate time for bulb replenishment has been allowed. Other factors, such as site and soil conditions are more likely to affect the long-term performance.

In a formal situation daffodils are most likely to be preceded and followed by other bulbs. As spring progresses so blossoms appear on the trees and other colours, which can be of considerable importance, are introduced into the picture. Bright golden daffodils under bare brown branches present a very different picture to that of yellow daffodils under pink cherries which can be rather harsh. Cherry blossom demands a sympathetic colour under it, such as that of creamy white daffodils. Bright yellow ones can be used provided you keep to early varieties that will have finished flowering by the time the cherry blossom is out. Other trees, such as weeping willows, have soft yellowish new leaves and golden daffodils here provide a harmonious picture.

In some gardens cow parsley in its various forms is encouraged as a foil for naturalizing bulbs, especially under trees. However, a word of warning. For the first few years the bulbs may look most attractive with the soft, ferny foliage of Queen Anne's lace, and it is very pretty in moderation. But if left unchecked this ''orrible umbel' spreads its progency so prodigiously that all but the very earliest and the very tallest bulbs fail to rise above it. Indeed, in time it may actually harm the smaller bulbs by choking them. However, seeding is easily controlled by removing the main stem once the flowers fade. Surplus plants can be dug out – a time-consuming job – so prevention is better than cure.

It is not necessary to have a large garden in order to have a truly wild patch as opposed to a few bulbs round a tree. Relatively small areas can be very effective if chosen carefully to fit naturally into the overall plan. It may also be a useful way of making a virtue of what would otherwise be a problem area.

One such example was a garden in Kent that I passed one day in early April. The front garden was bordered by a row of elderly lilacs which had grown into considerable thickets, casting quite deep shade over a damp, narrow strip of garden beside the entrance drive. The resulting patch of thin unkempt grass had been imaginatively planted with the lovely chequered snake's head fritillaries (*F. meleagris*). The native lady's smock (*Cardamine pratense*) had seeded in amongst them, the soft pink of the cardamine enhancing the deeper hues of the fritillaries, and a touch of brightness was provided by a scattering of white fritillaries. Other bulbs had been planted in this area for interest earlier in the year – snowdrops pushed right up to the multiple trunks of the lilacs, with primroses and daffodils in front of them.

I was once given a very pretty double form of the lady's smock (*Cardamine pratense* 'Flore Pleno') which is a great improvement on the wild form and well worth looking for. The flower heads of the double form are of a much more intense colour and the heads themselves have more substance. It spreads only modestly and is equally at home with the snake's head fritillaries, as it also needs cool, damp feet in order to be really happy. It is not by chance that the water meadows in Oxford and Suffolk have turned into complete carpets of fritillaries, although it is somewhat of a mystery as to why they are so localized a native. However, dampness is

not absolutely vital. My parents, in a dry limestone garden, have a very fine patch in an area of grass shaded by trees. Here the coolness is provided by the shade rather than an inherently damp soil.

One of the most famous plantings of *Fritillaria meleagris* must be at Great Dixter in Sussex. Here, an old, now dry moat is liberally planted with them. However, striking though this is, in its own quiet way, I found the area under the two trees flanking the entrance much more exciting. Here fritillaries were only one of a whole succession of small bulbs that made the area alive with interest from February until May. Snowdrops, with crocuses, were followed by wild daffodils (*N. pseudonarcissus*); wood anemones (*A. nemorosa*) jostled with purple dog's tooth violets (*Erythronium dens-canis*), and above them the nodding bells of fritillaries danced in the wind.

Another bulb not seen as often as it should be is the misnamed summer snowflake (*Leucojum aestivum*). Called summer snowflake to distinguish it from the early spring-flowering spring snowflake (*Leucojum vernum*), it does in fact flower in late March, normally around Easter, the taller and more vigorous *L. aestivum* 'Gravetye' being a week or so later. Although they tolerate dry conditions, and I am beginning to find them a weed on my very dry rock garden, they prefer a damp situation, and given a moist position they are certainly much more luxuriant and become quite bold and striking, whereas rather starved clumps have a slightly apologetic air. I once saw an old orchard where the clumps of daffodils were interspersed by clumps of leucojums – the white of the leucojums quite as bright as the yellow of the daffodils. The whole of the area around the larger clumps was dotted with *Fritillaria meleagris* and many wild meadow plants. The dry moat at Great Dixter also has a fine stand of *Leucojum aestivum* tumbling down its side.

In complete contrast to bulbs requiring moist soil, there are also less-common bulbs, requiring dry conditions, that could be tried in the grass. Many of our best plantings are pure serendipity. Having a nursery entails the continual moving of bulb stocks and inevitably some are overlooked and left behind. The smaller the bulb the more likely they are to be missed, and in this way I acquired a large patch of

Snake's head fritillaries, *F. meleagris*, naturalised in the dry moat at Great Dixter

Iris tuberosa (more correctly *Hermodactylus tuberosa* as according to the botanists it is not an iris at all). Its common name, black widow iris, sums up its unusual appearance as the sweetly scented flowers are pale green with almost black falls and are reminiscent of *Iris reticulata* in shape. It is usually recommended that they are planted at the foot of a dry, sunny wall in order to try and fool them into thinking that they are still in their Mediterranean home. However, they do produce an enormous amount of leaves, albeit thin ones, and having seen the way in which they have completely smothered a friend's rock garden I am not unnaturally a little wary of them, especially as they can be very shy to flower. I might forgive them their foliage if they could guarantee a fine display of flowers, but I am not prepared to have vast amounts of leaves for little return, although I did see one garden where they were underplanted by *C. tommasinianus* in a very narrow bed between a path and the lawn. The crocuses flowered under the iris leaves, followed by the iris flowers, and finally the gorgeous pink and yellow *Tulip saxatalis*, also from Greece. In this way three wanderers, all liking hot, dry conditions, were contained in their own little patch.

But I digress. We grow and flower *I. tuberosa* very successfully, under the canopy of a large oak. In this area of rough grass the untidy leaves do not matter and the irises do not seem to mind the odd accidental hair cut as the leaves are emerging. *Crocus tommasinianus* 'Whitewell Purple', also left behind, is mixed with it and provides a bold contrast to the shy charms of the iris.

It is not necessary to limit bulbs in grass to those more traditionally associated with this usage. I have met some very unusual bulbs used in this manner but which were still very effective in their own eccentric way. There is one large roundabout that has been imaginatively landscaped with outcrops of large rocks topped by clumps of birches. The surrounding grass was a mass of crocuses and late daffodils, but what caught my attention were the large hyacinths, of all colours, planted in front of this very natural scene. I rather presumed that they had done previous duty in the mayoral parlour and were now pensioned off. It should not have succeeded, but in fact it did work, a definite induce-ment to be willing to experiment, provided that you are prepared to look at the result critically and correct it if necessary.

The other unexpected sight was at Anglesea Abbey where a woodland glade was heavily planted with a wide assortment of spring bulbs, mostly daffodils, but once again including large hyacinths. At one side, beautifully set off by the dark yews behind, were clumps of the tall crown imperials (*Fritillaria imperialis*) that are more normally associated with herbaceous borders. These are natives of East Turkey and Iran but looked just at home in the wild English garden.

Surplus bulbs from other parts of the garden, as well as the ex-house plants, could easily be tried in the grass. They may not all succeed, but it is better than the compost heap and some results may be quite striking. At Kew I noticed the rather top-heavy intense blue heads of *Muscari* 'Blue Spike' growing in rough grass along with two lovely scented daffodils 'Sweet Pepper' and 'Suzy', both of which have bright yellow flowers and small orange-red cups. I presume that the grape hyacinth had previously seen service in one of the many formal bedding schemes but it was quite happy in its new home.

Banks can be very difficult parts of the garden to plant successfully, but I have seen very effective use made of bulbs to create a feature out of this problem area. One very simple, yet striking, planting involved the much-maligned common grape hyacinth (*Muscari armeniacum*). The whole of a 30 ft (10 m) hedge bank fronting the road was a mass of intense blue, well contrasted with the soft cream of primroses and the intense deep yellow of *Alyssum saxatile*. Sadly, the next year the owners had tried to be too clever and had removed the grass and, by adding other plants, had destroyed a simple, harmonious yet very effective, picture.

For a less formalized planting on a bank, a wide range of small bulbs could be used, such as *Anemone blanda*, *A. nemorosa*, crocuses, scillas, chionodoxas, and *Fritillaria meleagris*, provided that the bank receives full sun for much of the day. In shady situations snowdrops, *A. nemorosa*, and bluebells could be used, perhaps with a few clumps of the *N. cyclamineus* hybrid daffodils which will tolerate a certain amount of shade in the spring and almost full shade while they are dormant.

Late spring–early summer

By the middle of May most gardeners are intensely following the dying back of the bulb foliage and counting the days until the untidy areas can be safely returned to lawn once more. However, for those who have the space and/or the inclination, for wild gardening there are still some bulbs that will flower during the end of May and beginning of June, and, as a consequence, add touches of colour to the 'hay field' appearance of such areas.

One of the most delightful sights of May are the scarlet 'eyes' of the aptly named late pheasant's eye daffodil (*N. poeticus* 'Recurvus') peeping out from amongst the tall grasses, especially if they are planted on a slope or bank so that they can be viewed at eye-level. I always think that this daffodil is the exception to the rule that daffodils should always be planted in clumps. Although still attractive when planted in this way, they are somehow more natural when dotted through the area, either singly, or in twos or threes, where their bright-eyed faces add interest to an area that is otherwise tall grass and browning daffodil leaves.

There is a beautiful double-white form (*N. poeticus* 'Flore Pleno') that is like a pure white gardenia. It, too, can be planted in the grass, although the flower-heads tend to be a little top-heavy and can collapse. Both of these, flowering as they do in late May, can suffer from blindness. The buds form but then a sudden drought during April or May will cause them to abort and the bulb to go into premature retirement. Therefore they should be planted in a damp position, or given a few bucketfuls of water if there is a very warm, dry spell. The earlier-flowering hybrid 'Actaea', which is like a larger, more-rounded pheasant's eye, is much less prone to blindness but somehow lacks the charm of the little wild *N. poeticus*, although it is very good planted in clumps under trees, especially when seen with the light behind it and surrounded by the leaves of cow parsley.

However, as I have already warned, you must remember that those attractive ferny leaves of Queen Anne's lace, which are such a good background for early bulbs, turn, almost overnight, into towering 4 ft (1.3 m) giants which can easily swamp all the succeeding bulbs.

Tulips are not normally considered as naturalizing bulbs but it is possible to experiment with them and, if it succeeds, the results are most effective. Scarlet Darwin hybrids seem to adjust to this treatment, the flower size shrinks but I think they are more attractive like this, rather like poppies in a cornfield. 'Couleur Cardinal' seems to be a reliable variety of a good, strong red. In shady areas, where the grass is not too thick, you might also try that possible British native *T. sylvestris* with its slightly pointed yellow flowers. It is not a 'tidy' tulip and is best supported by other plants.

Drifts of bluebells in dappled sunlight under the bright, newly emerged leaves of beech trees are one of the most lovely sights of May. I know of no other bulb that has such a plethora of synonyms – *Scilla non-scripta* seems to be the current favourite, but you will find it in catalogues as *S. nutans*, *Endymion non-scriptus*, or *Hyacinthoides non-scripta*. It should not be confused with the much larger Spanish bluebell, *Scilla hispanica*, which is also variously known as *S. campanulata*, *Hyacinthoides hispanica*, and *Endymion hispanica*. However, the true bluebell in the garden must be treated with circumspection as it produces so much seed as to turn a dream into a nightmare. Along with the welcome aconites, we inherited bluebells on our rock garden and 16 years of pulling up the plants (the bulbs would need a major excavation to uncover) still have not deterred them, but it does at least control their seeding. They require a cool, shady position but will cope with sunshine as long as the soil is not too dry. Provided that the position is carefully chosen and the 'warning on the label' clearly understood, they are ideal for naturalizing in rough grass or under large trees or in hedge bottoms. They are particularly useful for planting among daffodils, under a large tree for example, where their flowers, appearing after the daffodils', distract the eye from the rather unsightly daffodil leaves. One of their few virtues – that their leaves die back quickly after flowering – means that the whole area is ready for cutting at the same time. I was amused to see that the areas of bulbs in grass in the

Royal Hospital grounds had been tidied up for the Chelsea Flower Show, and all the yellowing leaves had been raked flat, removing much of the loose foliage and leaving the rest to die in a dignified manner. It seemed an eminently sensible idea if one had the time.

An alternative to *Scilla non-scripta* is the more robust Spanish bluebell, *Scilla hispanica*. Unlike the English bluebell, its heads do not nod and the quite substantially larger flowers are spaced all around the stem. It is also available in pink and white, as well as the more normal blue, whereas the white true bluebell is not very often encountered. Sadly, it is just as difficult to eradicate should it be in the wrong place. However, unlike the wild bluebell which rapidly carpets an area, the Spanish blue-

bells form handsome clumps. I am thinking of trying a combination of blue and white ones, mixed with a large-leaved variegated ivy and perhaps *Vinca major* 'Variegata', under the north side of my large yew tree where it is very dry and little will grow. I have seen a delightful mixture of these along a road edge. As it was only in semi-shade the Welsh poppy (*Meconopsis cambrica*) had been allowed to seed at will, along with forget-me-nots, the whole forming a very harmonious grouping providing colour and interest over a long period.

Thus, bluebells can be useful in a slightly more formal situation, in areas that are problems rather than truly wild areas. My neighbours have a raised bank by their front gate under a large copper beech. This is heavily planted with cyclamen and colchicums for autumn interest, snowdrops and daffodils for early spring, and later the bed is filled with masses of bluebells. The contrast between the blue of the scillas and the fresh purple of the new beech foliage is quite magical in May. In summer the shade is so dense nothing but ivy will grow, not even weeds. That other bulb 'weed', a deep pink oxalis species, also seems to be quite happy despite the shade, and its strong colour adds a touch of brightness.

In a similar situation I once saw an unusual combination of the very formal *Bergenia cordifolia* appearing through massed bluebells. It should not have succeeded but it was in fact an arresting mixture of colours – the rather hard pink of the bergenia heads rearing up above a sea of blue. This might be an idea for a narrow, shady bed beside the house.

There are two British native bulbs I would never introduce into my garden. These are the native garlics, or *Allium*, to give them their Latin name. The first, *A. triquetrum*, is only truly a weed in the mild west, where it grows in its millions in the hedgerows of Cornwall. Indeed, for many years we supplied a Dutch wholesale firm with bulbs, as it does not grow well in the colder climate of Holland. We certainly do not find it uncontrolled, more undistinguished, but it might be considered for a cool damp corner where nothing else grows in June. The other, ramsomes (*A. ursinum*), brings back indelible memories of the river banks of my Yorkshire childhood home, with its overpowering onion smell, definitely not scent. It really is a weed of the first order and should be left on the river banks. But the allium family is an enormous one – I believe Turkey alone boasts 1000 species – of which I have met my fair share, as I once shared a journey with a Turkish botanist who was researching into them. Among such a host of often undistinguished members there are quite a number of truly garden-worthy plants. Unfortunately, as most of the more colourful and slightly better behaved ones come from the Middle East they require more sun and better drainage than is normally found in a wild patch in this country. Also, flowering as they do in June, they do delay the cutting of the grass even more. However, the golden garlic

(*A. moly*) – completely misnamed as it is not a garlic at all – likes a semi-shady site and will quite happily, sometimes too happily, colonize large areas under trees with its bright golden flowers. For more open positions, where by June the grass is reaching hay-field proportions, it might be rather fun to try the taller, vigorous *A. aflatunense*, with its drumstick head of purple stars. I always think these look rather naked and the grass heads would help to 'clothe' them.

Ornithogalum umbellatum, star of Bethlehem, is another good bulb for naturalizing in a dry, sunny place. Its cluster of brilliant white star-shaped flowers open wide in the sunshine, closing to reveal their green backs as soon as the light fades. However, being only 6 in (15 cm) tall they need to be in an area of short grass. We grow ours in rough grass on a sunny bank where it does not seem to mind very rough treatment from the lawn-mower. Indeed, it is the only place that I will allow in the garden, except for a single clump coming through pansies between paving stones on the terrace. Ornithogalums are very beautiful when viewed in the antiseptic surroundings of a flower show, but they can behave like bluebells and seed themselves vigorously, usually in the middle of a much treasured plant. I keep my solitary clump on the terrace under control by pulling the seed heads off as soon as they fade but, as they also increase vegetatively, clumps still expand quickly.

There are other, better behaved members of the same family that are suitable for naturalizing as well as for more general garden use. *O. nutans* has wonderful heads of nodding green and grey-white bells, and looks good under trees in a semi-shady position. The flowers are followed by preposterously swollen seed capsules which are quite distinctive in themselves.

I must admit a special partiality to *O. narbonense* since I once spent a memorable coffee-break sitting amongst it on Mount Ararat in East Turkey. Narrow, 14 in (36 cm) spikes of the white flowers of *O. narbonense* were dotted through the grass, with a deep purple gladiolus as a companion. It would be fun to try this ornithogalum with the hardy, reddish-purple *Gladiolus byzantinus* on a dry, sunny slope. Mixed with ox-eye daisies, the result would be very eye catching.

There are one or two other less common

bulbs that could be tried in a damper situation. These are the camassias and the English irises. The quamash bulbs, once eaten by the North American Indians, prefer a damp situation, such as a stream or pool-side, although we find that they still thrive in our light, sandy loam. The various blue camassias, *C. cusickii* (silvery-blue) and *C. quamash* (especially the deeper-blue 'Orion'), will naturalize well in grass and add a touch of stronger colour in June. I have also seen the rather stiff, cream *C. leichtlinii* 'Semi-plena' raise its stately head above the tall grass in a meadow. In a border it can flop, but here it stood stiff as the traditional ramrod. It is definitely a plant that needs to be planted singly rather than in clumps.

The English iris, *I. latifolium*, can also be naturalized in grass. Superficially it is similar to the well-known florist's or Dutch irises, and it gives a very exotic appearance to the grass, but this is how it would look in the wild, as it comes from the damp meadows of the Pyrenees. At Great Dixter it is naturalized in the meadow and looks particularly good with the ubiquitous clover.

Summer

It is difficult to decide whether the camassias, flowering in late May and early June, are really spring or summer bulbs, but there is no doubt about *Lilium martagon*. This trouble-free lily produces its spike of up to 50 recurved purple flowers in mid-June and, although one does not normally associate lilies with bulbs in grass, it is one of the few that are quite happy to do so, provided the conditions are right. It needs a rich, well-drained soil in semi-shade, but where there is a regular supply of water during its growing season.

The main drawback of including such bulbs in a naturalized planting is the length of time that the grass will have to be left uncut – from early March until August. For many people, gardening on a small scale, this is not a practical exercise, and the lilies are best in a shady border (q.v.), but where space does allow, a small clump of them, particularly when mixed with the white forms for contrast, are most attractive. The deeper flowered varieties stand out best, as martagons are not very showy and from a distance tend to merge into their background, particularly if it is full of tall grasses. The small-flowered yellow *L. pyrenaica* can also be planted in similar situations. Although leaving the seed heads does allow the clumps to slowly spread, it can be severely debilitating to the bulbs and result in blindness for a few years, so it is best to remove most of the seed pods as the flowers fade, only leaving one or two to mature.

The lilies apart, summer is the time of rest for most naturalized bulbs, even if it now means a period of protracted labour on the part of the gardener who must tackle the hay field that was once a lawn and attempt to bring it back to some semblance of order. Even when creating a much wilder area it is necessary to have a period of at least a few weeks in summer when the grass is short, allowing the soil to be warmed and the bulbs ripened. The raking up and removal of the grass cuttings will keep the soil relatively impoverished, which is necessary if wild flowers are to be encouraged. Excessive feeding will encourage the grasses and result in the swamping of the less vigorous, but usually more desirable, wild flowers. Regular mowing should be carried out until the first of the autumn crocuses put in an appearance and the seasonal cycle begins again.

Above: Ornithogalum umbellatum will naturalise in a dry, sunny situation

Left: Lilium martagon

Right: Gladiolus byzantinus can be naturalised in the warmer parts of the country

5 Bulbs for special places

So far we have examined the major parts of a garden where bulbs are most likely to be encountered and make their most dramatic impact, but there are certain other areas where bulbs can also find a place. Most of these involve specialist conditions or demand specialist bulbs, and there is therefore an element of self-limitation imposed upon the creative associations that may be possible, but even within these restrictions there is room for experimentation.

There is a danger that a chapter like this will turn into a list of plant names so I intend only to outline the salient points that must be considered when planting in these more specialized sites, and to give a brief summary of the main types of bulbs. More detailed lists of suitable varieties will be found at the end of the book.

Rock gardens

The rock garden, more commonly referred to as a rockery, must be one of the most popular features present, in one form or another, in nearly every garden. However, this rather vague term covers a multiplicity of garden features but they usually house only one of two very disparate collections of plants.

The first is the true alpine garden with carefully created soil and growing conditions, specially constructed to house a collection of alpine plants with very specific, often quite challenging, requirements. The second form is more frequently encountered and is normally an area, more or less constructed using rocks or stones, that is covered by brightly coloured low-growing plants – aubretia and alyssum spring to mind.

Both of these structures fulfil different functions and can be equally attractive, indeed they need not be mutually exclusive, but for many people the true alpine garden is neither a practical or even a desirable achievement. Therefore I propose to treat them separately although there can be, for the non-purist, considerable overlap and something approaching a happy medium can be created.

I do not propose to discuss how to build a rock garden, there are many excellent books on the subject, but the prime function of it, in whatever form it takes, is to create a specialist environment for low-growing plants, excellent drainage being the prime consideration and, preferably, a sunny site.

Although a rock garden will be planted primarily with low plants such as aubretia, pinks, and rock roses there are many dwarf bulbs that will also revel in sunny, well-drained conditions, the early varieties in particular being especially useful to extend the flowering season into early spring or even late winter.

Clumps of early flowering bulbs make one of the first bright splashes in the year, and I use them liberally, planting groups under low plants where they will push their way through and flower, but not leave an unsightly gap in the summer to be filled by weeds. However, great attention must be paid to the height of the bulb, and care taken that the supporting plant is neither too large nor too small. Nothing looks quite as ridiculous as a tiny daffodil struggling to rise above a smothering rock rose, except possibly the sight of a kaufmanniana tulip, although only 8 in (20 cm) tall, dwarfing a tiny 2 in (5 cm) androsace. A sense of scale is probably the most important factor to consider when planting any type of rock garden, but it is not necessary to keep to the shortest bulbs. Taller varieties may be useful to create focal points and avoid a general air of overall flatness. Although you may prefer this carpeting approach I like to add a few of the slightly taller, yet more delicate, tulips and daffodils, such as *Tulipa kolpakowskiana*, *T. clusiana*, *Narcissus* 'Hawera', *N.* 'Jack Snipe', and *N.* 'Jumblie' to create focal points.

These all have slender flowers on 12 in (30 cm) stems and associate well with the bolder rock plants, or even with one of the dwarf hebes such as *H. buchananii*.

Quite apart from the size of the flowers, it must be remembered that almost all leaves of bulbs expand after flowering (one of the few exceptions are the alliums where the leaves come well before the flowers and are virtually dead, or at least decaying, by the time the flowers appear). Some leaves, like those of *Iris reticulata*, remain upright, but most, particularly those of crocuses and daffodils, tend to flop and can cause quite considerable damage to a neighbouring plant if it is insufficiently sturdy to withstand this onslaught. It also looks very untidy, so once again scale is the most important consideration. If you are uncertain about the ultimate size of a bulb or plant, and neat little rock plants in a garden centre can easily trap the unwary into buying a rampaging thug as well as a very slow-growing cushion plant, then it is a good idea to place them beside each other so that you are able to assess their relative stature and, incidentally, the effectiveness of their association. The ideal is probably one clump of bulbs between three plants of the same, small rock plant. If the association is compatible, in time the plants will close the gap to form a carpet below the bulbs. If, on the other hand, the grouping does not work, then it is easily remedied in the autumn when either the bulbs, or the plants, can be moved.

Apart from their use as focal points, adding a little height, the main function of bulbs is to add colour and texture. The majority of bulbs, even the smallest, have larger flowers than most alpine plants so their impact is quite considerable. Early in the year when few plants are in flower the foliage forms a pleasing background to bulbs, often with sympathetic textures and colours. The blue *Iris reticulata* is excellent in small clumps either through or beside prostrate pinks (*Dianthus*); crocuses are excellent with sedums or mossy saxifrages; while that rather vigorous carpeter *Acaena* 'Blue Haze', with its mats of blue–grey ferny foliage, is well able to withstand the onslaught of any bulbs, but is particularly pleasing with blue crocuses such as *C. corsicus*.

There are many species of *Crocus* and it is great fun experimenting with different varieties, especially as only five or 10 bulbs are needed for a clump. Among my favourites are *C. corsicus*, with biscuit-coloured flowers opening to rich purple insides; *C. biflorus* subsp. *alexandri*, with its pure white petals each with a deep purple band on the outside; and *C. angustifolius* (*C. susianus*), which has bright golden flowers each striped brown, and a delightful habit of rolling them completely back when the sun shines.

Not many autumn bulbs are suitable for a rock garden but the autumn crocuses fulfil the same function as the spring ones and bring a touch of colour to the often bedraggled foliage of rock gardens. Some of the reliable species that could be tried are *C. speciosus* (blue), being relatively tall it is excellent when seen coming through grey-leaved rock roses (*Helianthemum*) *C. hadriaticus*, with its pure white flowers and startling red stigmas, is excellent beside a dark-leaved dwarf conifer; and *C. cancellatus*, which produces masses of small, pale blue flowers each heavily veined with purple, is good coming through flat, grey mats of pinks. In a sunny, sheltered corner you could also try the November-flowering *C. tournefortii*, which has the distinction of never closing its large, pale purple flowers once they have opened, and, lastly, the winter crocus *C. laevigatus*, which produces its flowers on any mild sunny day around New Year. In a good year they can continue well into January, linking up with the first of the spring crocuses. There are many more which can be found in the bulb catalogues.

However, as with all crocuses, the danger of their leaves, which appear in great profusion the following spring, must not be overlooked. A delicate carpeting plant may look charming with the haze of blue or purple crocuses hovering above it in September or October, but come spring the sea of grass-like foliage does nothing to improve either the visual effect or the health of the suffocating ground cover so, once again, thought must be given to the stature of their companions.

Bulbs may also be planted to provide contrasting colours to flowering plants. One of the most commonly encountered plants, and certainly among the boldest, is *Aubretia*. Its widespread, neat mats are invaluable for early colour but they are often the only plant in flower and the effect can be rather overpowering. On one housing estate where there were no formally

Left: An attractive group of spring bulbs on a rock garden *Erythronium* 'Pagoda', *Anemone blanda, Narcissus* 'Hawera' and *Muscari* 'Blue Spike'

Left: Iris reticulata 'Clairette'

Below: The lime-green bracts of *Euphorbia myrsinites* provide a bold contrast to the dark *Muscari latifolium*

delineated front gardens, a bank had been carpeted with *Aubretia*, but its rather harsh purple shades were softened by the addition of bold clumps of grape hyacinth and the softer lavender hues of *Primula denticulata*. I longed to tuck in a couple of clumps of a small, creamy daffodil like 'Jack Snipe' to add a little brightness to this otherwise harmonious picture.

Unless you are planting for a really bold effect or have a very large rock garden, the grape hyacinth (*M. armeniacum*) is probably too coarse and invasive, but there are some members of this family that are much better behaved, with smaller leaves that are truly herbaceous, unlike those of *M. armeniacum* which seems to be present virtually all year. *M. tubergeniana* has neat flowers of mid-blue, the top being lighter than the bottom. This contrast, which has given it the rather dubious name of the Oxford and Cambridge grape hyacinth, is only really noticeable as the flowers fade, and even then it is not really very striking. *M. latifolium*, on the other hand, has definite bi-coloured flowers with a pale blue top knot supported by an almost black base and needs a pale foil to be really effective. It is a relatively well-behaved grape hyacinth compared to many of its genus. In 16 years it has gently seeded itself over our rock garden and has now spread across an area of about 3½ sq. yd (3 sq. m). However, unwanted bulbs are easily removed as they are quickly recognizable by their single wide leaf.

Although traditionally thought of as being shades of blue, there are grape hyacinth available in different colours, the best being 'pearls of Spain' (*M. botryoides* 'Album') with its delicate, pure white flowers and neat foliage. This is completely trouble-free, only requiring a sunny, well-drained position, and has never seeded, to my knowledge, so it remains exactly where it is planted. It is excellent when planted through the completely prostrate *Cytisus decumbens*, perhaps with a *Saxifraga aizoon* for contrast and continuing interest. *M. comosum* 'Plumosum' produces strange, pinkish, sterile flowers in June and is a fascinating plant, causing much interest.

For bold effects there are many blue-flowered bulbs early in the year, the chionodoxas spring to mind, but one of the best groups are the scillas. They begin the year with one of the earliest bulbs of all, the delicate *Scilla mischtschenkoana* (*S. tubergeniana*). It pushes its first flower up in early February, and as it keeps its head down and begins flowering literally at ground level it should be placed where it can be seen. A dusting of fine gravel will help stop the flowers from becoming mud splashed, and they must be protected from slugs, unless you like the lace effect these pests quickly achieve. Each bulb produces a number of stems, each gradually lengthening to about 5 in (12 cm). Not only does it flower very early in the year, it will also tolerate partial or almost complete shade, as on the north side of our rock garden where it grows at the foot of a large plant of *Helleborus viridis* which is still dormant when the scilla flowers. The large leaves of the hellebore that appear late in the spring cover the dying scilla foliage most effectively.

Scilla bifolia is so tiny that it must be planted in tightly packed clumps and placed very carefully if it is not to be overlooked, but its brilliant blue flowers on gently arching stems are a delight in February. *S. sibirica*, on the other hand, is a much bolder plant and probably best planted at the foot of a shrub, but it is useful, especially in the form 'Spring Beauty' which has bigger and bolder flower spikes to give a patch of strong colour among the more vigorous rock plants. I am particularly fond of the delicate white form.

Another delicate bulb, that needs careful siting if it is not to be overlooked, is the pale blue *Puschkinia scilloides* (*P. libanotica*), likened by E. A. Bowles to 'the ghost of scilla'. It is excellent among the grey cushions of pinks or beside one of the prostrate phlox.

Soft, blending colours can be most attractive and some very pleasing effects can be achieved such as a cream mossy saxifrage with *Narcissus* 'Little Beauty' (4 in, 10 cm bi-coloured white and yellow) or the later flowering lemon *N.* 'Hawera'. One of my most successful, and entirely accidental, associations was a clump of the creamy *Tulipa batalinii* 'Bright Gem' planted at the edge of an almost white rock rose, the two colours being sufficiently different to give a pleasant contrast rather than an overall blandness.

However, such mistakes do not always have happy results, as I discovered to my cost when I planted the dwarf scarlet tulip, *T. maximowiczii*, under an aubretia. Unfortunately the aubretia, an unflowered seedling, produced a vast array of flowers of the most intense deep pink. When the sun shone and the tulips displayed their brilliant glistening red flowers beside the aubretia the result was strident, to say the least.

There are many excellent dwarf tulips that revel in the hot, dry conditions of a rock garden and can be left down from year to year. Some, like *T. fosteriana* 'Princeps' and 'Cantata', have relatively large flowers on short stems and should be used boldly to create patches of intense colour, scarlet in this instance. Others have much more delicate flowers and may, like the yellow *T. tarda* and *T. urumiensis*, produce more than one flower per bulb. Among my favourites is the primrose *T. batalinii* and its apricot-hued hybrids – 'Bronze Charm', 'Apricot Jewel' and 'Bright Gem'. Like all these smaller tulips they are relatively long lived, provided the bulbs are planted deeply in a very sunny, well-

drained position. I have had two neighbouring clumps of *T. batalinii* and *T. b.*
'Bronze Charm' on my rock garden for the
past 16 years and every year they produce
a magnificent display, the clumps having
expanded far beyond the original 10 bulbs.

The tulips mentioned so far spread vegetatively, and their seed pods should be
removed once the flower fades. *T. spren-
geri*, on the other hand, produces bulbs
relatively quickly from seed, taking three
or four years instead of the more usual
seven years. Although it is easy to grow,
and can spread its scarlet flowers so that a
whole rock garden is dotted with them in
late May or June, the bulbs are impossible
to harvest as it would involve a major
excavation to find them. Although very
tiny (only $\frac{1}{3}$ in (1 cm) long), they have
remarkable powers of penetration and can
be found more than 12 in (30 cm) below
the surface. Removing the seed-heads as
the flower fades will, of course, control
them, but they are so neat and well
behaved that I would not mind them as a
weed.

Not all bulbs are quite as easy and
reliable, and some may regularly fail in the
second year. One of the most frustrating
groups are the reticulata irises that push
up their neat blue or purple flowers in
February.

The main problem is that after flowering each bulb splits into masses of tiny
ones which will take some years before
they are of flowering size again. To try to
overcome this the bulbs should be planted
at least 6 in (15 cm) deep, or more on very
sandy soils, and then regularly watered
with a high-potash feed, one for tomatoes
is excellent, after flowering to encourage
the formation of a large bulb. One of the
most reliable is *Iris histrioides* 'Major',
which usually gives a regular performance,
and it is to be hoped that the superb new
hybrid *I. h.* 'George', with its widely flaring flowers of rich purple, will prove as
reliable. *I. reticulata* itself is also a good
repeat performer, although its dark blue–
purple flowers are rather poor compared
to some of the hybrids.

All reticulata irises can suffer from ink-
spot disease, which is a fungal infection
causing the destruction of a whole group
of irises in a very short space of time. Poor
drainage is a contributing factor, and this
should be improved and the irises watered
with Benlate or, alternatively, the bulbs
can be dipped in Benlate at planting time.
The lovely yellow *I. danfordiae* is rarely
perennial and it is probably best treated as
an annual, but it should be possible to
establish clumps of the many reticulata
hybrids, which range in colour from the
pale blue 'Clairette', mid-blue 'Harmony'
and 'Joyce', to the deep purple 'J. S. Dijt'
or 'Pauline'. At planting time the narrow,
square-sectioned leaves are relatively short
but they lengthen considerably after flowering and tend to remain stiffly upright.
Therefore they are difficult to hide on a
rock garden where everything is of small
stature, so it is best to distract attention
from them by planting them behind plants
that flower as the iris leaves fade. Many of
the rock pinks are particularly good as
they provide a neat grey cushion while the
early irises flower and then they flower in
turn and disguise the fading iris leaves. We
find *Erodium guttatum* with its mounds of
softly divided grey leaves a good partner
for reticulata irises, as is *Geranium ciner-
eum* 'Ballerina' or *G. c.* 'Lawrence Flat-
man'.

Some bulbs are not suitable for planting
under, or at the edge of, other plants as in
fact they are almost foliage plants in themselves. *Oxalis adenophylla* produces delightful compact buns of neat grey leaves
which in May become studded with little
pink flowers that open from furled buds
like little umbrellas. It is completely trouble-free, only requiring a position in full
sun, and deserves to be given a spot of its
own where it should be planted in groups
of three or more.

Anemone blanda is almost as important
for its foliage as for its flowers in early
spring. Its attractive leaves are produced
early in the year and it flowers intermit-
tently from February to April, with the
main flush in late March and early April.
The blue shades are excellent carpeters and
can become a bit of a nuisance, seeding
themselves everywhere, but the other coloured forms are excellent plants for the
rock garden. I love to see the large pure
white flowers of *A. b.* 'White Splendour'
tumbling between the rocks, perhaps with
a few of the magenta *A. b.* 'Radar' for
company and contrast. They provide excellent ground cover for other early spring
bulbs – such as chionodoxas with *A. b.*
'White Splendour', or *Narcissus* 'Tête a
Tête' with blue anemones.

The late-flowering Greek anemones,

A. hortensis and A. pavonina, bring a touch of the exotic to the rock garden. They need a well-drained position in full sun, and an open space where they can raise their brilliantly coloured flowers above the surrounding plants. The group, known as 'St Bavo' comes in all shades of pink and purple, while 'Annulata Grandiflora' is a brilliant scarlet with a white and black centre.

Some bulbs are such individuals that they deserve to be displayed on their own, uncluttered by surrounding plants. The juno irises are just such a group. The most commonly encountered one is *I. bucharica* which, despite its exotic appearance, is in fact completely hardy and trouble-free. The strange bulbs, with their large, fleshy roots, without which they will not grow, give rise to a series of alternating, folded leaves that sit one inside the other. The flowers cluster at the top of the stem and are unusual in that, unlike most irises, they have virtually no standards, just an apology for one tucked in at the base of the flower. *I. aucheriana* is similar, but instead of cream and yellow flowers, as in *I. bucharica*, it has pale blue ones. Both deserve to be much more widely grown.

The main problem with this group of bulbs, and the anemones, is that they leave empty gaps when they have died back. Ideally they need some neighbouring plant that can spread all over them for the summer months, to 'throw a veil of silver leaves and bright rose-coloured flowers over the summer sleep of the scillas' as E. A. Bowles puts it, describing *Convolvulus althaeoides*.

Although most rock garden bulbs flower throughout the spring, there are one or two small summer-flowering bulbs that will enjoy the sunny conditions. One of the brightest and easiest is *Allium oreophilum* (*A. ostrowskianum*), with its tight heads of bright pink flowers on 4 in (10 cm) stems. It is excellent with contrasting blue or white flowers, but is best kept away from yellow, or even other pinks if it is not an exact match.

In larger rock gardens, where there is a cooler, semi-shaded side, some of the dwarf lilies can be grown. These will have to be provided with a richer soil than the usual, rather starved fare that most rock plants prefer, but they will enjoy the excellent drainage and can be very striking in midsummer. Ones to try would be *Lilium*

Above: The early dwarf *Tulipa kaufmanniana* 'Hearts Delight' is an attractive foil for *Muscari botryoides* 'Album'

Right: The dwarf *Tulipa batalinii* 'Bronze Charm' is an excellent variety for the rock garden

amabile (yellow or red turk's cap), *L. pumilum* (syn. *tenuifolium*) (scarlet turk's cap), or *L. concolor* (upward-facing scarlet flowers).

So far I have been discussing bulbs suitable for the traditional rock garden where low plants are grown for colour throughout the year. I would now like to look briefly at the true alpine garden. This can be an elaborate construction involving landscaping, with huge rocks, but it may be on a much more modest scale, perhaps a low bank supported by rock walls, or a raised bed specially built to house a collection of alpines, or even a stone trough or maybe an old sink disguised by covering it with *hypertufa* (a mixture of cement and peat used to create a 'stone' effect). The main unifying feature is the nature of the soil. Most alpine plants need a very open, free-draining soil and the soil in these beds can be specially created to include a high proportion of sand and fine grit.

Such care and attention would be wasted on the bolder, larger bulbs and more vigorous plants, although I would include some of the more delicate of the larger bulbs to give a bolder touch of colour and shape. I know one gardener who would never allow the larger 'dwarf' bulbs into raised alpine beds, preferring the clinically precise arrangements of beautifully grown specimens of miniature plants. I am afraid that I tend towards the other extreme and add plants for height and interest, even if it does mean that some of my rarities are swamped in the process and that I have to replant some of the items.

People are always tempted by the small species daffodils, but with a few exceptions they are often not successful. However, chances of success can be greatly increased if they are grown in specially prepared raised beds. The earliest of all is *N. asturiensis* which is like a tiny version of our Lent lily. Although it is quite happy in semi-shaded woodland beds, it is probably best grown on a rock garden where it can be really appreciated and the predatory slugs kept at bay. Some of the *N. bulbocodium* hybrids flower almost as early as *N. asturiensis*, or even earlier in the case of the southern Spanish and North African *N. cantabricus*. The hybrid 'Nylon' always produces its creamy white hoop-petticoat flowers around New Year and, indeed, has been known to start flowering in October.

It seems to be completely hardy in all but the severest winters when the foliage can become so damaged that the bulb is severely weakened. All the bulbocodiums have narrow, grass-like leaves and are excellent for the alpine garden, looking particularly good against a grey rock, which is how I first encountered them in Spain, clinging to crevices in a cliff.

N. triandrus is probably best grown in a peat bed but its delicacy makes it suitable for a peaty pocket on the rock garden.

The jonquils come from southern Europe and need a much drier summer than ours to ripen the bulbs, therefore they, too, are eminently suited to the rock garden. The taller species, *N. jonquilla*, and its hybrids 'Sundial', 'Lintie', and 'Bobbysoxer' are all suitable subjects for the more traditional rock garden, but some of the small species such as *N. juncifolius*, *N. rupicola* and *N. scaberulus* need a well-drained pocket, and their tiny size, 2–3 in (5–8 cm), makes them ideal companions for the smaller alpines. I grow *N. scaberulus* very successfully in the corner of a large stone trough. Some of the smaller hybrids, such as 'Sundisc' and 'Segovia', and also some of the hybrids based on *N. asturiensis*, 'Little Beauty' and 'Little Gem' for instance, are also probably small enough and delicate enough to be considered for this kind of gardening.

I also grow the tiny *Iris hyrcana* in one of my troughs. This is like a miniature reticulata iris in a deep blue, occasionally purple, and is unusual in that it usually produces two flowers to each bulb. Once again, scale is probably the single most important factor when choosing bulbs to associate with the smaller alpine plants. I would certainly include some of the more unusual crocuses, such as *C. minimus*, with its tiny, purple flowers, each heavily marked with deep purple on the outsides; *C. sieberi* 'Bowles White', which has glistening, pure white flowers produced early in the year; and *C. s.* forma *tricolor*, with its purple flowers, each with a yellow band above a deep purple centre. Superficially similar to the crocuses are the romuleas and it is worth trying the easiest of the species, *Romulea bulbocodium*, on a very dry sunny spot. It may not be very long-lived but it is a delightful plant with mid-purple flowers, each with recurved petals. I have seen it coming through a small mossy saxifrage on the very top of a raised bed where it looked delightful.

Adjacent to the romulea, and looking very exotic indeed, was one of the dwarf fritillaries. These, with their usually chequered flowers, often in subdued shades of brown or greeny creams, are often considered too difficult, but some take well to the open garden, revelling in a good soil, excellent drainage, and a sunny situation. Among the most reliable are *Fritillaria acmopetala*, with good-sized green flowers with brown inner petals, *F. pontica*, with 2–4 greenish-brown flowers; *F. uva-vulpis* (*F. asyraica*), with small chocolate brown flowers; and *F. involucrata*, with lightly chequered, green flowers. This is very much the tip of the iceberg, and as more of the species become freely available so experiments in growing them outside are increasing and the number suitable grows each year.

Although the majority of tulips are too big to be included in this type of gardening, I do find some of them useful for troughs or to make a slightly bolder impact. White is a relatively uncommon colour in tulips, yellow being the normal albino form, but I would not be without *Tulipa turkestanica*, and the similar *T. bifolia*, which produce creamy white, yellow-centred flowers very early in the year and are very reliable, as is *T. pulchella* in its various forms. This produces intense purplish–pink flowers in February and March and can be followed by the softer, rose-coloured *T. aucheriana*.

To conclude, in all rock gardens scale is the prime factor to be taken into consideration. The same small crocus that dwarfs a tiny androsace can equally well be lost under a large rock rose. I am always surprised how often people find heights in a catalogue deceptive. A 8 in (20 cm) daffodil or tulip is often considered too tall but, quite apart from the fact that the slightly taller hybrid daffodils are much more reliable than the very tiny species ones, you must bear in mind that the majority of rock garden plants do not cling to the rocks like a second skin – they too have substance, usually 3–4 in (7–10 cm). Therefore, if the bulbs are going to be seen at all, they must be at least as tall or a little taller than the surrounding plants. Indeed, if the rock garden is a large feature or backed by a solid structure like a wall or hedge, then even taller bulbs could be used effectively. The range avail-

able is overwhelming but chosen with care, a bulb can be found to enhance almost all types of rock garden feature.

Bulbs in containers

I have already briefly discussed gardening in one type of container in the section on rock gardens. These are troughs, which can be beautifully cut from stone or may just be cement, or cement disguising an old, deep kitchen sink. No matter what material they are made from, they all have one thing in common – they are planted, so as to create miniature gardens, where truly dwarf daffodils flower next to tiny alpines. Two big advantages of these are that it is possible to vary the soil within them, to suit specific plants, and that they are, with difficulty (six log-rollers and a gang of willing children in our case), relatively mobile. Thus they can be filled with an acid, peaty soil and placed in a semi-shady position for *Narcissus cyclamineus* and dwarf rhododendrons, or placed in the sun and given a very open, limy soil with plenty of grit for a large range of tiny bulbs and alpines.

As they are not so much garden ornaments as miniature gardens in themselves, with the same plants remaining in them for many years, snails and God willing, they are, of course, a very permanent feature and can be landscaped into the surrounding garden. This is probably easier with troughs in shady situations, where small ferns and perhaps erythroniums (especially 'Pagoda' and 'White Beauty') could be planted at one side to soften the line and form a gentle transition from the surrounding garden to the trough. This is especially useful where the trough is filled with an acid soil for calcifuge plants (those that hate lime, like rhododendrons) in the context of a limy garden. It is very important to check the scale of such plants and make sure that they complement the trough and do not either dwarf or detract from it.

This can be especially true of plants surrounding a trough in a sunny situation

Above: A large pot of *Tulipa* 'Apricot Beauty' associates well with pots of grey-leaved plants to define this Somerset terrace

year with a succession of plants and bulbs. In order to make a strong visual impact, containers are, by their very nature, bold garden features, and they need bold handling if they are to fulfil this primary function properly.

Once again, it is necessary to begin with the garden and decide where a container will be useful, and then to choose a suitable one for that situation. Traditionally, pots are placed by the front door or scattered around the edge of the terrace to add a touch of colour, which is fine, but with a little imagination they can be used even more effectively. Groups of pots, mixing bulbs and annual or herbaceous plants are much more effective than a single pot. They also provide a mini microclimate and can help reduce frost damage in winter. In periods of severe weather sacks filled with straw can be tied round the pots to help protect them.

Single pots of tulips can be placed among pots of grey-leaved plants on the end of a terrace, or at the edge of a path to make a focal point. The smaller hybrid tulips – variously found in catalogues under the names fosteriana, kaufmanniana, and greigii, are all excellent for containers. All have neat, relatively large brightly coloured flowers on short 6–9 in (15–23 cm) stems, and many have the added bonus of attractively mottled leaves. Traditionally, tulips are mixed with pansies or grape hyacinths to soften their often stiff, upright stance. Daffodils, on the other hand, are prone to flop and are probably best on their own, the pot being packed with bulbs as tightly as possible for a really dramatic effect.

When choosing daffodils for pots it is best to choose varieties with relatively large heads and not-too-tall stems for maximum impact. The true dwarf daffodils are usually perfectly proportioned miniatures and are best placed in troughs or rock gardens, where their delicacy can be appreciated. The size of the pot is also of utmost importance. It defeats the object of the exercise to have very small daffodils peeping coyly out of a very large pot. The *N. cyclamineus* hybrids are all good subjects for pots, especially 'February Gold', the bi-coloured 'Jack Snipe' or 'Jenny', and the lemon 'Charity May'. One of my favourites is the lovely *N. triandrus* hybrid 'Liberty Bells', which has beautiful twin flowers of the clearest lemon that nod in a

where they can be easily overwhelmed by adjacent injudicious plantings. Pansies seed themselves at will around my terrace and do not detract from the troughs but I feel that anything larger would spoil the overall effect. Indeed, you may prefer the more clinical isolated appearance or rely upon the alpines themselves to soften the sides.

Delightful though they may be, troughs are not the kind of containers that normally spring to mind when this type of gardening is discussed. For most people a container means a wide range of objects from huge stone urns and terracotta vases to old beer barrels or even tyres turned half inside-out.

The one thing they have in common is that they are bedded out throughout the

delightful way.

For scent and sturdiness 'Geranium', a multi-headed variety with pure white petals and orange cup, is difficult to beat. It is also good for indoor culture.

The classic spot for containers is beside the front door, especially if this looks out directly onto a path with no beds alongside the house wall. Provided that there is sun for at least part of the day there are many bulbs that can be used to brighten these areas – hyacinths, as much for their scent as their colour, and the large-flowered dwarf tulips spring to mind. *Tulipa fosteriana* 'Cantata' and 'Princeps' are excellent for this usage, as is *T. greigii* 'Red Riding Hood', with its large scarlet flowers above beautifully striped leaves.

However, it is also possible to use the pots in a more architectural way. Shallow urns, whether of real stone or one of the very good imitation ones, are very useful to define the ends of low walls, as at the top of the steps. These plots may be very beautiful but they are frequently rather impractical, being very shallow and therefore only suitable for the smaller bulbs, and even then they will require very careful watering. I fill mine with hyacinths every year, and the blue ones look particularly good against the grey stone of the container.

Containers should not only be individually attractive, but attractive when viewed in the overall context of the garden, and once again, the background becomes important. Often it is neutral, such as grass or a path, which is why a pot is placed there in the first place, in order to add a little colour; but looking at it from another angle a very different picture can emerge and it becomes obvious that a different colour combination would look better. It is important to remember that what looks good looking up the garden must also look good when walking back down it again.

I know one garden where the path round the house is edged by a low brick wall to separate it from the lawn beyond. On either side of the gap leading through to the grass there is a low stone urn. On the sunny April day I visited the garden they were filled with *Tulipa greigii* 'Red Riding Hood' and blue pansies. Each pot was a brilliant splash of colour and delightful on their own, but even more so in the context of the garden when they were the only touch of colour against a green background. As you approached the side of the

house they brought the quiet lawn and its shrub beds beyond to life, making you want to continue round the corner and explore further. The walls were clad in a large-leaved variegated ivy which added to the interest.

Having decided upon the location, you must then decide upon the type of container. This is a very personal choice, but one thing must always be remembered and that is that there must be sufficient depth for an ample root run for either bulbs or plants, otherwise they will develop poorly. Shallow containers also dry out very quickly and will need regular watering and feeding.

When it comes to the choice of bulb, scale is once again very important, as not only must the bulbs not swamp the pot,

Above: Tulipa greigii 'Red Riding Hood' with blue pansies

they themselves must not be dwarfed by their container. It is also important to consider the location. Many pots are placed in exposed positions and it is therefore better to choose a short tulip or daffodil than a taller one that may well be damaged by the wind. The main advantage of bulbs is that they flower early in the year, before most bedding plants, and are therefore useful to extend the season. It is also advisable to choose early flowering varieties if you wish to replace them with summer bedding.

It is not necessary to use only one variety of bulb, they can, of course, be mixed with others. We have an old Victorian cast-iron jardinière that is filled with *Anemone blanda* 'White Splendour' which begins flowering in early March and provides a soft, ferny carpet of leaves for the creamy *Tulipa fosteriana* 'White Emperor', in April. Alternatively, one of the shorter scarlet tulips could be used, to provide a very striking grouping. We leave the bulbs there from one year to the next, only replacing the tulips every two or three years when they deteriorate, but the usual practice is to lift the bulbs as they fade and replace them with summer bedding. Summer-flowering bulbs, like lilies, that must be planted early in the year, are best on their own, although they can be mixed with other plants that will provide interest as the lilies grow, provided the container is large enough.

Lilies are ideal subjects for pots and tubs. I know one gardener who graphically describes her garden as '3″ of soil over 700 feet of clay – the type you model with'. Lilies, with their need for excellent drainage, are a complete failure in the open garden here, so she plants them in pots and then plunges them, pot and all, in the border where a little extra height or colour is needed. Once they have finished flowering they are removed to the kitchen garden where they can be given careful attention to build up the bulbs for the following year. I always plant two or three 12 in (30 cm) pots of *Lilium regale* to mix with my fuchsias and geraniums on the terrace in the summer. Some good, reliable lilies for pots are 'Bright Star' (white with a yellow centre), 'Enchantment' (easy, orange), 'Connecticut King' (yellow), and 'Green Magic'.

Bulbs, of course, need not be planted in isolation or only with other bulbs, they can be very effectively mixed with other plants. In a London square I saw two rectangular pots flanking an imposing front door that looked out directly to the street. The troughs were filled with a collection of silver-leaved plants, mostly artemesias, and every year white daffodils and tulips were followed in the summer by white petunias, making a continual display. In an adjacent street there was a small, very gloomy basement that caught my eye one evening. Two large tubs were completely smothered by a variegated ivy, through which rose two clumps of *Narcissus* 'February Gold', that really did bring a touch of golden warmth to that otherwise dismal place. Behind the daffodils was a clematis trained up the wall for colour throughout the summer.

On a not much larger scale, but at ground level this time, was a rather small, gloomy courtyard immediately outside a back door and overlooked by the kitchen window. It only received direct sun during the afternoon, but it was a thoroughfare that was constantly in use and continually observed from the kitchen sink. The walls of the courtyard had been painted white to reflect as much light as possible and it was home to four enormous wooden tubs, each raised on four bricks and painted black, and each filled to overflowing. A climbing rose scrambled out of one and up the wall behind, fighting for space with lilies, herbaceous geraniums, and trailing lobelia, (never mind if the trailing one is not available, they all flop over the edge of pots in a very satisfactory manner, but do make sure it is a true blue and not a muddy mauve). One of the tubs was a complete symphony of blue and cream. Dwarf lavender and tiny cream roses fought for space, while above and through them arched the perfect blue pom-poms of *Allium caeruleum*, more frequently encountered under its equally descriptive name of *A. azureum*. Towards the back of the tub there were three golden lilies to continue interest through July.

The choice of container is not important, they can be lead, stone, concrete, or even plastic, provided they are planted well and placed carefully in the garden the eventual effect will be much the same. After all, the plant does not mind whether it is a genuine antique or a Woolworth's copy it is growing in so long as the growing conditions are suitable.

The first consideration is depth in relation to the size of plant you hope to grow. Small bulbs, such as crocuses or the dwarf tulips and daffodils, will accept a relatively shallow root run of 6–9 in (15–23 cm), but taller daffodils and tulips require at least 12 in (30 cm). Lilies, especially if stem rooting, need at least 6–8 in (15–20 cm) of soil above the bulb and almost as much below. In smaller containers lilies will grow the first year but will be of little value in subsequent ones. They also tend to become top-heavy and are at risk of aborting their flowers due to a shortage of water.

Having chosen the container, the size of the bulb suitable, and the type of bulb for a particular season it is worth considering the colour of the container. Grey stone, or its imitations, blend with all colours, but certain strident terracottas do not look comfortable with pale pinks, but look stunning with deep, bronzy reds, such as that of the dwarf *Tulipa kaufmanniana* 'Showwinner'.

When it comes to actually planting the container I must reiterate once again the cry of drainage. The first thing is to check that the container has adequate drainage holes and then to cover them with crocks so that the soil cannot seep through and block them. Nothing will kill a bulb faster than drought, except a waterlogged soil. In wet soils root production is poor and the bulb quickly becomes unstable, even if it does not rot completely, and this is especially noticeable with hyacinths where there is a large head to support. I usually place 2 in (5 cm) of broken crocks or small stones in the bottom of my pots, followed by a shallow layer of peat to keep some moisture at the bottom where it is needed, and then fill the remainder with a good potting compost.

The actual compost is relatively unimportant, especially if the bulbs are going to be discarded after flowering, but the soil should be open and gritty to allow for good drainage and should contain a balanced fertilizer. Old potting compost is ideal, but any good, sandy loam will do. In areas of heavy clay it is perhaps best to buy some John Innes No. 2, adding some more sand if it seems a little sticky, although this should not be necessary. Ideally, the bulbs should be planted as soon as they are obtained. The container, with its layer of drainage material, should be filled to half way with compost, making sure that it is firmed down but not compressed too much. The bulbs should then be lightly pushed onto the surface and the container filled to the very top, as the soil will soon settle. The pots should then be thoroughly watered, until water runs through the bottom. It will not normally be necessary to water again until spring.

For summer-flowering bulbs very regular watering must take place from late spring in order to maintain regular active growth, as any irregularity in water supply will result in poor performance. If you are mixing herbaceous or annual plants with bulbs, tulips with pansies for example, then the annuals can be planted into the urn at any suitable time, even just before the bulbs flower.

There is, of course, a danger of damage by frost to all bulbs in containers; even very hardy ones will not tolerate being completely frozen for any length of time, and I have known severe frosts over successive weeks to completely rot bulbs planted in relatively shallow urns. However, it is possible to take some precautions against such adverse conditions. The best method, if the container is movable, is to put it under cover for the duration, but most are far too heavy. In such emergencies a cardboard box packed with crumpled newspaper and placed on the pot provides a simple but effective protection. However, you must remember to remove it once the frost eases, or it rains, otherwise it will collapse in a soggy heap. Large groups of pots, or pots that are movable but with nowhere under cover to store them, can be packed closely together and the gaps filled with straw or newspaper and the whole covered by a net. It is a little unsightly perhaps but it is none the less effective.

If the containers are large enough, they can be lined with thin sheets of polystyrene and the bulbs planted deep in the middle, but this only really works for rectangular shapes. I must admit that I favour the policy of filling my urns with cheap bulbs, making sure that they are in scale and then keeping my fingers crossed that we will have a mild winter. If really bad weather destroys the bulbs then I quickly visit my local nursery and plant the containers with pansies – 'King John' is my favourite. If the pots are needed for a special occasion, such as a wedding, then I would recommend taking the precaution of planting

spare bulbs in small pots and keeping these under cover to bring out if and when the need should arise.

As with troughs, it may be desirable to blend a container into its surroundings, and this can be done in such a way that the architectural value of the container is not sacrificed. One simple method for relatively tall urns is to place them upon a small plinth made from four hollow concrete wall blocks, containing a simple flower design, supporting a fifth, placed diagonally in the middle, upon which the urn stands. The lower blocks make an effective container for other small bulbs, grape hyacinths in the example I saw. I have a very large 'stone' urn on a gravel path and a plant of *Alchemilla mollis* (lady's mantle), has seeded under it. Its lime-green flowers and blue-green foliage are most attractive against the grey of the urn, which is filled with silver-leaved plants and deep-red tulips, *Tulipa eichleri*, around a red phormium (New Zealand flax). In the summer the tulips are replaced by white petunias.

Window boxes

Although window boxes are essentially containers in virtually all respects, and they can be treated in the same way, especially regarding compost and planting, they often fulfil a very different function and this demands an essentially different type of bulb. Some are purely for external decoration, one immediately thinks of the waterfalls of ivy-leaved geraniums tumbling down from Alpine chalets, and are therefore, like most containers, concerned with making impact and are principally intended to be seen from outside. In this instance the shorter bulbs with large flower-heads will provide the bold splash of colour necessary. However, for many the window box is more of a miniature garden, especially when it is the only, or virtually the only, garden. Under these circumstances they are observed from both inside the house at eye-level, and from the garden at possibly ten feet below. When viewed in such an intimate way scale once again becomes important, and many of the smaller bulbs that would be planted on the rock garden could usefully find a home here where their delicate charms can be closely examined and fully appreciated.

It is possible to plant a window box so that there is a continuous succession of interest from late winter right through to May when annuals replace the bulbs. The first thing to remember is that as the boxes are looked at from inside the house, the earlier bulbs should be planted on the outside edge so that their fading leaves are masked by the succeeding flowers. Once again, it is possible to mix early and late varieties in the same space, provided that their leaves are compatible. As there is an almost endless range of possible combinations I will just give details of one plan to give the general idea.

Anemone blanda, blue and white, but not pink if yellow daffodils are to be included, can be planted virtually throughout the box, primarily to give a soft ferny background to the other bulbs, although, of course, their flowers are most attractive in their own right. I would then put one or two clumps of early crocuses, varieties of *Crocus chrysanthus* are excellent, on the outer edge, with a clump of one of the reticulata irises between them for height. One or two small groups of one of the dwarf daffodils such as 'Tête a Tête' or 'Sundial' would follow the crocuses and accompany the anemones, or a dwarf red tulip such as *Tulipa praestans* 'Fusilier' may be preferred, to flower with the white anemone. To hide the fading leaves and continue the interest into April or early May, I would tuck in a few of the dwarf tulips such as *T. maximowiczii* or *T. batalinii*, perhaps with the delicate *Narcissus* 'Hawera' or the fabulously scented *N. jonquilla* to complete the picture and season. There is such a huge range of dwarf bulbs available that there is an almost endless list of possible combinations.

Once the last bulbs begin to fade they can all be removed and the boxes replanted with summer bedding. Then the fading bulbs should be heeled in the garden and well watered. It may be possible to use some of the bulbs again the following spring, but many dislike container cultivation and it is probably better to buy new ones each season to ensure a good display. However, not everyone has a garden, in which case the bulbs must be thrown or given away, but if the box is deep enough, it is possible to leave the bulbs there from one year to the next, planting summer plants on top of them. Not all bulbs will tolerate the inevitable watering of the summer bedding but, provided they are planted almost at the bottom of the box, and with ample drainage, some bulbs will persist. The most likely to succeed are crocuses, anemones, chionodoxas, grape hyacinths, and some of the daffodils, but not the jonquil hybrids as they need a very dry dormant period. Similarly, tulips and reticulata irises will not persist.

One method that facilitates the change from bulbs to bedding plants without actually disturbing either is to make a removable liner for a window box or trough. As this will have to support a great weight it must be of wood or plastic. Preferably, it should have handles, rope is ideal for easy handling, and the whole internal container complete with fading bulbs, can be lifted out and replaced by another, already planted for the next season, or it can just be moved to a suitable place for emptying and replanting.

Warm, sheltered borders

So far, I have only discussed bulbs that are completely hardy and will flower well in the main garden, but there is a group of bulbs, mostly autumn-flowering, that, although hardy, require a warm, sunny position before they will flower well. Their flowers also tend not to be frost hardy and, as they flower rather late in the year, they are very vulnerable unless grown in a sheltered position. Indeed, a warm, sheltered wall, facing south or west, against the house, or even a greenhouse, can have a unique microclimate that, as well as a full range of normal bulbs, will allow an exciting range of others to be grown. There is inevitably great competition for space in such choice aspects but it is usually possible to squeeze a few bulbs in. As these bulbs all require the maximum amount of sun on them while they are dormant, in order to ripen their bulbs and encourage flowering, it is not possible to disguise the gaps they leave when dormant by overplanting. Therefore, it is best to plant quite small clumps, and, indeed, these are often much more effective than massed beds of one exotic plant where the sheer quantity becomes overpowering and they almost degenerate into bedding plants, albeit superior ones. To my mind, a small clump of nerines carefully placed is much more beautiful than an enormous mass of them lining a wall, dramatic though that is.

I would always plant a few clumps of crocuses along the edge of these beds. Although they do not need these special conditions, they will revel in the dryness and reward you with an eye-catching display early in the year. Later in the spring there is a magnificent tulip from Crete. *T. saxatilis*, that needs a very dry, sunny place where it can be left undisturbed. It has shiny, apple-green leaves and glorious rich pink flowers, up to four on a stem, which open wide to reveal their golden eye. They are stoloniferous, and mine have slowly spread to form quite a large patch which is quite spectacular in late April. *T. bakeri* is a deeper, purplish pink, and *T. b.* 'Lilac Wonder' probably has the richest colouring. These tulips need to be left uncovered during the summer and are best in front of a shrub where the gap they leave is less noticeable, although mine have coped well with the invasion of one of the dwarf campanulas.

Although the name scilla is usually associated with the smaller spring bulbs, bluebells in particular, there is one southern European species that is definitely not small, indeed it can be one of the most architectural bulbs in the garden. The large triangular heads of deep blue flowers of *S. peruviana* are very striking, and a clump of them beside a step or at the corner of a raised bed is an arresting sight in May and June. *S. peruviana* requires a well-drained position and, although completely hardy (we grow it as a field crop and even its overwintering leaves survived severe freezing), it flowers best in a sunny bed and deserves to be placed where it can dominate the surrounding plants. It is excellent with low, grey-leaved plants.

As spring advances and the temperature rises so the so-called hardy gladioli begin to flower. These have the added attraction of being more dwarf in habit and much less 'stiff' in appearance than the florist varieties, and consequently, are useful additions to the garden. All gladioli are sun-lovers, requiring a well-drained position, and especially liking an alkaline soil. Out-

side favoured areas they are best given the protection of a wall and, indeed, they are at home with other sun-loving bulbs such as *Nerine* and *Amaryllis belladonna*. They should be planted quite deeply, 3–4 in (8–10 cm), to avoid frost damage to the corms. They also have a tendency to produce leaves during the winter months, and these can be damaged by late frosts, weakening the bulb or even killing it outright. Consequently, they are not suitable for areas with long winters, and their growth cycle makes them unsuitable for lifting and storing through the winter months in the same way as the taller hybrids. Given the right conditions of soil and aspect, however, they suffer from few pests and will, if happy, seed themselves freely, even becoming a nuisance, as has happened in the bulb fields of the Scilly Isles, where the bright cerise flowers of *Gladiolus byzantinus* are to be found mixed with many crops.

Gladiolus tristis, the earliest to flower (in late April or May), is also one of the least hardy, requiring a very warm sheltered spot under a wall or against a greenhouse. It is very beautiful, producing a succession of pale, creamy green flowers with bright brown splashes on the lower petals, and it is most attractive when combined with flowers and foliage of similar creamy shades, such as *Sisyrinchium striatum* (especially the variegated form) or *Camassia leichtlinii* 'Semi-plena'. Unlike the florist's gladioli, *G. tristis* is reluctant to follow a straight line, its wiry stems bending into the most delightful contortions, as I know to my cost when trying to cut them for an arrangement at the Chelsea Flower Show. It is also heavily scented, but only at night – so plant it with white stocks under a bedroom window for an overpowering effect. Sadly, *G. tristis* does begin to produce its leaves in the autumn, so they should be given a generous covering of straw and bracken to protect them during the hardest frosts, but do remember to remove this once the worst weather is over as it does not appreciate a waterlogged blanket which will, if left in position, cause rotting of the foliage, and cause as much damage as the frost it was protecting against.

Succeeding the rather tender South African *G. tristis*, is the much hardier southern European *G. byzantinus*. Its much stiffer habit and rather strong purple–cerise colouring lend it to planting in clumps, where it is most attractive among grey-leaved plants, especially those with soft pink flowers, such as the smaller flowered pinks, or plants from its native Mediterranean home, such as cistuses, rock roses or rosemary. All these can be combined with *Tulipa saxatilis* to make a most attractive feature in front of a sunny wall. It is also useful tucked into odd, dry, sunny corners where it can provide a bright splash of colour. We have a large clump at the back of a small bed beside our front door, where it is behind *Bergenia* 'Silberlicht' at the foot of an enormous rose, 'Lady Hillingdon'. It produces its flowers after the bergenia is past its best and just before the rose comes into flower, adding a splash of vivid colour to an extremely dry and rather impoverished site. Indeed, it is so happy there that its seedlings are becoming a problem in the gravel drive. Although *G. byzantinus* is the species most likely to be encountered, occasionally the similar · *G. communis*, *G. imbricatus*, or *G. italicus* are offered in specialist catalogues. These are smaller and more delicate and the flowers less striking than *G. byzantinus* but they are suitable for similar positions in the garden.

I am very fond of another little South African bulb, *Anomatheca laxa* (*Lapeirousia cruenta*). Its fans of leaves are overtopped by a succession of salmon-red flowers, each having a deeper red blotch on the lower petals. It flowers for most of the summer and its tiny stature makes it ideal for the front of a border. It seems able to withstand quite low temperatures but, being winter dormant, is easily lifted if required. There is also a superb pure white one which is lovely with silver-foliaged plants, or as a contrast to the red one. Unusually, its seed-head is also attractive, having relatively large, very conspicuous, deep orange–red seeds that are displayed for quite a long period.

However, it is in the autumn, particularly following that rare commodity, a hot, dry summer, that these narrow borders really give their best display. The sudden appearance of the golden, crocus-like flowers of *Sternbergia lutea* is one of the most welcome sights of early autumn. *S. lutea* flowers with its leaves, is reliably hardy, and usually does well in a warm, dry position, especially on alkaline soils; while the similar *S. l.* var. *angustifolia* and

S. sicula are both very vigorous and have narrower foliage than *S. lutea*. They, too, need a sunny, well-drained situation, as does the Middle Eastern *S. clusiana*, which is often encountered masquerading as *S. lutea*. *S. clusiana* has much larger flowers, slightly ragged at the tips, and flowers before its leaves, which appear later in the year. We grew it for many years on our very dry raised rock garden, but it did not survive the very severe prolonged frosts of one winter.

Another crocus-like bulb, but this time originating on the other side of the Atlantic Ocean in Argentina, is *Zephryanthes candida*. This bulb is evergreen, producing a rather untidy clump of leaves above which are carried, in late August and September, a succession of pure white flowers. When happy the clumps quickly increase and can be divided easily. As it is rather drab and untidy for much of the year it should be planted beside a brightly coloured plant that will detract attention from it, but preferably not one that flowers in the autumn if it is not to completely overshadow the zephryanthes.

Nerines, on the other hand, deserve to be carefully framed so that their intense-pink flowers, each reminiscent of a small lily, can form a truly eye-catching picture. Their pink shade is a difficult one to match sympathetically, and they are probably best against a neutral foliage background, especially one of silver-leaved plants such as artemisias. However, do not be tempted to try and mask their naked stems by putting other plants too close. The idea of pink nerines rising above a carpet of artemisia might be one that works on the show bench but in reality it is not so successful. Nerines need sun on the bulbs to ripen them and they only perform really well when they are congested. When we were first planting our garden I put a new hybrid against one of my walls where all the plants were small. Over the years the surrounding plants expanded until the nerines were lost from view and I forgot about them, as of course, they never flowered. Last year, when I decided to remove a rather bedraggled ceanothus I discovered the most enormous clump of nerines completely swamped by the plants around them. I have now moved them to a much more open situation where they can receive as much sun as our unpredictable summers provide, and hopefully I will be

encourage flowering, and my mother-in-law always recommended giving nerines a good soaking in June.

Like many bulbs that need a similar sun-baked position, they can be left undisturbed for many years, and only need dividing when bulbs are pushed out of the clumps. Then it is best to tackle only part of the clump at a time, lifting and replanting. The newly replanted bulbs will take a couple of seasons to settle down and flower.

As I mentioned earlier, nerines are best framed against a sympathetic background. However, this is not always possible and, sadly, deep pink nerines against a bright-orange brick wall is not the most beautiful combination, as I know from experience. However, it is possible to disguise the wall by planting an evergreen shrub or climber on it and training it behind the nerines.

All plants against walls naturally lean outwards and it is possible to exploit this trait, especially when the wall is approached from the side as well as from the front, by planting sympathetic plants beyond. We have a grey-leaved daisy bush *Olearia* × *scilloniensis*, behind my very pale pink hybrid, and I once saw the more intense pink *N. b.* 'Pink Triumph' beautifully backed by a variegated fuchsia, the arching stems of the fuchsia forming the perfect background to the arching stems of the nerines. Not all combinations succeed quite as well in practice as in theory. Some of the delicate silvery grasses could also be good companions for nerines but do take care to choose a well-behaved one, or the nerines, like those in one garden I know, will be destined to flower within a grey veil – very beautiful but not quite what was planned.

Unlike *N. bowdenii* which is hardy over most of the country, the other autumn lily, *Amaryllis belladonna* is not so hardy and needs protection from frost for its leaves during winter – a layer of bracken or straw is ideal. Once again, deep planting, about 4 in (10 cm), in a dry, very sunny position is necessary, with an application of bone-meal in the spring. It, too, must be left undisturbed and unshaded during the summer and will only flower really well when congested. My clump is between two plants of *Iris unguicularis* (*I. stylosa*), which enjoys a similar spartan fare. Although it flowers only irregularly it is well worth the wait, as each bulb produces

rewarded with flowers again. It is possible to plant very low plants, such as *Artemisia schmidtii*, in front of them or let one of my favourites, the annual toadflax, *Linaria nevadensis*, seed around the same area. It likes the same dry conditions and it is too small to affect the nerines. *N. bowdenii* is the hardiest species and it should be planted 2 in (5 cm) below the surface, not at the surface as is often recommended. I was once give a bag of nerine offsets which I planted against a wall as a stock bed. During the severe winters that followed most of the bulbs were killed but the few that were well below the surface survived. The leaves are produced during the late winter or early spring, dying before the flowers appear in October. A dusting of bone-meal or a high-potash fertilizer will

relatively large, lightly scented, pale pink flowers which are suffused by a deeper shade.

If amaryllis give an exotic air to the garden, then the other group of autumn-flowering bulbs, eucomis, impart an almost tropical atmosphere. The pine-apple flower, given its name for the tuft of leaves above the flower-spike, has only recently 'escaped' from the greenhouse and is proving much hardier than at first thought. In the mildest counties it can be grown in the open garden, and at Knights-hayes Court in Devon plants have sur-vived in the woodland garden for many years, but for colder districts they need the protection of a warm wall.

Eucomis have a quiet charm, slightly marred by often rather untidy, strap-like leaves and a tendency for the flower-spike to collapse as the buds open. In one garden this relaxed habit was masked by a dense planting of fuchsias, *Osteospermum* (*Dimorphotheca*), *Agapanthus*, and *Amar-yllis*, with *Clematis tangutica* scrambling over the wall behind them. They also make excellent subjects for large pots, but in this instance they must be brought under cover during the winter. In the garden the bulbs should be planted 6 in (15 cm) deep.

It can be seen, therefore, that there is a wide range of bulbs that will revel in the hot, dry conditions of these borders and that can be used to turn them into truly exotic features.

Above: Nerine bowdenii massed against a house wall

6 Afterthoughts

Propagation

Given good growing conditions most bulbs will increase vegetatively with no help from the gardener, small bulbs (offsets) forming naturally alongside the parent bulb until, eventually, large clumps are formed. Should these become so overcrowded that flowering is impaired, or you wish to start a new group elsewhere, the clumps should be lifted while dormant, the bulbs gently prised apart, and then replanted into newly prepared soil. Any bulbs that are damaged in this process should be discarded as the damaged tissue could become infected by Botrytis.

Although most bulbs are easily lifted while dormant, certain genera should be tackled very carefully, almost in a manner approaching an archaeological dig. Erythroniums must be among the worst to move. We try to lift all ours once every two years because, if left much longer than that, the bulbs may be as much as 10 in (25 cm) deep and it is very easy to damage the top of the bulb if it is where one thinks the bottom should be. E. A. Bowles advocated digging a large hole beside the clump and then making trial tunnels in towards it, in order to locate the level at which the bulbs are. Once found they can be lifted safely, carefully prised apart, and replanted, when they will sulk for a couple of years while they settle at their most comfortable depth.

It is not always necessary, or indeed desirable, to divide bulbs while they are dormant. Provided that they are replanted immediately, traditionally difficult subjects such as snowdrops and leucojums can be moved while dormant, but it is more normal to move them while they are in active growth. In this case it is best to divide large clumps into several smaller ones, rather than into individual bulbs. Not only does this look more natural but there is less risk of damaging the roots. All newly replanted bulbs should be well watered.

Although division is the easiest and the best method of increasing bulbs, not all bulbs produce offsets and for these, *Cycla-men* in particular, seed is the only way. It is also an ideal method of producing a large number of bulbs relatively cheaply, or of propagating the rarer varieties. Snake's-head fritillaries and erythroniums are good examples of this. The seed should be collected as soon as it is ripe and sown immediately. If the bulbs are ultimately quite large, such as lilies, galtonias, or alliums, then they are best sown directly into specially prepared seed beds. Smaller quantities of seed, or more specialist varieties, should be sown into deep seed-trays where they must be kept cool and damp. It is very important that the young seedlings should be allowed to grow for as long as possible to encourage the formation of a bulb, therefore they must be protected from pests, particularly slugs and aphids, and from competition from weeds which may easily smother them. It is also necessary to provide a suitable compost for the seeds, this should always have free drainage but care must be taken over the acidity and humus content when growing certain varieties.

The seedlings, which may take two years to appear, should be left undisturbed for two or three years, at which time they should be large enough to handle and they can either be moved to a new nursery bed, or planted out in their permanent home. Some bulbs flower relatively quickly, but most take between five and seven years to reach flowering size, so patience will be needed.

Although many of the bulbs commonly grown in our gardens are species, and will come true from seed, many are hybrids, particularly daffodils, tulips, and lilies. It is possible to grow these from seed, indeed this is how they were created, but their offspring will not resemble them, so it is probably best to remove the seed heads and concentrate upon vegetative increase, although growing new hybrids from seed can be great fun and is a fascinating, albeit a time- and space-consuming hobby.

Plants such as the wood anemone have rhizomes rather than bulbs and spread to form large patches of interlocking roots. Propagation of these is simply a matter of lifting the clumps in the early autumn and gently breaking off small pieces, making sure that each has a small, white, growing shoot visible. They should be replanted as soon as possible into a humus-rich soil, where it will take a couple of years before they once again set out to conquer the garden.

Lilies offer two other methods of increase, apart from natural division and seed. Certain species have tiny bulbils in the axils where the leaves join the stem. These can be carefully removed from the stem in the autumn and either potted up or, if large enough, planted out directly into the garden in well-prepared nursery beds.

The bulbs of a lily comprises a number of scales attached to a basal plate and each of these is also capable of producing a new bulblet. The scales should be carefully detached from the bulb and placed in a plastic bag of sterile peat and sand, sealed tightly, and placed in a warm cupboard – an airing cupboard is ideal. After a few weeks tiny bulblets will have formed at the base of the scales. They should be potted on into a sterile, humus-rich compost.

Trouble-shooting

Provided that they are grown under good conditions, most bulbs are trouble-free subjects, but like any other plant they can be struck down by a wide range of pests and diseases. I do not wish to be discouraging, as most gardeners will never encounter these problems, but it may be helpful to outline very briefly some of the more common ones that might occur.

The most obvious pest is one that we all have to contend with, the slug. Probably more damage is caused by this than any other problem. Not only do they attack the leaves, the succulent young stems of lilies being a particular favourite, keeled slugs also eat the bulb and its roots. Colchicums are frequently eaten by them, and not only does this damage weaken the bulb, either by destroying the leaves that will replenish it for another season or by actually eating part of it, this damaged tissue is also very vulnerable to attack by various forms of rot that will quickly finish what the slug has started. I find that colchicums, lilies, tulips, and fritillaries are especially prone to often fatal attacks by slugs, possibly because they, too, prefer the slightly moist, heavier soils that suit these bulbs. Chemical methods can be used in an attempt to control slugs, but the addition of sharp sand to the soil is probably the best deterrent. It also provides the good drainage favoured by most bulbs.

Aphids can damage bulbs by attacking the leaves, weakening and distorting them, but the main damage they inflict is to spread virus diseases from one plant to another previously healthy one. This is a special problem among lilies, and whole colonies can be destroyed in this way. Therefore, careful watch should be kept and the plants sprayed at the first sign of an aphid infestation.

The last main pest of bulbs is primarily one of greenhouses or among plants kept in pots. This is the vine weevil and it can devastate whole collections of cyclamen and lilies in particular. Each beetle is capable of laying 1000 eggs, and the small white grubs feed on the roots of plants, quickly destroying them. Unfortunately there is no complete chemical answer, although HCH dust may help. Scrupulous hygiene and the replanting into sterile soil is the best method of control. Fortunately, it is rarely a problem in the garden, although it can occasionally be temporarily introduced by placing an infested plant, usually a primula, near to a clump of vulnerable bulbs, such as lilies or cyclamen.

Larger animals, too, can cause physical damage, the most common pests being mice that frequently eat crocus corms as fast as they are planted. Although laborious, one reliable method of deterring them, and other animals such as rabbits and squirrels that scratch up the bulbs, is to place narrow ($\frac{1}{4}$ in, 7 mm) mesh wire over the corms and just below the soil surface. It also helps if the bulbs are planted deeply and firmly, all loose tunics being carefully removed.

The sudden demise of a clump of daffodils or their non-appearance usually indicates the presence of much more serious problems that need immediate investigation. There are two possible causes: one is the narcissus fly and the other a fungal disease, basal rot. Both result in a soft bulb with a completely rotted centre, but if it has been caused by the narcissus fly then the whitish larvae will be found in the middle of the bulb if you squeeze it.

Infected bulbs should be immediately destroyed by burning, taking care that none are left behind. The fly lays its eggs in the hole left by the dying leaves and the best method of control is to rake up the dying leaves and fill in the holes. Basal rot occurs in poorly drained soils, and improving the drainage by adding sand should help, although it is advisable to leave an infected area empty for a few seasons.

There is little that can be done to control virus diseases, usually shown as yellow streaking on the leaves, and any badly infected bulbs should be destroyed to prevent the spread of virus to healthy plants.

The final group of diseases, the various rots, can occur in poor growing conditions. Basal rot has already been mentioned as a problem of daffodils in poorly drained soils, but tulip fire can also spread rapidly in damp weather as does Botrytis on lilies. An improvement in the drainage and the circulation of air around the bulbs will do much to control these diseases, but it may be necessary to resort to one of the chemicals based on benomyl (Benlate for example). This has proved to be very useful as a dip for dormant bulbs and is especially useful to control ink disease in *Iris reticulata*.

I will conclude by emphasizing once again the importance of preparing the ground thoroughly before planting the bulbs, taking special care over the question of drainage, and the importance of choosing varieties suitable for your particular border. A strong, healthy bulb is less likely to be attacked by disease and is better able to resist it than a weak one. Given good growing conditions, bulbs are among the most trouble-free plants for the garden, with an enormous range of colours, shapes, and flowering seasons, and capable of giving many years of interest and delight.

Sunny borders

Variety	Description	Flowering time	Height (cm)	Planting depth (cm)	Distance apart (cm)	Planting season	Comments	Other uses
WINTER/EARLY SPRING								
Anemone								
blanda	Dissected leaves, blue, white or pink flowers	Feb/Mar	8	8	8	Aut		N R
Crocus								
angustifolius	Deep yellow, brown reverse	Feb	8	10	5–8	Aut		R
chrysanthus hybrids	Rounded flowers in various colours, often striped	Feb	8	10	5–8	Aut		R
corsicus	Soft purple, deeper veins	Feb/Mar	8	10	5–8	Aut		R
etruscus Zwanenburg	Lilac with silver outside	Feb/Mar	8	10	5–8	Aut		R
imperati	Violet inside, biscuit outside	Jan	8	10	5–8	Aut		R
sieberi 'Firefly'	Soft violet	Feb/Mar	8	10	5–8	Aut		N R
sieberi 'Violet Queen'	Violet-blue, yellow centre	Feb/Mar	8	10	5–8	Aut		N R
Eranthis [winter aconite]								
cilicica	Yellow with bronze leaves	Mar	8	10	5–8	Aut	Or in growth in spring	N R S
hyemalis	Yellow, green leaves	Feb	8	10	5–8	Aut	As above	N R S
Galanthus [Snowdrop]								
nivalis	Common snowdrop	Feb/Mar	10	10	5–8	Aut	Or in growth in spring	N S
nivalis Plenus	Double snowdrop	Feb/Mar	10	10	5–8	Aut	As above	N S
'Atkinsii'	Tall with large flowers	Feb	20	10	8	Aut		S
Scilla								
tubergeniana [mischtschenkoana]	Steel-blue flowers	Feb	10	10	8	Aut		R
MID SPRING								
Anemone								
nemorosa Alba Plena	Small double white flowers	Mar/Apr	10	5	5	Aut	Humus rich	S N
Chionodoxa								
luciliae, gigantea, sardensis	Blue with white eye	Mar	12	10	5	Aut		N R S
Fritillaria								
imperialis [crown imperial]	Nodding bells of yellow [lutea] or orange [rubra]	Apr	60	20	20	Aut		N
persica	Tall spikes of plum-coloured bells	Apr	90	20	20	Aut	Must be very well drained	
Hyacinthus								
orientalis hybrids	Bedding hyacinths in pink, white, purple, blue and cream	Mar/Apr	25	15	10	Aut		N
Ipheion								
uniflorum	Blue star-shaped flowers	Feb/Apr	12	10	2	Aut		R
Muscari								
grape hyacinths	In shades of blue and white	Mar/Apr	12–20	10	5	Aut		N R W C
Narcissus [daffodils]								
any garden hybrids	Wide variety of colours and shapes	Mar/Apr	20–45	15	10	Aut		N R C
Scilla								
hispanica La Grandesse	White Spanish bluebell	Apr/May	37	10	7	Aut		N S
sibirica	Electric-blue flowers	Mar/Apr	20	10	7	Aut		R S

Key: B = sunny borders   S = shady borders   N = growing in grass   R = rock gardens   W = window boxes   C = containers

Variety	Description	Flowering time	Height (cm)	Planting depth (cm)	Distance apart (cm)	Planting season	Comments	Other uses
Tulipa								
fosteriana hybrids	Early large flowers, red, white, yellow, etc.	Apr	45	20	10	Aut		R C
greigii hybrids	Large flowers often with patterned leaves	Apr	20	20	15	Aut		R C
kaufmanniana hybrids	Various colours often with patterned leaves	Feb/Mar	15–20	20	10	Aut		R C
tarda	2/3 cream flowers with yellow centres	Apr	15	15	7	Aut		R W
urumiensis	2/3 golden flowers with bronze exterior	Apr	15	15	7	Aut		R W
LATE SPRING/EARLY SUMMER								
Camassia	Spikes of silvery blue or creamy white flowers	Jun	60	15	10	Aut	Likes a moister position than many bulbs	N
Eremurus								
foxtail lily	Tall spikes in white, yellow, orange, pink, etc.	Jun/Jul	1–2 m		70–1 m	Aut	Plant crown at soil level. Protect from wind and cover in winter in cold districts	
Narcissus								
Actea	Large pure white flowers with tiny red cup	Apr/May	40	15	10	Aut		N
poeticus 'Recurvus'	Pheasant's eye, white with tiny red cup, scented	May	40	15	10	Aut		N
poeticus 'Flore Pleno'	Double white flowers, scented	May	40	15	10	Aut		N
Tulipa								
Single Early	Tall tulips with well-formed egg-shaped flowers, long lasting	Early Apr	30–35	20	12	Late Aut	Best on limy soils	C
Double Early	Double peony-like flowers in a wide range of colours	Apr	15–20	20	12	Late Aut	As above	C
Triumph	Strong growing and long lasting	Mid-Apr	40–45	20	12	Aut	As above	
Darwin hybrids	Very vigorous with enormous flowers	Apr/May	50–60	20	12	Aut	As above	
May flowering tulips	Oval flowers, slightly square in shape	May	55–65	20	12	Aut	As above	
Lily flowered	Pointed petals, reflexed at tips	May	55–65	20	12	Aut	As above	
Late Double	Large fully double flowers	May	40–45	20	12	Aut	As above	
Fancy tulips	Fringed, Parrot, Viridiflora, Rembrandt, etc.	May	50–60	20	12	Aut	As above	
SUMMER								
Allium [ornamental onions]								
aflatunense	Dense cluster of purple-lilac flowers in a ball	May/Jun	35	15	15	Aut		
albopilosum [christophii]	Huge heads of star-like flowers, lilac	Jun	60	15	20	Aut		
caeruleum [azureum]	Small dense balls of deep sky blue	Jun/Jul	45	15	10	Aut		
karataviense	Broad leaves like hosta, dull pink flowers	May/Jun	20	15	10	Aut		
Crinum								
× powellii	Heads of nodding pink trumpet flowers	Aug/Sep	75	at soil level	1 m	Spr	Protect in winter in cold districts	
Galtonia								
candicans	Sweetly scented large white bells	Aug	75	10	15	Spr	Lift for winter in cold districts	
princeps	Deep green bells	Aug	40	10	15	Spr	As above	
viridiflora	Pale green bells	Aug	65	10	15	Spr	As above	

Key: B = sunny borders   S = shady borders   N = growing in grass   R = rock gardens   W = window boxes   C = containers

Variety	Description	Flowering time	Height (cm)	Planting depth (cm)	Distance apart (cm)	Planting season	Comments	Other uses
Gladiolus								
Hybrids – Large Flowered	Large flowers in wide range of colours	Jul/Sep	1.3 m	12	10–15	Spr	Lift and store during winter	
Butterfly	Smaller flowers with deep central marking	Jul/Sep	1 m	12	10–15	Spr	As above	
Primulinus	Delicate hooded flowers widely spread along stem	Jul/Sep	1 m	12	10–15	Spr	As above	
Miniature	Like a small version of the large flowered hybrids with frilled flowers	Jul/Sep	45–90	12	10–15	Spr	As above	
Nanus [including colvillei and tubergenii hybrids]	Small flowers, often with deeper flashes on lower petals	Jul/Sep	45–60	10	10–15	Aut/ Spr	Hardy in sheltered positions	
Iris								
latifolium	English irises with flaring flowers of purple, blue or white	Jun/Jul	50	10	10–15	Aut	Should not be too dry in summer	N
xiphium [Spanish iris]	Slender flowers in white, blue, yellow, violet and purple	Jun	40	10	10–15	Aut	Lift and dry after flowering unless in warm position	
Dutch iris [florist iris]	Blue, white, bronze and yellow	Jun	50–60	10	10–15	Aut	As above	
Lilium								
Species								
candidum [madonna lily]	Pure white scented flowers, semi-evergreen foliage	Jun/Jul	1.5 m		20	Aug	Plant just below the surface Prefers lime	
hansonii	Golden yellow recurved flowers spotted with brown	Jun/Jul	1– 1.5 m	20	20	Nov/ Apr	Lime tolerant Stem rooting	
henryi	Orange-yellow turk's cap flowers with green central line	Jun/Jul	1.5– 2 m	20	20	Nov/ Apr	As above	
regale	Pure white scented trumpets with yellow throats and purple-shaded outsides	Jun/Jul	1– 1.5 m	20	20	Nov/ Apr	As above	
Hybrid lilies	These are available in a wide range of colours and flower shapes	May/Oct	90– 2 m	10–20	15–20	Nov/ Apr	Conditions vary from hybrid to hybrid	
AUTUMN								
Colchicum								
agrippinum	Small star-like flowers, strongly chequered	Aug/Sep	10	7	5	Aug		R
garden hybrids	Usually large flowered in shades of violet or mauve	Sep/Nov	10–20	10	10	Aug		S N
Crocosmia								
Emberglow	Hooded burnt orange flowers	Aug	50	15	10	Spr		S N
Lucifer	Brilliant flame-red flowers and wide sword-like leaves	Jul/Aug	1 m	15	10	Spr		S
Solfaterre	Apricot flowers with bronzed leaves	Aug/Sep	50	15	10	Spr	Only hardy in sheltered districts	
Crocus								
speciosus	Lilac-blue flowers with deeper veins	Sep/Nov	17	10	5	Aug		N S
Tritonia								
rubrolucens [rosea]	Small pink flowers on wiry stems	Aug/Sep	60	10	5	Spr		

Key: B = sunny borders   S = shady borders   N = growing in grass   R = rock gardens   W = window boxes   C = containers

Shady borders

Variety	Description	Flowering time	Height (cm)	Planting depth (cm)	Distance apart (cm)	Planting season	Comments	Other uses
AUTUMN								
Colchicum								
autumnale	7/9 small soft lilac or white [Alba] flowers	Sep/Oct	10	10	7	Aug		N B
bornmuelleri	2/3 large lilac flowers	Sep	20	10	10	Aug		N
byzantinum	7/9 small soft lilac flowers	Sep	15	10	10	Aug		N
speciosum	2/3 large goblet-shaped flowers of rich violet or white [Album]	Oct	17	10	10	Aug		N
Garden hybrids	Usually large flowered in shades of violet or mauve	Sep/Nov	10–20	10	10	Aug		
Crocus								
banaticus [iridiflorus]	Lilac-blue with small pale inner petals	Sep/Oct	7	7	5	Aug		
medius	Rounded rich purple flowers produced with leaves	Oct	10	10	7	Aug		N R
nudiflorus	Deep purple flowers on long stems	Sep/Oct	17	10	7	Aug	Stoloniferous	N
ochroleucus	Small white flowers with golden throats	Oct/Nov	7	10	5	Aug		N
serotinus salzmannii	Lilac flowers produced with leaves	Oct/Nov	10	10	5	Aug		R
speciosus	Lilac-blue flowers with deeper veins, reliable	Sep/Nov	17	10	5	Aug		N R B
Cyclamen								
cilicium	Small shell-pink flowers and marbled leaves	Sep/Nov	5	3	10		Best moved in growth, must be well drained	
hederifolium [neapolitanum]	Pink or white flowers followed by marbled leaves	Aug/Sep	10	3	20		As above	N
purpurascens [europaeum]	Scented deep carmine flowers	Jul/Oct	10	3	10		As above	
Galanthus [snowdrops]								
reginae-olgae	Small white flowers produced before the leaves	Sep/Oct	10	10	5		Best moved in growth	
WINTER								
Anemone								
blanda	Dissected leaves with blue flowers	Feb/Mar	7	7	7	Aut		N B R
Crocus								
laevigatus Fontenayi	Soft violet-blue with purple lines on the outside	Dec	7	10	5	Aut		N R
tommasinianus	Soft lavender flowers; prolific	Feb	10	10	5	Aut		N
Cyclamen								
coum	Small pink, white or crimson flowers with round leaves	Jan/Feb	10	3	10		Best planted in growth	
Eranthis [winter aconite]								
cilicica	Yellow with bronze leaves	Mar	7	10	7	Aut	Or in growth in spring	N R B
hyemalis	Yellow with green dissected leaves	Feb	7	10	7	Aut	As above	N R B
Galanthus [snowdrops]								
caucasicus	Large flowers with wide grey leaves	Feb	10	10	5		Galanthus are best planted in growth	
elwesii	Small flowers with large grey leaves	Feb	20	10	5			
nivalis	Common snowdrop	Feb	10	10	5			N
nivalis Plenus	Double common snowdrop	Feb	10	10	5			N
plicatus	Small flowers with folded green leaves	Feb	15	10	5			
Hybrid snowdrops	Large single and double flowers, some marked green on the outer petals	Jan/Mar	10–20	10	5			

Key: B = sunny borders   S = shady borders   N = growing in grass   R = rock gardens   W = window boxes   C = containers

Variety	Description	Flowering time	Height (cm)	Planting depth (cm)	Distance apart (cm)	Planting season	Comments	Other uses
SPRING								
Anemone								
apennina	Sky-blue or white flowers	Mar/Apr	15	5	7	Aut		N
nemorosa [wood anemone]	Single or double flowers in white or shades of blue	Apr	15	5	7	Aut		N B
ranunculoides	Yellow wood anemone	Apr	15	5	7	Aut		
Arisarum								
proboscidium	Curious arum flowers like round tailed mice	May/Jun	7	15	5	Aut		
Arum								
italicum Pictum	Deep green leaves, marbled with white, all winter	May/Jun	30	15	10	Aut/Spr		
Corydalis								
ambigua	Brilliant blue or purple snap dragon flowers	Mar/Apr	7	15	10	Aut	Peaty soil	
caucasica Alba	Pure white	Apr	7	15	10	Aut	Peaty soil	
solida	Pinkish-purple flowers in a dense spike. Easy	Apr	15	15	10	Aut		
Cyclamen								
repandum	Deep pink flowers with twisted petals	Apr/May	10	10	10		Plant in growth in peaty soil	
Erythronium								
dens canis [dog's tooth violet]	Pink or white flowers above darkly marbled leaves	Mar/Apr	7	15	5	Aut		N
revolutum	Tall flowers in shades of pink	Apr	20	15	10	Aut		
tuolumnense	Small brilliant yellow flowers and apple-green leaves	Mar/Apr	25	15	10	Aut		
tuolumnense Pagoda	Large sulphur-yellow flowers with marbled leaves	Apr	25	15	10	Aut		
White Beauty	Large cream flowers with yellow centres, marbled leaves	Mar/Apr	20	15	10	Aut		
Fritillaria								
camschatcensis	Almost black bell-like flowers	May	25	15	15	Aut	Peaty soil	
meleagris [snake's head]	Large chequered flowers in purple or white	Apr/May	20	15	10	Aut		N
pyrenaica	Large deep purple bells green on the inside	Apr	30	15	10	Aut		
Leucojum [snowflake]								
aestivum	Clusters of small white, green-tipped flowers	Apr	35	15	10	Aut	Or in growth in spring	N
aestivum Gravetye Giant	Much larger-flowered form of the above	Apr/May	55	15	10	Aut	As above	
vernum	Large white bell-shaped flowers with green tips	Feb/Mar	25	15	10	Aut	As above	
Narcissus [daffodils]								
cyclamineus	Long narrow golden trumpet with swept back petals	Mar	13	10	5	Aut	Acid peaty soil, moist	
cyclamineus hybrids	Various colours	Feb/Apr	15–40	15	10	Aut	N B R C	
triandrus	Milk-white nodding flowers with reflexed petals	Mar	10	10	5	Aut	Well-drained acid soil	R
Ornithogalum								
nutans	Silvery white with broad green stripe outside	Apr/May	30	15	5	Aut		N B R
Scilla								
bithynica	Small blue flowers in a dense spike	Mar/Apr	15	15	5	Aut		N
hispanica	Spanish bluebells in blue, pink or white	May	35	15	10	Aut		N B
non-scripta	Bluebell	May	30	15	10	Aut		N
sibirica	Rich deep blue flowers	Mar/Apr	15	15	5	Aut		B R

Key: B = sunny borders S = shady borders N = growing in grass R = rock gardens W = window boxes C = containers

Variety	Description	Flowering time	Height (cm)	Planting depth (cm)	Distance apart (cm)	Planting season	Comments	Other uses
Trillium								
cernuum	Nodding white flowers with deep purple anthers	Apr	45	10	10	Win/Spr		
cuneatum [sessile]	Long dark purple erect flowers, long lasting	Apr	25	10	10	Win/Spr		
luteum	Upright greenish-yellow flowers	Apr/May	25	10	10	Win/Spr		
grandiflorum	Large white flowers fading to rose	Apr	30	10	10	Win/Spr		
Tulipa								
Sylvestris	Nodding yellow flowers	Apr	35	15	10	Aut		N
SUMMER								
Arisaema								
candidissimum	White flower spathes, broadly striped pink	May/Jun	30–50	15–25	15	Spr		
consanguineum	Deep purple and white flower spathes, leaves like a lupin	Jun/Jul	45	15–25	15	Spr		
triphyllum	Green flower spathes with deep brown stripes	Jun	30–50	15–25	15	Spr		
Cardiocrinum								
giganteum	Huge white trumpet flowers	Jul/Aug	1.8–2.5 m	5	40	Win/Spr	Bulb dies after flowering	
Crocosmia								
Citronella	Clear golden flowers	Aug/Sep	75	15	10	Spr		N B
Emberglow	Hooded burnt orange flowers, vigorous	Jul/Aug	75	15	10	Spr		B
Emily McKenzie	Large orange flowers with mahogany blotch	Aug/Sep	60	15	10	Spr		B
Jackanapes	Flowers with alternate yellow and orange petals	Aug/Sep	60	15	10	Spr		B
masonorum	Horizontal spikes of orange-scarlet flowers	Aug/Sep	60	15	10	Spr		N B
Lilium								
martagon	Up to 30 purple or white spotted turk's cap flowers	Jun	1 m	20	20	Win/Spr	Lime tolerant stem rooting	N
monadelphum	Pale straw-yellow turk's cap flowers, scented	Jun	1 m	20	20	Win/Spr	As above	
pardalinum [panther lily]	Bright orange, brown spotted turk's cap flowers	Jul	1.5 m	20	20	Win/Spr	Damp humus-rich soil	
pyrenaicum	Small bright yellow turk's cap flowers	May	65	20	20	Win/Spr	Lime tolerant stem rooting	N
speciosum	Recurved flower strongly flushed with reddish-pink, heavily scented	Aug/Sep	1 m	20	20	Win/Spr	Needs acid soil	
szovitsianum	Golden turk's cap flowers with dark spots	Jun	1.5 m	20	20	Win/Spr	Lime tolerant; prefers heavy soil; stem rooting	N
tigrinum [tiger lily]	Robust easily grown lily with spotted turk's cap flowers in shades of orange, yellow or red	Aug	1 m	20	20	Win/Spr	Acid soil stem rooting	

Key: B = sunny borders　S = shady borders　N = growing in grass　R = rock gardens　W = window boxes　C = containers

Bulbs in grass

Variety	Description	Flowering time	Height (cm)	Planting depth (cm)	Distance apart (cm)	Planting season	Comments	Other uses
AUTUMN								
Colchicum								
autumnale	7/9 small soft lilac flowers	Sep/Oct	10	10	7	Aug		S B
byzantinum	7/9 small soft lilac flowers [larger than autumnale]	Sep	20	10	10	Aug		S
Crocus								
nudiflorus	Deep purple flowers on long stems	Sep/Oct	17	10	7	Aug	Stoloniferous	S
pulchellus	Pale lilac with white anthers	Sep/Oct	15	10	5	Aug		S R
Cyclamen								
hederifolium [neapolitanum]	Pink or white flowers followed by marbled leaves	Aug/Sep	10	3	20		Best moved in growth; plant in thin grass only	S
WINTER/EARLY SPRING								
Anemone								
blanda	Dissected leaves with blue flowers	Feb/Mar	7	7	7	Aut		S B R
Crocus								
laevigatus Fontenayi	Soft violet blue with purple lines on the outside	Dec	7	10	5	Aut		S R
tommasinianus	Masses of small flowers of soft lavender or deep purple [Whitewell Purple]	Feb	10	10	5	Aut		S
Eranthis [Winter Aconite]								
cilicica	Yellow flowers with bronze leaves	Mar	7	10	7	Aut	Or in growth in spring	S R B
hyemalis	Yellow flowers with dissected green leaves	Feb	7	10	7	Aut	As above	S R B
Galanthus [Snowdrops]								
nivalis	Common snowdrop	Feb	10	10	5		Best planted in growth	S
nivalis Plenus	Double snowdrop	Feb	10	10	5		As above	S
Hybrids	Some of the more vigorous hybrids such as Atkinsii or S. Arnott could also be used	Feb	15–20	10	5			S
MID SPRING								
Anemone								
apennina	Sky blue or white flowers	Mar/Apr	15	5	7	Aut		S
nemerosa [wood anemone]	White or shades of blue	Apr	15	5	7	Aut		B S
Chionodoxa								
luciliae, gigantea, sardensis	Blue with a white 'eye'	Mar	12	10	5	Aut		S R B
Crocus								
chrysanthus hybrids	Rounded flowers in various colours, often striped on the outside	Feb	7	10	5	Aut		S R B
Dutch crocus	Large flowers of blue, purple, yellow and white	Mar	12	10	5	Aut		B
sieberi	Rounded flowers of soft lilac	Feb/Mar	7	10	5	Aut		R B
Erythronium								
dens-canis [dog's tooth violet]	Pink and white flowers above darkly marbled leaves	Mar/Apr	7	15	5	Aut		S

Key: B = sunny borders   S = shady borders   N = growing in grass   R = rock gardens   W = window boxes   C = containers

Variety	Description	Flowering time	Height (cm)	Planting depth (cm)	Distance apart (cm)	Planting season	Comments	Other uses
Fritillaria								
imperialis [crown imperial]	Nodding bells of yellow [lutea] or orange [rubra]	Apr	60	20	20	Aut		S
meleagris [snake's head]	Large chequered flowers in purple or white	Apr/May	20	15	10	Aut		S
Hermodactylus								
tuberosa [black widow iris]	Greenish-black iris flowers	Mar/Apr	20	15	5	Aut	Must be dry	R
Leucojum [snowflake]								
aestivum	Clusters of small white, green-tipped flowers	Apr	35	15	10	Aut	Or in growth in spring	S
Muscari [grape hyacinth]								
armenaicum 'Blue Spike'	Large heads of blue flowers	Mar/Apr	15	10	7	Aut		B R
Narcissus								
cyclamineus	Long trumpet with swept back petals	Mar	13	10	5	Aut	Moist acid soil	S
pseudonarcissus [Lent lily]	Pale yellow trumpet and narrow white petals	Mar	15	10	7	Aut		
obvallaris [Tenby daffodil]	Neat golden flowers	Mar	20	10	7	Aut		
Tall garden hybrid daffodils		Mar/Apr	15	10	7	Aut		B
Scilla								
bifolia	Tiny bright blue flowers	Feb/Mar	10	10	5	Aut		B R
LATE SPRING								
Allium								
moly	Clusters of bright golden yellow flowers	Jun	25	10	5	Aut		S
Camassia								
cusickii	Spikes of silvery blue	May/Jun	60	10	10	Aut	Likes moist soil	B
leichtlinii	Tall spikes of blue or cream flowers	Jun	60–90	10	10	Aut	Likes moist soil	B
quamash	Deep blue flowers	Jun	40	10	10	Aut	Likes moist soil	B
Iris								
latifolium [English iris]	Wide flowers in purple, blue or white	Jun/Jul	50	15	10	Aut		B
Narcissus								
poeticus [pheasant's eye]	Small white flowers with tiny red cups, scented	May	40	15	10	Aut		B
poeticus Flore Pleno	Pure white double flowers, scented	May	40	15	10	Aut		B
Ornithogalum								
narbonense	Tall spikes of white flowers	May/Jun	35	10	10	Aut	Must be well drained	B
nutans	Silvery white flowers with broad green stripe outside	Apr/May	30	15	5	Aut		S
umbellatum [star of Bethlehem]	Large pure white flowers which open with sun	May	10	10	5	Aut		B
Scilla								
hispanica	Spanish bluebell in blue, pink or white	May	35	15	10	Aut		S B
non-scripta	Common bluebell	May	30	15	10	Aut		S
Tulipa								
sylvestris	Nodding yellow flowers	Apr	35	15	10	Aut		S
SUMMER								
Lilium								
martagon	Up to 30 purple or white turk's cap flowers	Jun	1 m	20	20	Nov/ Apr	Lime tolerant	S
pyrenaicum	Small bright yellow turk's cap flowers	Jun	65	20	20	Nov/ Apr	Lime tolerant	S

Key: B = sunny borders S = shady borders N = growing in grass R = rock gardens W = window boxes C = containers

Bulbs for special places

Variety	Description	Flowering time	Height (cm)	Planting depth (cm)	Distance apart (cm)	Planting season	Comments	Other uses
ROCK GARDENS								
Allium								
oreophilum [ostrowskianum]	Dense heads of bright rose	Jun	15	10	5	Aut		
Anemone								
blanda White Splendour	Large flowers of pure white	Apr	10	10	5	Aut		B C
pavonina St Bavo	Long-stemmed anemones in subtle shades of rose and lavender	Apr/May	25	5	5	Aut		B N
Crocus	Any autumn or spring crocus except the large Dutch crocus	Sep/Mar	5–15	10	5	Aug/ Nov		B S N
Fritillaria								
acmopetala	Large green and brown bells	Apr	30	10	5	Aut		
uva-vulpis	Small chocolate-brown bells	Apr	20	10	5	Aut		
Iris								
aucheri	A Juno iris with pale blue flowers	Mar/Apr	25	12	10	Aut	The fleshy roots must not be damaged	
bucharica	A creamy yellow Juno iris	Mar/Apr	30	12	10	Aut	As above	
danfordiae	Yellow flowers, spotted green	Feb/Mar	10	10	5	Aut		
histrioides Major	Large blue flowers, reliable	Feb/Mar	10	10	5	Aut		
reticulata and hybrids	Variable shades of blue and purple	Feb/Mar	10	10	5	Aut		
Leucojum								
autumnale	2/3 small pinkish bells	Sep	15	7	5	Aut	Or in growth in spring	
Lilium								
amabile	Deep red and yellow turk's cap flowers	Jun/Jul	60	15	15	Nov/ Apr	Lime tolerant; stem rooting	
tenuifolium [pumilum]	Small scarlet turk's cap flowers	Jun/Jul	45	15	15	Nov/ Apr	As above	
Muscari	Grape hyacinths in shades of blue, violet and white	Mar/May	12–25	10	5	Aut		B N C
Narcissus								
asturiensis	Tiny golden trumpet daffodil	Feb/Mar	7	5	5	Aut	Protect from slugs	
bulbocodium	Hoop petticoat daffodils in yellow or white	Jan/Mar	12	5	5	Aut	Needs excellent drainage	
jonquilla	Up to 6 sweetly scented golden flowers	Apr/May	30	7	5	Aut	As above	
juncifolius	Several tiny sweet-scented flowers	Mar/Apr	7	5	5	Aut	As above	
triandrus	Nodding creamy flowers with reflexed petals	Mar	10	5	5	Aut	As above	
dwarf hybrids such as	Bobbysoxer, Hawera, Jack Snipe, Jumblie, Little Beauty, Linte, Sundial, Tête a Tête, etc.	Feb/May	15–30	10	5–10	Aut		
Oxalis								
adenophylla	Buns of grey-green foliage and pink flowers	Apr/May	10	5	5	Aut		
Puschkinia								
scilloides [libanotica]	Dense clusters of silvery blue flowers	Mar/Apr	10	7	5	Aut		

Key: B = sunny borders   S = shady borders   N = growing in grass   R = rock gardens   W = window boxes   C = containers

Variety	Description	Flowering time	Height (cm)	Planting depth (cm)	Distance apart (cm)	Planting season	Comments	Other uses
Scilla								
bifolia	Starry deep blue flowers	Feb/Mar	10	10	5	Aut		N
mischtschenkoana [tubergeniana]	Pale silvery blue	Feb	10	10	7	Aut		
sibirica	Rich deep blue bells	Mar/Apr	15	15	5	Aut		
Tulipa								
aucheriana	Deep rose pink with prostrate foliage	Apr/May	10	10	7	Aut		
batalinii	Delicate primrose or apricot flowers	May	12	10	5	Aut		
clusiana [lady tulip]	Slender white flowers with red stripe	Apr	25	10	5	Aut		
fosteriana	Dwarf hybrids such as Cantata and Princeps	Apr	25	10	10	Aut		C B
greigii hybrids	Large flowers in a wide range of colours with striped leaves	Apr	20–25	15	10	Aut		C B
kaufmanniana and hybrids	Large flowers in a wide range of colours	Feb/Mar	15–25	15	10	Aut		C B
maximowiczii [or linifolia]	Small scarlet flowers	Apr/May	12	10	5	Aut		
pulchella	Bright violet-pink flowers	Feb/Mar	7	10	5	Aut		
sprengeri	Scarlet-shaded bronze	May	35	15	7	Aut		
tarda	Several creamy flowers with yellow centre	Apr	15	10	7	Aut		B
turkestanica	5/9 creamy white flowers	Feb/Mar	20	10	7	Aut		
urumiensis	Several yellow flowers with bronze exteriors	Apr	15	10	7	Aut		B

CONTAINERS

Variety	Description	Flowering time	Height (cm)	Planting depth (cm)	Distance apart (cm)	Planting season	Comments	Other uses
Anemone								
blanda White Splendour	Large white flowers	Apr	10	10	5	Aut	Use as a carpeting plant	R
Hyacinthus								
orientalis hybrids	Bedding hyacinth in white, pink, cream or blue	Mar/Apr	25	15	10	Aut		B
Lilium								
regale	Pure white scented trumpets	Jun/Jul	1.2 m	20	20	Nov/Apr	Lime tolerant; stem rooting	B S
hybrids esp. Enchantment, Connecticut King, Citronella, Bright Star, etc., and trumpet hybrids		Jul/Aug	90–1.5 m	20	20	Nov/Apr	Variable	B S
Muscari	Grape hyacinths in blue and white	Mar/Apr	12–	10	5	Aut		B S R
Narcissus								
dwarf hybrids such as	February Gold, February Silver, Charity May, Little Witch, Jenny, Jack Snipe, Liberty Bells, Geranium, etc.	Feb/Apr	15–35	10	5	Aut		B R
Tulipa								
Double Early	Peony-like flowers in a wide range of colours	Apr	15–20	15–20	12	Aut		B
eichleri	Scarlet flowers with black and yellow centres and grey leaves	Apr/May	25	15	10	Aut		B R
fosteriana hybrids	Large early flowers in red, yellow, white, etc.	Apr	45	15–20	10	Aut		B
greigii hybrids	Large flowers and striped leaves	Apr	20	15	10	Aut		B R
kaufmanniana hybrids	Early flowering with large short flowers	Feb/Mar	15	15	10	Aut		B R
praestans fusilier	Two or three orange-red flowers per stem	Apr	20	15	10	Aut		R

WINDOW BOXES
Many of the bulbs listed under rock gardens can be used to create miniature gardens or use the shortest of the container bulbs for bold effects.

Key: B = sunny borders   S = shady borders   N = growing in grass   R = rock gardens   W = window boxes   C = containers

Variety	Description	Flowering time	Height (cm)	Planting depth (cm)	Distance apart (cm)	Planting season	Comments	Other uses
SHELTERED WARM BORDERS								
Amaryllis								
belladonna	Clusters of pink lily-like flowers on naked stems	Sep/Nov	45		10	Spr	When planting top of bulb to be 5–10 cm below surface; must have sun on the bulbs to ripen them	
Anomatheca								
laxa [cruenta]	Small carmine flowers with darker blotches	Jun/Sep	17	5	5	Spr		
Crinum								
× powellii	Large heads of pale pink or white [Alba] trumpet flowers above large leaves	Aug/Sep	90	at soil level	1 m	Spr	Protect in winter in cold districts	B
Eucomis								
'pineapple flower'	Spikes of creamy green flowers often tinged with purple with a tuft of leaves above.	Jul/Sep	20–40	10	15	Spr	Keep frost free in winter	C
Gladiolus								
byzantinus	Fairly large purple-red flowers	Jun	60	10	7	Aut	In milder counties	N B
tristis	A few sulphur-yellow, night-scented flowers on wiry stems	May	65	10	5	Aut	Hardy in mild districts only	
Hermodactylus								
tuberosa [snake's head iris]	Sweetly scented green flowers with almost black falls	Apr	30	7	5	Aut	In sunny dry position	N
Nerine								
bowdenii	Umbels of deep pink lily flowers	Oct	60		10	Spr	When planting top of bulb to be 5 cm below surface	
undulata [crispa]	Small heads of delicate pink flowers with wavy edges	Oct/Nov	45		5	Spr	As above; only hardy in very sheltered areas	
Scilla								
peruviana	Large triangular heads of blue flowers	May/Jun	25		10	Aut	When planting top of bulb to be at soil level	
Sternbergia								
clusiana	Large yellow crocus-like flowers	Sep	12	10	5	Aug		
lutea	The yellow crocus-like flowers are produced with the leaves	Sep	10	10	5	Aug		
sicula [and angustifolia]	Very free flowering with golden flowers and narrow leaves	Sep	10	10	5	Aug		
Tulipa								
Lilac Wonder	Clear lilac flowers with yellow centres	Mar/Apr	30	10–15	5–10	Aut		R
saxatalis	Pink flowers with yellow centre and apple-green leaves	Mar/Apr	30	10–15	5–10	Aut	Stoloniferous	R
Zephyranthes								
candida	Pure white crocus-like flowers with narrow evergreen foliage	Sep/Oct	15	5	5	Spr		

Key: B = sunny borders   S = shady borders   N = growing in grass   R = rock gardens   W = window boxes   C = containers

Index

Page references in italics are to illustrations